It's About Time

Jan Ruhe

It's About Time

Copyright © 2008 by Jan Ruhe

ISBN 978-1-60530-636-0
LCCN 2007942138

Cover Design and Graphic Art
by Sarah Rose McKinley

Copyright © 2008 by Jan Ruhe
Published by Proteus Press
300 Puppy Smith, Suite 205-290, Aspen, CO 81611
tel. 970-927-9380 fax 970-927-0112

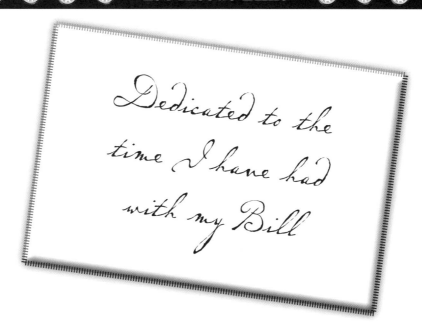

Dedicated to the time I have had with my Bill

Love is a journey that knows no end.

"It's not my place to tell anyone on earth what they should or should not do with their time. I do believe that by providing an example of what can be accomplished if you apply your thoughts, time and energy with great determination, you will make the first attempt toward some distant goal."

Jan Ruhe

"It is a funny thing about life; if you refuse to accept anything but the best, you very often get it."
-Somerset Maugham

Table of Contents It's About Time

Introduction

In all of my readings, studies, world travels, attending seminars, teaching seminars worldwide, writing 12 books and being a wife and a mother of three children, what I have learned most is the value of time. Time does not wait on any of us. Don't wait until...to use your best china, silver, crystal, jewels...use it now! It's later than you think. We are truly dancing on this earth for such a short time. I don't remember when it hit me that I would not live forever...or that while I was on earth that I wanted to make a contribution to those who live long after I am gone. But when that reality hit me, that was when I began to really live...to pay more attention to sunrises, sunsets, the changing of the seasons, of breathing, of adventure, of risks, of quick forgiveness, of deep love and cherished memories with close friends and family. Many years ago, I began gathering stories, poems, quotes and ideas about the importance of time and now have put them together in this one book for those who value time. We all value different things, but the one thing we all have in common is 24 hours a day. Why is it that only 3% of the people reach their dreams in life? Don't you think its about time that you stop what you are doing to fill your time with time wasters and really begin to master that which is most important to you in life? My intent in writing this book is to stimulate your desire to walk away from the 97% of the people who have no goals, no dreams, no drive, no vision and join the 3% who are making use of the rest of the time they have left on earth. I believe in you,

After everything that I have experienced in my life, the thing that has impressed me the most is this poem about living your dash...

The Dash

I read of a man who stood to speak
At the funeral of a friend
He referred to the dates on her tombstone
From the beginning-to the end.
He noted that first came her date of birth
Spoke the following date with tears,
But he said what mattered most of all
Was the dash between those years.
For that dash represented all the time
That she spent alive on earth...
And now only those who loved her
Know what that little time is worth.
For it matters not, how much we own,
The cars...the house...the cash,
What matters is how we live and love
And how we spend our dash.
So think about this long and hard...
Are there things you'd like to change?
For you never know how much time is left,
That can still be rearranged.
If we could just slow down enough
To consider what's true and real
And always try to understand
The way other people feel.
And be less quick to anger,
Show appreciation more
And love the people in our lives
Like we've never loved before.
If we treat each other with respect,
And more often wear a smile.
Remembering that this special dash
Might last but a little while.
So, when your eulogy's being read
Life's actions to rehash...
Would you be proud of the things they say
About how you spent your dash?
-Linda Ellis

Don't you think it's about time that you get control of what is going on in your life and the way you're spending your time? Starting now. Right now. And don't you want those you love to stop going in the wrong direction in life? If you say it, they doubt it, but what about an entire book to read again and again to help them sort out what they need to do. It truly is about time.

To get all there is out of living, employ your time wisely, never be in too much of a hurry to stop and sip life, but never losing the sense of the enormous value of a minute. Today, be aware of how you are spending your 1,440 beautiful moments...make sure you spend them wisely. Why? Because it's about time that you do.

Do you sometimes feel like the rabbit from Alice in Wonderland? One of the most memorable scenes was that frantic rabbit hysterically shouting, "I'm late, I'm late, I'm late-- for a very important date".

You are Old, Father William

"You are old, father William", the young man said, *"and your hair has become very white; and yet you incessantly stand on your head- Do you think, at your age, it is right?"*
"In my youth", father William replied to his son, *"I feared it might injure the brain; but, now that I'm perfectly sure I have none, why, I do it again and again."*
"You are old", said the youth, *"as I mentioned before, and you have grown most uncommonly fat; yet you turned a back-somersault at the door- Pray what is the reason for that?"*
"In my youth", said the sage, as he shook his grey locks, *"I kept all my limbs very supple by the use of this ointment-one shilling a box-allow me to sell you a couple?"*
"You are old", said the youth, *"and your jaws are too weak for anything tougher than suet; yet you finished the goose, with the bones and the beak-pray, how did you manage to do it?"*
"In my youth", said his father, *"I took to the law and argued each case with my wife; and the muscular strength, which it gave to my jaw, has lasted the rest of my life."*
"You are old", said the youth, *"one would hardly suppose that your eye was as steady as ever; yet you balanced an eel on the end of your nose- what made you so awfully clever?"*
"I have answered three questions and that is enough", said his father. *"Don't give yourself airs! Do you think I can listen all day to such stuff? Be off, or I'll kick you down the stairs."*
-Lewis Carroll

We all must suffer one of two pains no matter what so it is imperative to make the right choice. You either suffer the pain of discipline or the pain of regret. Choose discipline because discipline, you will learn, weighs ounces while regret weighs tons.

Excerpted from Arnold Bennett's *How to Live on 24 hours a Day,* published in 1907, containing his wise advice on how best to use the most valuable asset we all possess, time. You must learn how to invest your time wisely or you will never be able to achieve anywhere near your full potential. Philosophers have not explained time. With it, all is possible; without it, nothing is possible. The supply of time is truly a daily miracle, an affair genuinely astonishing when you examine it. You wake up in the morning and your day is filled with 24 hours. It is yours. It is the most precious of possessions. Yet, no one can take it from you. It is unstealable. No one received either more or less that you received. In the realm of time there is no aristocracy of wealth and no aristocracy of intellect. Genius is never rewarded by even an extra hour a day. It has been said that time is money. Time is a great deal more than money, usually. Though you might have the wealth of royalty you cannot buy yourself a minute more time than I have or the cat by the fireplace has. There is no punishment with time. Waste your infinitely precious commodity as much as you will and the supply will still not be withheld from you. You cannot draw on the future. It is impossible to get into debt! You cannot waste tomorrow; it is kept for you. You cannot waste the next hour, it is kept for you. You have to live on 24 hours of daily time. Out of it you have to spin health, pleasure, money, content, respect and the evolution of your immortal soul. Strange that the newspapers and magazines are not full of *"How to live on a given income of time"*, instead of *"How to live on a given income of money!"* Money is far commoner than time. Which person says, *"I shall this or that when I have a little more time?"* Failures always seem to act as if they had a thousand years to live. They drink too much, party too much, sleep too much, play too much and constantly assure us that they will take care of all of their duties tomorrow. There is no such thing as a calendar with a *"tomorrow"* on it. There is dissatisfaction in the feeling that you are every day leaving undone something which you would like to do and which you are always hoping to do when you have *"more time"*. You will never have *"more time"*, since you already have all the time there is. The most important preliminary to the task of arranging your life so that you may live fully and comfortably within your daily budget of 24 hours is the calm realization of the extreme difficulty of the task, of the sacrifices and the endless effort which it demands. Next year, the next day, the next hour are lying ready for you unspoiled as if you had never wasted or misapplied a single moment in all your life. No object is served in waiting till next week or even until tomorrow. Allow for accidents. Allow for human nature, especially your own. Everyone gets the same amount of time per day, rich people do not get more than poor people. It's not possible to go to the store and buy time. Say your day is already full to overflowing. How? You actually spend in earning your livelihood how much? Seven hours, on the average? In actual sleep, seven? You persist in looking upon those hours from 10-6 as *the day,* to which the ten hours preceding them and the six hours following them are nothing but a prologue and epilogue. Such an attitude, unconscious though it is, of course kills his interest in the odd 16 hours, with the result that, even if he does not waste them, he does not count them; he regards them simply as margin. This attitude is utterly illogical and unhealthy, since it formally gives the central prominence to a patch of time and a bunch of activities which the man's one idea is to *get through* and have *done with.* You are not the Shah of time. You have no more time than I have. Six hours are normally wasted in the evening, probably more, are gone--gone like a dream, gone like magic, unaccountably gone! At 6:00 p.m. look facts in the face and admit that you are not tired (because you are not, you know) and arrange your evening so that it is not cut in the middle by a meal. By so doing you will have a clear expanse of at least three hours. Employ an hour and a half every other evening in some important and consecutive cultivation of the mind. You will still be left with three evenings for friends, bridge, tennis, domestic scenes, odd reading, gardening and prize competitions. If you persevere you will soon want to pass four evenings and perhaps five, in some sustained endeavor to be genuinely alive. You will fall out of that habit of muttering to yourself at 11:15 p.m., *Time to be thinking about going to bed.* Those 90 nocturnal minutes thrice a week must be the most important minutes in the 10,080. They must be sacred. You practice physical exercises for a mere ten minutes. You may have spent your time badly, but you did spend it; you did do something with it, however ill-advised that something may have been. You are thinking... *"it may be well enough for some folks to want to use their free time in such a way, but it isn't for me".* It is for you. You are the very man I am aiming at. Throw away the suggestion and you throw away the most precious suggestion that was ever offered to you. It is the suggestion of the most sensible, practical, hard-headed people who have walked the earth. See how the process cures worry, that miserable, avoidable, shameful disease--worry! Many people pursue a regular and uninterrupted course of idleness in the evenings because they think that there is no alternative to idleness. This is a great mistake. When you set forth on the enterprise of using all of your time, it is just as well to remember that your own time and not other people's time, is the material with which you have to deal; that the earth rolled on pretty comfortably before you began to balance a budget of the hours and that it will continue to roll on pretty comfortably whether or not you succeed in your new role of chancellor of the exchequer of time. We know men whose lives are a burden to themselves and a distressing burden to their relatives and friends simply because they have failed to appreciate the obvious. *"Oh, no",* I have heard the martyred wife exclaim, *"Arthur always takes the dog out for exercise at 8:00 p.m. and he always begins to read at a quarter to nine. So it's quite out of the question that we should..." etc., etc.* The note of absolute finality in that plaintive voice reveals the unsuspected and ridiculous tragedy of a career. Don't develop a policy of rush, of being gradually more and more obsessed by what you have to do next. In this way, you may come to exist as in a prison and your life may cease to be your own. There are people who come to like a constant breathless hurry of endeavor. Of them it may be said, that a constant breathless hurry is better than an eternal doze.

Always strive to be better than you are. You must surpass yourself. You are what you are now but in an hour you must be more than you are now. We are architects of the minutes. We build ourselves every moment. What you are this minute is the result of what you were building during the thousands of minutes that have already passed in your life. What you will be in a minute from now depends upon what you are now, plus what you are mentally demanding that this present moment shall add. With every turn around of the clock's second hand you are building yourself anew, are you changing, altering, revising, remaking, increasing? You are the product of minutes. Each minute is an opportunity to build for growth, advance, gain, supremacy and conquest. It all rests with you.

Keep your eyes on the minutes.

"Lost: somewhere between sunrise and sunset, two golden hours, each set with sixty diamond minutes. No rewards are offered, for they are gone forever."
-Horace Mann

Looking at time is like trying to see air

the world
stands
aside to
let those
pass who
know where
they are going.

Self-Management is the Key

Self-Management or Time-Management is not a hard subject to understand. But unless you are committed to building Time-Management techniques into your daily routine you'll only achieve partial (or no) results and then make comments such as *"I tried time-management once and it doesn't work for me"*. Unfortunately the term *Time-Management* creates a false impression of what a person is able to do. Time can't be managed, time is uncontrollable we can only manage ourselves and our use of time. Time-Management is actually Self-Management. It's interesting that the skills you need to manage others are the same skills you need to manage yourself: the ability to plan, delegate, organize, direct and control.

Be a Serious Student of Self-Management

Self-Management is important to those who want to accomplish something in life. You can ignore the subject of Self-Management and that is a valid approach. But, why not be a student of Self-Management and design your personal life? So many people plan their vacation in detail and yet leave their life time to drift along.

Humans are the only creatures on earth who have multiple choices. You can be sure of one thing; four years from now you will be four years older. *Will you just let the time slip by? Or will you focus on each hour, each day and each week and make the most of it? And what is the best way to measure time?* You will know because you manage your time with a written plan and you know the exact role time plays toward accomplishing your goals and the design of the rest of your life.

The idea is to get more from yourself so you can accomplish in an hour what used to take you a week. The big challenge is to get control of your time. It is so very easy to be distracted by things that take up or waste time but do not help in accomplishing your goals. It's not the hours you put in to what you wish to accomplish but what you put into the hours that count. Don't mistake movement for achievement or activity for results.

A rocking horse and a rocking chair both move but never get anywhere.

TIME SPENT DEBATING THE IMPOSSIBLE SUBTRACTS FROM THE TIME DURING WHICH YOU CAN TRY TO ACCOMPLISH IT.

26 Strategies to Increase Your Self-Management

Keep in mind that your goal is to increase your self-management. These are the best ways to achieve this:

1. **Always define your objectives as clearly as possible:** Do you find you are not doing what you want because your goals have not been set? One of the factors which mark successful people is their ability to work out what they want to achieve and have written goals which they can review constantly.

2. **Analyze your use of time:** Are you spending enough time on the projects, which although may not be urgent now, are the things you need to do to develop yourself or your career? If you are constantly asking yourself, *"What is the most important use of my time, right now?"*, it will help you to focus on *important tasks* and stop reacting to tasks which seem urgent (or pleasant to do) but carry no importance toward your goals.

3. **Have a plan:** How can you achieve your goals without a plan? Most people know what they want but have no plan to achieve it except by sheer hard work. Your yearly plan should be reviewed daily and reset as your achievements are met. Successful people make lists constantly. It enables them to stay on top of priorities and enables them to remain flexible to changing priorities. This should be done for both personal and business goals.

4. **Action plan analysis:** Challenges will always occur, the value of a good plan is to identify them early and seek out solutions.

5. **Quit *Trying*:** You've claimed that you've tried and tried to do this or that. Take *"try"* out of your vocabulary and take the steps to do what you need to do. Once you set goals for yourself, you'll be very clear on what you should spend your time doing.

> *"There is no try..."*
> -Yoda

6. **Decide to decide:** Get to work on spending your time better and be more productive.

7. **Get determined:** Chance favors only the prepared mind. Decide what you want, decide what you are willing to exchange for it. Establish your priorities and go to work. Each indecision brings its own delays and days are lost lamenting over lost days...What you can do or think you can do; begin it. For boldness has magic, power and genius in it. Even if you are on the right track, you will get run over if you just sit there. Few people have any next, they live from hand to mouth without a plan and are always at the end of their line.

> "If you want a thing bad enough
> To go out and fight for it,
> Work day and night for it,
> Give up your time and your peace
> and your sleep for it,
> If only desire of it makes you quite mad
> enough never to tire of it, makes you hold
> all other things tawdry and cheap for it,
> If life seems all empty and useless
> without it and all that you scheme
> and you dream is about it,
> If gladly you'll sweat for it,
> Fret for it, plan for it,
> Lose all your terror of God or man for it,
> If you'll simply go after that
> thing that you want with all your capacity,
> Strength and sagacity, faith, hope and
> confidence, stern pertinacity,
> If neither cold, poverty, famished and gaunt
> Nor sickness nor pain of body and brain
> Can turn you away from the thing
> that you want, if dogged and grim you
> besiege and beset it, you'll get it."
> -Berton Bradley

it's easier to build boys than to mend men

8. **Get a sense of urgency:** It is time for us all to stand and cheer for the doer, the achiever. So many people are not willing to even get started. Time is marching forth. What you do today will pay off the rest of your life...your life will bring you grand results if you get going on achieving your goals. It's about time.

9. **Get a philosophy:** Lead me, follow me or get out of my way.

10. **Make time:** You don't find time for important things, you make it. If you haven't got time to do it right, you don't have time to do it wrong.

11. **Learn to cut time short:** *"I'm in the middle of something now..."* Start with *"I only have 5 minutes."* - you can always extend this. Stand up, head to a door, compliment, thank, shake hands. Look at your watch.

12. **Quit wasting other people's time:** Ask yourself...*What do I do that wastes others' time? Are you hanging on the phone for way too long? Do you need to tell your sales field to pick up sales? Can you increase your own value during the time that you are wasting others' time?*

13. **Meetings:** Most meetings are a waste of time. Always ask for an agenda prior to the meeting. Make sure that when the meeting starts you are not interrupted. Turn off cell phones. Most people can focus for twenty minutes before they need a break. Remember that people digest information differently in rnonochronic and polychronic time. Have someone take notes. Don't agree to doing something and then forget it because you didn't jot it down. Decide who is responsible for what, by when. Always announce the next meeting. Studies have shown that the average manager spends about 17 hours a week in meetings, about six hours in the planning time and untold hours in the follow up. It is widely acknowledged that about as much as a third of the time spent in meetings is wasted due to poor meeting management and lack of planning.

14. **Laptop computer:** You can scavenge time and work anywhere.

15. **Only touch a piece of paper once:** Read it, file it, or toss it.

16. **E-Mail Tips:** Save all of it; no exceptions, except for spam. Get a great spam blocker. You cannot E-mail passion or excitement. If you want somebody to do something, make them the only recipient, otherwise, you have diffusion of responsibility. Give a concrete request/task and a deadline. If you really want somebody to do something, CC someone powerful.

17. **Calendar:** Get a day timer or PDA. Write things down. When is our next meeting? What's my goal to have done by then? Who to turn to for help?

18. **Shifting priorities and crisis management:** Peter Drucker says that *"crisis management is actually the form of management preferred by most managers"*. The irony is that actions taken prior to the crisis could have prevented the crisis in the first place.

19. **The telephone:** The telephone-our greatest communication tool can be our biggest enemy to effectiveness if you don't know how to control its hold over you. I suggest you read Make That Call available at www.janruhe.com.

20. **Don't have a lack of purpose priorities/objectives:** This is probably the biggest, most important time stealer. It affects all you do, both professionally and personally. **Those who accomplish the most in a day know exactly what they want to accomplish.** Unfortunately too many think that goals and objectives are yearly things and not dai-

ly considerations. This results in too much time spent on the minor things and not on the things which are important to our work/lives. Keep your focus on the main thing.

21. **Don't attempt too much:** Many people today feel that they have to accomplish everything yesterday and don't give themselves enough time to do things properly. This leads only to half finished projects and no feeling of achievement.

22. **Drop in visitors:** The five deadliest words that rob your time are *"Have you got a minute?"* Everyone's the culprit-friends, children, spouses, colleagues, the boss, the coach, or your peers. Knowing how to deal with interruptions is one of the best skills you can learn.

Sign for your office:

If you have nothing else to do, don't do it here!

23. **Arguing, debating, correcting, criticizing:** When you get your weight where you want it, your hair like you want it, your skincare like you want it, your bills paid, your credit cards paid off, the car you want to drive, your home in order, your children's behavior in order, THEN you can criticize others. Arguing, debating, and correcting are a huge waste of life time. Ask yourself: Who made you the judge and jury? Who made you the coach, the Monday morning quarterback? King? Queen? Who made you in control of others? Don't stay up all night arguing with your teenager, you need your rest. Teenagers will rage on and on wanting

you to *"hear them"*. Remember that you are the parent, they are the child. Tell them you will resume the debate in the morning if necessary but that you need your rest. Anger is one letter short of danger. The greatest remedy for anger is delay.

When looking for faults use a mirror, not a telescope

24. **Field Trips, Working in the lunchroom, Home Room Mothers, Scout Leaders:** Your children will not remember if you were one of these. When you take on these leadership roles or support roles, you are choosing to put your time there. You are actually not doing it for the children...you are doing it to give yourself some feeling that you require. If you are going for your dreams and goals, there are many other people who will take over these time taking roles in life.

25. **Get passionate:** Fall in love with what you are doing and you will find that time will fly. If you are miserable in how you are spending your time you will live a life of regrets. We only have this one life to live, stop hating your life. Do what you can to be passionate about. You will never regret spending time doing that which brings you joy and happiness.

26. **Vacations:** Phone callers should get two options: *"If this can't wait, contact Suzie Creamcheese at 555-1212 otherwise, please call back June 1."* This works for E-mail too! Vacations should be vacation, it's not a vacation if you're reading E-mail. Turn off your television (How badly do you want to use your time wisely?) Eat, sleep and exercise.

> *"Why should you be content with so little? Why shouldn't you reach out for something big?"*
> -Charles L. Allen

The Daffodil Principle

Several times my daughter, Julie, had phoned to say, *"Mom, you must come see the daffodils before they are over"*. It was a long drive from my place to her mountain home. *"I will come next Tuesday"*, I promised. Tuesday dawned cold and rainy as I got in the car and began the long drive. When I walked into Julie's home and hugged and greeted my grandchildren, I said, *"Forget the daffodils, Julie! The road is invisible in the fog!* My daughter smiled, *"We drive in this all the time, Mom"*. *"Well, you won't get me back on the road until it clears!"* I said. *" Mom, I was hoping you'd take me over to the garage to pick up my car"*, Julie said. *"How far will we have to drive?"* *"Just a few blocks, I'll drive ... I'm used to this."* After a few minutes, I asked *"Where are we going? This isn't the way to the garage!"* *"We're going to the garage the long way...by way of the daffodils."* *"Julie"*. I said, *"please turn around"*. *"It's all right, Mom, I promise, you will never forgive yourself if you miss this experience."* Soon we turned onto a gravel road and I saw a church. On the far side of the church I saw a sign...

Daffodil Garden.

We got out of the car and each took a child's hand and I followed Julie down the path. As we turned a corner of the path I looked up and gasped. Before me lay the most glorious sight. The flowers were planted in majestic, swirling patterns, great ribbons and swaths of deep orange, white, lemon yellow, salmon pink, saffron and butter yellow. Five acres of the most beautiful flowers I had ever seen! *"Who planted all these?"* I asked Julie. *"It's just one woman"*, Julie answered, *"She lives on the property. That's her home"* and she pointed to a modest home in the midst of all that glory. We walked up to the house and on the patio we saw a poster ...

Answers to the Questions I Know You Are Asking
50,000 bulbs
one at a time
by one woman
2 hands, 2 feet
and very little brain
Began in 1958

There it was...*"The Daffodil Principle"* That moment was a life-changing experience. I thought of this woman, who, more than 35 years before, had begun one bulb at a time-to bring her vision of beauty and joy to an obscure mountain top. She had forever changed the world in which she lived by creating something of magnificent beauty and inspiration. The principle her daffodil garden taught is one of the greatest principles of time: learning to move toward our goals and desires one step at a time, (often just one baby-step at a time) learning to love the doing, learning to use the accumulation of time. When we multiply tiny pieces of time with small increments of daily effort, we too will find we can accomplish magnificent things. *"It makes me sad in a way"*, I said to Julie, *"What might I have accomplished if I had thought of a wonderful goal 35 years ago and had worked away at it 'one bulb at a time' through all those years. Just think what I might have been able to achieve!"* Julie said, *"Start tomorrow, Mom. It's so pointless to think of the lost hours of our yesterdays. The way to make learning a lesson, a celebration instead of a cause for regret, is to only ask...How can I put this to use today?"*

-Jaroldeen Asplund Edwards

chapter 1

**In this Chapter
you will learn about:**

- Personal Time Foundation
- Leaving a Legacy
- Dump the Slump
- Do Not Panic
- Priorities

Chapter One

Personal Time Foundation

Imagine if you could wake up every morning excited about the prospects of the day? What if you no longer found yourself just handling life's challenges but actively creating a fulfilling and ideal life? What if you no longer reacted to small annoying things or to large pressing conflicts? What if your relationships, with yourself and others were as fulfilling as you hoped they could be in your life?

If it is your goal to use your lifetime to improve your ability to coach others, significantly increase your income, deepen your relationships with friends and family and more, then study and learn the art of *Personal Foundation*. When you do you will increase your self confidence and expand your ability to become more open and more able to attract great people into your business.

Just when you think you have learned it all, you will realize there is more to learn and such a short time in life to learn all the lessons you want to learn. Review these lessons on an annual basis as you continue to raise the bar on the quality of your life and work. When you work on your *Personal Foundation* you want more value from your time on earth because you want to contribute more and you understand that you will grow from being connected more in life.

i AM GOING TO GAiN BACK MY LiFE TiME. STARTiNG TODAY!

"Ya gotta do what ya gotta do."
-Sylvester Stallone in the movie Rocky IV, 1985

"The penalty of using your time wisely and becoming successful is to he bored by the people who used to snub you."
-Lady Astor (1897-1964)

It's my life and I am going to prove it!

What is Personal Foundation?

Personal Foundation is your structural base to support you in living an exceptional life. Just like a house being built, the foundation of your life must be strong so your life doesn't collapse. Your *Personal Foundation* is composed of three elements, the body, spirit and mind or *the What, the Who* and *the How*. If things aren't working at home, they probably are not working professionally. If you are experiencing professional challenges, there most likely exist personal challenges as well.

Personal Foundation Work is the Right Place to Start

Beginning at the foundation will certainly end a lot of start and stops that you might have encountered in wasting time previously on your path of self-development. Maybe this is the book that will open your eyes to an opportunity to deepen your core of who you are. You are free to make the choices that lead to personal fulfillment that comes from aligning your actions and your time with your pride, passion and purpose. When you move forward with a strong foundation, many of the challenges that you have had can now be prevented or entirely eliminated. It's time to focus fully on using your unique gifts, talents, strengths and wisdom. It's time to restore yourself, heal from past experiences and start getting your *Personal Foundation* stronger.

Raise your standards of how you use your time until you feel terrific!

Leave a Legacy-Pay It Forward

When you have a strong foundation, you will ultimately leave a legacy. Everyone is on a unique path and personal timetable in personal growth. Building a strong *Personal Foundation* is not created overnight, it takes time and energy, but it is about time. Many of the changes that it is time to make you have been living with for a very long time. No one makes it alone. You may be by yourself when you achieve something but look behind you to see the people who have made your success possible: parents, coaches, friends and fans. They have given you so much and they ask for so little in return. You can leave them with memories of a true champion who cared enough for what he did with his time to give something back. People will soon forget the records you create. What they will remember is the way you hustled, the poise you had under pressure and the class you showed. You can never fully pay back those who have helped you. What you can do is follow their example and help others get started. Take your knowledge, experience and enthusiasm and share it with others. Teach them everything you were taught about achieving that which you spent your time on in life. Teach them about class. Teach them how to overcome adversity and criticism. A few words of wisdom to someone eager to be a success might make their road to the top a bit easier. You may help someone you don't even know to solve or even avoid some challenges. Reach out to as many people as you can. Your impact on others can be significant. When you touch their lives this way, you will never go to bed discouraged, be depressed or worry about getting old. The way you feel inside about the people you have helped and about yourself is a huge payoff. By helping others you also help yourself. As others grow emotionally, physically and spiritually, so will you. There isn't any amount of money that can replace the pure self satisfaction of knowing that your love, your time and your inner strength have helped someone else on their path in life. If you really enjoy what you are doing, you will enjoy teaching it to others. One of the greatest thrills in life is working with people, watching them improve and knowing that you played a significant part in their growth and success. Have a feeling of leaving something behind, pay it forward. What a better way than by passing your knowledge on to those coming up behind you. Help others live their dream just as you lived yours. This is the stuff that dreams are made of. Leave a great deal of generosity and tenderness when your life is concluded.

Integrity first, needs second, wants third.

It's Time to Grow

If you are not where you want to be in life, if you want more, you know that it is time to make certain changes in your life in order to get more of what you really want...then *it's about time* that you accelerate your time to maximize the rest of your life on earth. Become very focused on yourself to internalize the changes that you must make to take yourself from where you are today to where you want to be.

You will accomplish more, more easily when you take the time to work on strengthening your *Personal Foundation*. Progress naturally. No need to completely stop what you are doing in life; just start paying attention to adding in ideas to help you build your foundation stronger than ever before.

Who doesn't want to accomplish more with their time? Don't you want more time to enjoy a life filled with prosperity and abundance? Don't you want more money? More love? More personal satisfaction? Most people search for all of this instead of attracting it.

"It's the iron will to do it and the steady sticking to it. So whatever your task, go to it. And life's purpose you will win."
-Unknown

The next six months, watch my smoke!

OUT OF CONTROL? START CONTROLLING WHAT YOU CAN!

If it weren't for the last minute, nothing would get done!

Build a Solid Foundation

A strong *Personal Foundation* includes 10 stepping stones that link together to provide a solid, personalized foundation on which to spend your time. And a way to naturally attract every single thing you want. You don't want your life built on quick sand nor shifting sand. A skyscraper doesn't start at the street level. The taller the building, the deeper the foundation. This is true for people, too. You want a solid, dependable, stable, secure foundation. *Are you ready?* Will you take the time to make building your *Personal Foundation* a priority? What do you need to remove from your schedule or sacrifice in order to take time to make changes in your life?

The 10 Stepping Stones of Personal Foundation

1. A past that is complete and over.
2. A life that is based fully on who you are.
3. Your needs identified and met.
4. Boundaries that you set and adhere to.
5. Standards that let you be the best you can be.
6. Not settling.
7. A choice to spend your time in a positive place.
8. A family, team or group to nurture you.
9. A community where you are safe to develop your talents.
10. A life that includes your values.

Start attracting instead of striving

Day by day, it's something new!

7 Tips to a Strong Foundation

The following information includes some tips for developing yourself.

1. **A *Personal Foundation* is an investment in your personal infrastructure:** To grow in life, you want to be anchored in personal growth, studying and moving forward.
2. **Major changes will happen during this process:** Starting now you want to tell and live the truth and not feel guilty about putting yourself first. You want to start now re-prioritizing how you spend your time. You will want to warn people around you that you are going to be smarter in how you spend your time.
3. **It's okay to complain as long as you are working:** Do your very best to get in control of your time. You can complain but only if you are making every effort to change, grow and prosper.
4. **Get over the *"So far"* mentality:** When making changes, don't attach the *"So far; so good"* mentality. Don't rush making huge changes with your time, but keep going steadily. Make sure whatever you are choosing to do does not crumble. Faith that fizzles was faulty from the first. Get in control of your time even though that means you might make mistakes. Use your own plan to get in control of your time, not anyone else's.
5. **Focus on The 10 Stepping Stones daily:** Set aside time each week to go over the stepping stones to see how you are doing.
6. **Don't settle:** You will know you are getting stronger when you stop putting up with things you have been tolerating. Get away from the people who drain, disturb, diminish and destroy you. Don't put up with silly, immature behavior that wastes your time. You will find yourself growing and making changes on how you use your time.
7. **Your environment matters:** Get rid of the clutter. Less is more. Get organized. Throw out what you don't need. The environment which energizes and invites one side of the brain seems to tire and frustrate the other side of the brain and the reverse is also true.

The What

The *What* is how the world sees you when it looks at how you spend or have spent your time. It is your behavior, your public self and what you show others.

The Who

This is the part of you *who* is easily understood, the real you, the core of *who* you are when you are by yourself and with those who know and understand you. This is your spirit, it is *who* you are when you leave a room.

The How

This is the process and values that drive your behavior, it's *how* you spend your time and it's *how* you go about your life every day, every moment.

What is *Personal Growth?*

Personal growth is the overall process of becoming the person you wish to be to express your values and purpose in life.

What is *Integrity?*

Integrity is who you are in any moment and it is the important relationship that you maintain between purpose and path. You want to be vigilant in working to be better, to develop yourself to be the best you can be to your calling in life. It is not something to achieve, but rather a state of being.

What are *Needs?*

Needs are the emotional part of you that drives you to do what you do. Your needs direct major life decisions and you will not stop until they are met. Everyone needs air, food, water, shelter and certainty.

What is *Attraction?*

The Law of Attraction is that you will attract that which you wish to become. You will be drawn to it and it to you.

What are *Wants?*

Wanting something means you desire it or wish for it. You will not necessarily spend time getting it. They are optional. If you get it great, if not, great. If you want something badly enough, you will spend time on working to get it.

What are *Goals?*

Goals are dreams with a deadline. Goals can be simple or very complex. It is what you will spend time working to achieve which turn out to be your goals.

What are *Priorities?*

A priority is something that you place your time and attention on above all else.

What is *Discernment?*

You are able to recognize good and bad, happy and sad, right and wrong, timely or untimely, truth and lies, truth or false.

What is *Vision?*

Vision is something you can see before it happens. It includes anticipation, perception, conception and desire. You can close your eyes and see it clearly. It is a scene of something happening in the future.

What are *Shifts?*

Shifts happen in life. You realize that what you are doing with your time is not working and you had better do something else with your time. It can take years to make a shift or it can happen suddenly. You can tell when someone goes into a shift in life because of their results or their behavior.

Shifts Happen

*I am sick and tired of my results,
it's about time I take control of my time.*

What is *Strategy?*

A strategy is a way or plan of how you are going to achieve your goal. It really is how you are planning on using your time to achieve your goals.

What is a *Leap?*

A leap is what happens when you decide to take your time to take off from where you are right now to where you know you want to be. A leap is sudden and quick in personal growth. You decide to read and feed your mind. You become a student of what you are interested in learning. You begin to study and build your own library. You cannot quench your thirst for knowledge. You quit making excuses and you leap into the future, you are sick and tired of being sick and tired.

What is *Motivation?*

Motivation comes only from within. You cannot motivate anyone to do anything. You can get inspired and then motivated but you must motivate yourself. Once you are motivated you go into massive action. You stay motivated for as long as it takes. You become unstoppable and you get an attitude of stick-to-it for as long as it takes. You become results oriented. You cannot stop until you reach your goal. Real motivation is lasting. You don't start and stop.

What is *Forgiveness?*

You don't have to forget what someone did to you or how they made you feel but your time on earth is better served to forgive them and move on. In fact, as time goes by, you will probably thank those who hurt you because whatever they did to you, you became a stronger person. I have never found that you can forgive *and* forget. But I am clear on the forgiveness part. Let go. Let *karma* get those who have hurt you. *Karma* will get them. Count on it.

> *"Whatever does not destroy me makes me stronger."*
> -Friedrich Wilhelm Nietzsche

What is *Focus?*

Focus is what you spend time doing. You get exactly what you focus on. Nothing less, nothing more *So, why are you not focused on what you truly want?* Because you just don't think you want it bad enough! That's fine but don't get all upset when you are not at the point that you would like to be in your life. Don't complain to others that you wish things were different for you and don't sit around feeling sorry for yourself. In the end it is you who makes the choices that you make with the time in your life and it is you who must live with the consequences of your decisions. So if you want things to change then you simply must find that drive from within you (trust me it is in there somewhere) and release it from its cage.

Consider the following hypothetical scenario: A messenger from the future has come to warn you that you will die within 30 days if you do not accomplish a specific goal. How would this situation effect you and what would you do? The answer is simple. You would do everything and just about anything you had to do in order to achieve your goal. Think about this. When faced with the appropriate challenge you are able to find the passion and burning drive to reach your goal which means that we all have it within us all the time! We just don't choose to tap into it. This just goes to show you that if you want something bad enough you will do what it takes to get it. Take this opportunity to ask yourself...Do I want what I want badly enough? If you are not where you want to be in your life then you know what the answer to the question is.

Don't let anyone or any person or situation distract you from achieving your goal.

What is *Avoidance?*

You know what you need to spend time doing. You even know exactly when you should do it. When you learn about procrastination, better self-image, how to be a self-starter and those things you don't have time for, you will realize that you DO have time for them, you have just been avoiding doing what you need to do.

What are *Strengths?*

Strengths are a source of personal power, a collection of attributes and the part of you that excels at doing.

What is *Toleration?*

To tolerate means to permit or endure something or to put up with something which distracts you from your focus. It might be something you cannot stand and it drains your core of your being. It might be a huge time waster in life that is less than ideal. You want to be aware of what you are tolerating. Do not settle in life. You do not have to tolerate where you are in life, your life time is something you and you alone own. Be careful of who influences you.

Zap the tolerations: Remove that which is limiting your growth in life. Every toleration is worth fixing. As you fix each one, you will lighten up and free up more time to achieve your goals. You have better things to do than tolerate. Stop trying to manage situations that drain your energy and really do not be a part of how you spend your time. The sooner you let go of what you are tolerating the less distracted you will be. You don't have to put up with what is not useful to you. You are stunting your future by tolerating what is annoying you.

Why do I have tolerations in my life?
How do they really work for me?
Are they draining a lot of time out of my life?

What are *Values?*

Values are what is important to what you spend your time doing. People act congruent with their personal values or what they deem to be important. It is your meaning in life which propels you in everything you do which promotes well-being or prevents harm. Everyone has them. They are specific and individual, however, people can share different values. Values are our guidelines for what is acceptable. They are emotional beliefs in principles regarded as particularly favorable or important for you. Values are the scales we use to weigh our choices for our actions, whether to move towards or away from something. Our values associate emotions to our experiences to guide our choices, decisions and actions. William James, identified that *"When the will and the emotions are in conflict, the emotions most often win"*. Consequently, a person's actions rarely conflict with their values and distress is felt when they do conflict. A person's observations of their environment are filtered through their values to determine whether or not they should expend energy to do something about their experiences. A person that values gold and sees a large pot of gold (a positive value) in their path as they walk will be motivated to reach down and pick it up. A person that values their life and knows about venomous snakes will retreat from the sound of a rattlesnake (a negative value) nearby when they are walking in the desert.

Not all values have the same weight or priority. Some are more important than others and must be satisfied before others can be addressed. Survival has a higher priority than security, which has a higher priority than social acceptance. Self-esteem can only be addressed to the degree that social acceptance is fulfilled. Similarly, self-actualization can only be pursued to the degree that self-esteem has been satisfied.

My way, all the way

Never let life become an ongoing emergency.

"While serving as chaplain at the U.S. Naval Academy, I remember a young man who came to my office wanting to resign. He had been there about two weeks. "I can't take 300 days of this", he said. I asked him whether he could stand it until tomorrow. He said he could and I told him to come back to see me. The next day I asked him if he could stand it for one more day, explaining to him that he doesn't have to handle all 300 days at once. Only one day at a time. He got the point and got through it, all 300 days of it, one day at a time."
-The Reverend Chuck Greenwood
Captain (Chaplain), U.S. Navy Retired

"You don't want a million answers as much as you want a few forever questions. The questions are diamonds you hold in the light. Study a lifetime and you will see different colors from the same jewel."
-Richard Bach, <u>Running from Safety</u>

The future is something which everyone reaches at the rate of sixty minutes an hour, whatever he does, whoever they are.

Purge from your thinking all notion of the **good old days.** If you think there were greater opportunities in the times past, you will find it difficult to recognize the opportunities before you now. These are the **good old days,** if you take the time to make them so.

Mankind has a far greater need to be reminded than informed.

"He who stops being better stops being good."
-Oliver Cromwell

God doesn't call the equipped, he equips the called.

Think of change as life's number one inevitability and number one opportunity.

I NEVER SEE FAILURE AS FAILURE, ONLY AS A LEARNING OPPORTUNITY.

Never let a day go by without enthusiastically celebrating something.

WE ARE NOT HUMAN BEINGS HAVING A SPIRITUAL EXPERIENCE. WE ARE SPIRITUAL BEINGS HAVING A HUMAN EXPERIENCE.

"If you succeed in life, you must do it in spite of the efforts of others to pull you down. There is nothing in the idea that people are willing to help those who help themselves. People are willing to help a man who can't help himself, but as soon as a man is able to help himself, they join in making his life as uncomfortable as possible."
-Edgar W. Howe

"Twenty years from now you will be more disappointed by the things that you didn't do, than by the ones that you did do. So throw off the bowlines. Sail away from the safe harbor Catch the trade winds. Explore, Dream, Discover."
-Mark Twain

Allow Yourself a YAWN

Since yawning has a bad reputation, you may want to wait until no one else is around. But yawning **FEELS GREAT.** It relieves tension, fatigue and boredom. Just open your mouth wide and yawn. Stretch your arms over your head. After the first few your yawns will roll out more easily.

Dim the Lights

Bright lighting is important in the office, but soft lighting enhances relaxation in the bedroom or meditation space. Use dimmer switches to decrease energy use and soothe your mood.

Walk in the Mountains, on the Beach or in the Woods

A walk in the mountains will provide you with a cardiovascular boost and satisfy you visually. So put on some sturdy boots and grab your day pack to benefit from this great stress reliever.

Candle Meditation

Sit in a comfortable place. Light a candle on a small table in front of you at eye level. Take a couple of deep breaths. Let the tension flow out of your body. With your eyes half open, gaze at the candle flame. Let the candle have all of your attention. When your mind wanders, gently return to watching the flame. After five minutes, close your eyes and look at the images behind your eyelids. Slowly count to 20 and open your eyes.

Weekend Warrior Syndrome

Beware the ways of the *weekend warrior.* Extra chores and active sports on those couple of days off often result in the pains of over exertion. **SOOTHE** away muscle soreness with homeopathic arnica gel found in health food stores and natural pharmacies. Always have a tube of aloe vera jelly in your home for any minor cuts or burns.

Dump the Slump

If you are in a slump, you are probably experiencing: **Poor self-esteem.** Before you can begin to improve your self-esteem you must first believe that you can change it. Change doesn't necessarily happen quickly or easily, but it can happen. You are not powerless! Once you have accepted, or are at least willing to entertain the possibility that you are not powerless, there are three steps you can take to begin to change your self-esteem:

Step 1: Rebut the Inner Critic
Step 2: Practice Self-Nurturing
Step 3: Get Help from Others

Poor Work Habits: People do not want to be or need to be educated about what you know. They want answers to how you can improve their life. They do not want solutions. They want answers. They do not want to take their time to hear about you. If they give you time, it better be about them. Which do you think is more important to others... what you did 30 years ago or answers to the challenges in their current life? **Not sold on what you are doing:** So many people are unfulfilled in what they spend time doing. Stop right now and decide if you are happy with your current situation, if not CHANGE IT.

Peer pressure or family pressure: It's really hard to want to do something with your time when the people you love the most ridicule you, laugh or tease you. Most of the time when people don't want you to do that which you wish to do they are scared that they will lose you, or that you will change, or that you will not need them in your life anymore. Or they think they know what is best for you. However, if you know what you want to do, do not let anyone kill your dream.

Poor personal habits: It is up to you to change your habits. Life is ticking by.

Too much pressure from a boss: If you are in a job where you are getting a lot of pressure, stop and ask yourself if this is really how you want to spend your time. Some people have the temperament to thrive on pressure. Pressure is not good for the human body. Think carefully if you should stay in that job. Even if you are making a fortune, if you are miserable, get out.

Events that happen that discourage you: Everyone has setbacks. Make setbacks pave the way for great comebacks. If your heart has been broken, give love a chance. If you have been fired, be thankful for that because now you can do something else with your time. If you have gone through a painful divorce, another love awaits you. If you have lost a big order or someone has hurt you or criticized you, spray yourself off with invisible Teflon and carry on. The clock is ticking.

Losing a Loved One: This is one of the hardest parts of life. Losing those we cherish, saying goodbye to those who are so very important to us. Go through the stages of grief but don't stay in each stage too long. Life is for the living. Hold on to the precious memories, think of those you have lost to death as your guardian angels.

Turn off the TV: How many people achieve their dreams only watching TV? TV can waste a lot of your lifetime. Turn it off.

Depression: There are times in life when depression hits. Everything is going wrong. Try everything you can BUT medication. The side effects of some medicine is worse than the cure. Be careful running to drugs and alcohol to help you through your trying times. Instead, try self-talk. Dump the slump.

Blaming: Stop blaming other people for your lack of success. How you use your time is your choice.

PLAN YOUR WORK, WORK YOUR PLAN

Time cannot be managed, but what can be managed are our activities and how we "spend" time. By knowing what is important for us, planning our work and working our plan, we become wise self-managers.

"A rich world of wonder awaits."
-Carl Sagan

The Big Aha Clue

If you want something badly enough and are willing to ardently desire it and work for it day and night, it must ultimately come to pass. You will change everything you need to change to attract the person of your dreams, to create success, to see the world or whatever you really want. Take time to dream.

Why Are so Many People Lazy?

Why won't most people put forth the effort to get from where they are to where they want to be? Because most people float through life believing that the government owes them, you owe them, their spouse owes them, they deserve more for working less and they blame and make excuses.

You Become What You Think About

If that is true, why are you waiting and letting time pass to get what you want in life? What are you thinking about? Perhaps you need to change your thinking now.

We live in a world of negative thinking and conditioning. The big three things that motivate everyone are: greed, fear and vanity.

YOU CAN EITHER LEARN FROM FAILURE OR IGNORE IT.

Do Not Panic

When things go badly in your life and you find yourself in a slump it is not the time to panic. It is just a big clue in your life that you must fix it. Once you accept the fact that you **can change your situation** you can begin to recover. Believe in the most important person in the entire world. You. Here is how:

1. **Go back to basics:** Uncomplicate the slump. Then take action. Start over. It's always too soon to quit.

2. **Make a new plan for success:** Don't ignore that you are in a slump. Identify it and then figure out what you need to do to change your circumstances.

3. **Master your presentation:** Get the Master Presentation Guide at www.janruhe.com for great ideas.

4. **Get clear what YOU need to do to change:** If you are sending out brochures about YOU, forget it, they are being thrown away. Change what you send out to include information on how they can profit, produce more or succeed in what THEY want to achieve in life. They will devour every word.

5. **Get a mentor:** You don't have to even be in touch with your mentor on a regular basis. Learn everything you can from them. Find someone you admire who is living the life that you want and learn every single thing you can from them.

6. **Give your customers what they want:** More sales, increased productivity, increased profit, better image, more clients, loyal workers, increased happiness, morale, less hassle, more free time, better science, notoriety, safety, use value, more vacation time, better health, smarter children, security. People buy with their emotions and then justify with logic. The heart is attached to the wallet.

7. **Stay away from the black clouds:** Truly stay away from those who gossip or who drain you. They are a colossal waste of time. Ignore idiots and zealots: Don't let anyone rain on your parade by discouraging you...just remember that they don't have a parade that anyone can rain on. Get away from them, far away and stay away from them. Don't be a part of a rain cloud of negative people. There are a lot of jealous people in the world and you must ignore them.

8. **Realize that you are probably joy starved.** Bring more joy into your life.

9. **Spend at least 30 minutes reading positive attitude books:** Listen to attitude CD's and have a positive attitude book in every room you go into during the day. Read something positive every day.

10. **Sing:** Singing is so good for the soul. It doesn't matter if you can carry a tune. Sing. The birds always chirp and sing after the rain.

11. **Decrease clutter:** Get some large sacks and throw away everything that is not beautiful or meaningful or useful to you. Create a vacuum and replace the tacky old things with only those things that you love.

12. **Video your presentation or put your presentation on CD and listen to it:** Although, when you are in a slump it is hard to watch yourself or listen to yourself, it will help you realize that you need to change the direction in the course you are going. Your slump might be something finite that you can change by listening or watching yourself.

13. **Spend time with someone who has achieved that which you wish to achieve:** Did you know that your income is the average of the five people you spend time with the most.

14. **Ask for help. Don't give up:** There is absolutely nothing wrong with asking for help. But ask a professional. Don't take advice from someone more messed up than you are.

15. **Get fired or get fired up:** In life, enthusiasm pays the most, magnetizes abundance and prosperity. If you are not fired up in life, change direction now.

16. **Don't focus on selling someone something:** Price lasts for a moment, profit and value can last for a life-time. Sell the benefits...the money will follow.

Your life is either a warning or a message...
it's up to you how you spend your time.

Quit Whining

Don't whine that your boss is difficult, get a new boss. Don't complain that your children are at a difficult age, what age ISN'T difficult? Don't whine that you can't make calls, read <u>Make That Call</u> and learn some scripts. Don't whine that your spouse is not supportive. If your spouse sees you succeeding your spouse will change their tune. Don't whine that you don't have a car or a computer, get busy in life working for that which you need to take you to the next level.

> *"How beautiful it is to do nothing and rest afterwards."*
> -Spanish Proverb

The 6 Reactions to Failure

1. Curse it. Get mad about it.
2. Deny it.
3. Avoid it.
4. Make an excuse about it.
5. Blame others or the economy or government.
6. Quit. The only way to fail in using your lifetime is to give up or quit. When and if you get to the quit stage do the following: Look at the failure as an event, not a person. Look for why something happened and review it calmly. List possibilities. Discover what you learned from the experience. Say *"Oh well..."* and move on. Say, *"Some will, some won't, so what...next...someone is waiting"*. Don't mope around with others who have failed. Ever. Change your environment. Get away from negative family members and friends. Seek out positive people.

> Change *"I failed"*, for
> *"I learned what never to do again."*

It's Okay to Make Mistakes

Learn from your failures. Look at failure as a valuable learning experience. You can see the glass as half-full rather than half-empty. Perspective is a habit. Tweak your long-standing negative patterns.

People with optimistic outlooks live longer and healthier lives than do pessimists.

The Key to a Better Life

"Man or woman...wherever these words have found you, turn away from your travail and struggles of the hour and give me your hand. Come with me on a mission of exploration, a journey of the mind that may help you to change your life for the better. We are not, you and I, searching for gold or silver or oil but for something far more valuable, a key, a simple key that will unlock our prison door and free us from our hell of unhappiness, insecurity and failure so that we can at least have the opportunity to fulfill our dreams. That same key, if we find it, will unlock the greatest puzzle box of humanity and unveil the answer to a question that has haunted and occupied most of mankind for centuries...Is there a better way to live? There is a better way to live! When we were given dominion over the world, we were also given dominion over ourselves. God is not our navigator. It was never HIS intention to chart a course for each of us and thus place us all under HIS bondage. Instead, He bestowed each of us with intellect and talent and vision to map our own way, to write our own Book of Life in any manner that we choose. Choice! The key is choice. You have options. You need not spend your life wallowing in failure, ignorance, grief, poverty, shame and self-pity. Who would be fool enough to choose failure over success, ignorance over knowledge, poverty over wealth? No one!"
-Unknown

PRIORITIZE, WHAT IS IMPORTANT?

Prioritize Ruthlessly

The secret to booking your time effectively boils down to knowing what's important and what can wait. Ask questions that help you determine the level of urgency. Negotiate longer lead times whenever you can and don't give into the *"instant-and-immediate answer"* syndrome. Treating everything as top priority is draining and depleting.

M=Most
I=Important
N=Now

What should I be doing NOW? Is what I am doing right now getting me closer to my goal?

They key to setting priorities, the order in which you must accomplish things, is to ask yourself, What is my payoff in doing this activity? How does this fit in with my long-term objectives?

Hello, Welcome to the Psychiatric Hotline

If you are obsessive-compulsive, press 1 repeatedly. If you are co-dependent, please ask someone else to press 2. If you have multiple personalities, press 3,4,5 and 6. If you are paranoid-delusional, we know who you are and what you want; just stay on the line so we can trace the call. If you are schizophrenic, listen carefully and a little voice will tell you which number to press. If you are manic-depressive, it doesn't matter which number you press, no-one will answer.

You Will Win

It's the steady, constant driving to the goal for which you're striving, not the speed with which you travel that will make the victory sure. It's the everlasting gaining, without whimper or complaining at the burdens. It's the holding to a purpose and the never giving in, it's the cutting down the distance by the little that you win.

I AM GOING TO TAKE CONTROL OF MY TIME

Add Up the Rights of Time Use

Everyone knows the basic difference between right and wrong. If you can put more rights than wrongs on your side of the ledger, then you will succeed. If you can achieve that, while at the same time lead by example, you will end up influencing a lot of people in a positive way.

> *"We have left undone those things which we ought to have done; and we have done those things which ought not to have done."*
> -The Book of Common Prayer

I am not a businesswoman,
I am a business, woman.

Set BAGS
Big Audacious Goals

Most people don't have
a driving reason to get up in
the morning. Win the battle of
the bed. Put mind over mattress.
Get up and get going.

PROSPERITY AND ABUNDANCE ARE COMING MY WAY

Don't shrink your dreams to what
a mediocre income can bring you,
instead expand your income so you
can achieve your dreams.

IF YOU MESSED UP THE
LAST SIX YEARS IN
YOUR LIFE, YOU DON'T
HAVE TIME TO MESS UP
THE NEXT SIX YEARS.

Time is passing! Use it wisely!

Life is not meant to be miserable.

"Everyone of us will die. But so few really live."
-Braveheart

General George Patton, Jr. said about the determination you need to overcome the tug of people against you as you reach for high goals:

- You have to be single minded.
- Drive only for one thing on which you have decided.
- And if it looks as if you might be getting there, all kinds of people, including some you thought were your loyal friends, will suddenly show up to trip you, blacken you and break your spirit.

At the end of the
day you are alone
with your thoughts.
Ask yourself,
"Did I do everything
I could do today to
make my life better for
myself and those I love?"
If the answer is no, then
you had better take action.

"For a long time it had seemed to me that
life was about to begin. But there was always
some obstacle in the way, something to be
gotten through first, some unfinished business,
time still to be served, a debt to be paid. Then
life would begin. At last it dawned on me
that these obstacles were my life."
-Alfred D. Souza

chapter 2

Chapter Two

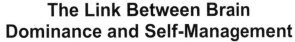

The Link Between Brain Dominance and Self-Management

Research about the brain explains a great deal of your two frontal hemispheres. Each functions in a separate, almost directly opposite way. Right-brain controls creativity and left-brain controls logic. You are constantly in touch with both sides of your brain. However, certain tasks are primarily requiring the work of one or the other side of the brain.

In the first five years of life you are primarily a dominate right-brained thinker (the creative side). Observe the typical behavior of a three year old and you will see the effect of many right-brained characteristics clearly in action. Do you think you can reason with a three year old about why she or he should eat all the vegetables on their dinner plate? Logic is not the most effective way to persuade a preschooler to take any action. Early in life, children spend a lot of time being playful, enjoying fantasy and having a massive imagination.

Children are natural artists, dancers, musicians and actors normally with a huge amount of self-confidence until or unless someone interferes...which they normally do. Give a three year old a supply of paint or crayons, brushes and paper. Even without the paper they will be creative by painting or coloring spontaneously and they most likely believe that what they have created is magnificent.

No one has to teach a child. They just explore and discover a way to make a masterpiece until someone comes along and says something *like...Let ME show you how to paint, to color.* You put this finger on the middle C and you color in the lines of the coloring book and then and guess what happens? The magic is gone and the child begins to learn...oh yes, the REAL way to play, to sing, dance, create or paint. Adults rob children of their natural visual language way too soon in life by offering them coloring books or patterns or stencils so their art will LOOK RIGHT. Soon chil-

dren get the message loud and clear. Real art should look like the coloring books look like. Soon you will hear a young child say apologetically, *"I can't draw, will you do it for me?"*

Instead, children should not be taught there is only one way to do something, instead, make it clear that there is another way to dance or sing, rather than THE ONLY WAY IS MY WAY. All the leaders in the world have in common one thing...being rule breakers. They each made a major creative contribution mainly because...

they departed from the ONLY WAY mentality and discovered their own way.

Perhaps they moved from their left-brained way of thinking and performing to a whole-brained way of thinking. When you use creativity (right-brain) to find new ways of connecting ideas and processes you call upon a lot of your left-brained skills that you have learned to get the job done. So you don't stay just in your left brain...move to whole brain thinking.

When you have no destination, any road will do, but if you fix your mind on the direction you are going and put the time in and stick to your plan, failure is out of the question.

‖‖‖‖‖‖ We don't stop playing because ‖‖‖‖‖‖
‖‖‖‖‖ we grow old. We grow old because ‖‖‖‖‖
‖‖‖‖‖ we stop playing. Play more! ‖‖‖‖‖

Make Peace Peace With Your Past

Cultivating forgiveness is complex. Forgive yourself for any regrets, but don't force yourself into a resolution. Forgiveness will help you let go of guilt, anger, anxiety and fear. Remember, you are more affected by negative feelings and memories than the other person involved.

99% of all children are highly creative until age five. Then within two years, the number drops to 10%. Only one year later, only 2% are left to supply the inspiration for the other 98%. The survivors somehow developed an ability to shed criticism.

The Early Years

At school, teachers emphasize the left-brain development. Children are often labeled as *"problem children"*, *"ADD"* or *"disruptive"* when they think or act independently using their right brain. Children are hammered with facts, rules, order, systems, symbols, language, math, reading and logical learning. Here is where children begin to conform.

No talking, no running, no chewing gum, no laughing, no interrupting, color inside the lines, anything worth doing is worth doing well, act your age, big boys and girls don't cry, don't wear your feelings on your sleeve, suck it up, sit up, get over it, deal with it, finish one thing before you start another, don't be a quitter, cleanliness is next to Godliness, What's the matter with you, sit down, raise your hand, hurry up, you are out of time get in line, good children do as they are told, don't reinvent the wheel.

As children learn all of these new thought processes they are also learning to discount all the fantastic birth-brain processes that had been so strong in early childhood. It in some ways is very sad.

What happened to that creative child in such a short time?

Negative value is placed on those who won't conform, or be obedient and controlled. Just watch what happens if your child thinks independently, creatively, thinks for themselves, creating new and unique options for their behavior. Most children grow into adults who mismanage their time because they follow rules that are not appropriate or necessary in certain situations instead of evaluating every situation individually and then applying their best skills to resolve the situation.

Inner Permission is Key

Adults have high inner permission to work for hours to get a job completed. Most adults have a low inner permission to play. Research shows that most adults in jail never played games as children. If you want your children to come home when they are adults, play table top games at home as a family with them. Show them as an adult it is okay to play. Many adults will have fun at first at their job or occupation and will stick with it long after the fun has gone out of it, seeing it through to the end. It's important to give yourself the inner permission to refresh and rejuvenate yourself. Children have a high inner permission to have fun and put their own needs first. Most schools are set up to teach in a left-brain situation which makes school very difficult for the right brained children.

People learn in different ways. People digest information in different ways. People study in different ways.

The right-brain child wants to see, feel, or touch the real object. Right-brain students may have had trouble learning to read using phonics. They prefer to see words in context, to see how the formula works. To use your right- brain, create opportunities for hands-on activities, use something real whenever possible. You may also want to draw out a math problem or illustrate your notes.

Right-Brain

1. **Illogical:** They do not analyze situations. They think with emotions, not logic. If they want something, they will justify it even if it makes no sense.
2. **Irrational:** There is no way to rationalize with them until they have been heard. They will say the craziest things that are not rational but just let them get their point across and they will become somewhat rational.
3. **Intuition:** They are intuitive and can make decisions with very little facts.
4. **Fantasy:** They crave fantasy, love movies that take them to another era or into the future.
5. **Playful:** They are fun loving people and love to have a good laugh. They are funny, witty and gravitate to other fun people. They crave happiness.
6. **Holistic:** They start with the answer. They see the big picture first, not the details. If you are right-brained, you may have difficulty following a lecture unless you are given the big picture first.
7. **Spontaneous:** Right-brained people like to do things at the drop of a hat. They can get ready fast if they want to. They don't have to have a plan.
8. **Flexibility:** They are flexible. They will organize their day around what is important to them. They can change plans easily and don't think twice about it.
9. **Common Sense:** They can make snap decisions and they know the difference between right and wrong.
10. **Creativity:** They are very creative and strive to find creativity in their lives. These are the interior decorators, the artists, the musicians, the actors.
11. **Have a heart:** Right-brained people have a massive heart. They think before they speak and they work hard not to offend anyone or hurt people's feelings. They are considerate and think of others.
12. **The Arts:** They love museums, the symphony, the live theatre, live concerts, the ballet, art classes, etc.
13. **Spelling:** The mention of spelling makes them cringe. Use the dictionary and use the spell check on their computer.

Left-Brain

1. **Logical:** Everything needs to make sense. Bottom line is their mantra. Do it by the book.
2. **Rational:** They have to have all the facts, statistics and understanding of why something must be done before they can make a decision.
3. **Knowledge:** They seek to learn. They are the ongoing students in life.
4. **Facts:** They seek facts before making any decisions. They need proof.
5. **Serious:** Left-brained people tend to be more serious about their time and their decisions.
6. **Linear, Sequential:** They take pieces, line them up and arrange them in a logical order; then draw conclusions. They are list makers. If you are left-brained, you enjoy making master schedules and daily planning. You complete tasks in order and take pleasure in checking them off when they are accomplished. Learning things in sequence is relatively easy for you. Spelling involves sequencing - if you are left-brained, you are probably a good speller. The left-brain is also good at work in following directions.
7. **Math, Language:** They understand the concepts of math and language. They do very well as accountants.
8. **Rules, Order:** They have expectations that when they put something away or down, that it will be where they put it when they need it again. They cannot stand everything out of order. They are the judges who say what is and is not going to happen.
9. ***"But, we have always done it this way."*** If they have traditions, it is almost impossible to get them to be flexible.
10. **Question:** It's in their nature to question, debate, disagree, argue and make their point.
11. **Punctual:** They are on time and expect you to be on time.
12. **Expectations:** They have expectations of those who are in their lives. They expect you to keep your word, to be in integrity, to work hard, to contribute to what is the goal.

Right/Left-Brain Thinking

Most Time-Management courses, programs and leaders who try to teach Time-Management don't work because unless you understand the brain dominance you can't help people. Most people who teach Time-Management are left-brained dominate and most Time-Management systems are designed for the left-brain dominate people. The right-brain dominant people are made to feel guilty because they have taken the class, attended the seminar, read the books, tried the systems and they still can't get organized. Instead of heaping more guilt on the right-brain person, here are some important clues to help you help yourself. Right brained gifted people gravitate to situations which include:

> Bright colors, smells, lots of textures, a variety of sounds, events of all kinds, people and different cultures, activity, play, toys, new ideas, novelty, fantasy, innovation, the arts, non-conformity, gimmicks and divergent thinking.

You cannot ask or expect a mainly right-brained person to conform to that which you expect them to do. They will frustrate you to bits if you try to make them conform. They will try, but it just won't work. The right-brained personality will move away from the kinds of environments that attract most left-brained dominant people, such as...routine, order, neat and sparse furnishings and decorations (less is more), quiet, systems, rules, reading, calculation, logic, abstract thinking, low-key.

An hour or more in church might sooth a left-brained gifted adult but tire and totally frustrate a right-brained personality. An adventure park filled with action and bright colors and texture and loads of people might be the most fun place in the world for right-brained dominant people but the left-brained person would be miserable.

INVENT YOUR OWN WHEEL

Don't be afraid to be different!

reward me regularly for the joy i bring to your life, for my creativity and sense of humor

I LOVE TO-DO LISTS.
I LOVE TO HAVE PRIORITIES.
I NEED A SCHEDULE.
I AM TIED TO MY CALENDAR.
TELL ME WHAT TO DO.

Many have been conditioned by instruction, rules and discipline that they stay in their left-brain. As the human develops they mainly develop toward a dominance of one side of the brain or the other. Just as you develop using your right or left hand. And when this happens...

You are discounting the opposite ways of thinking from your dominant preference so in effect, you are choosing to be half-brained.

Left-brain dominant thinkers will find helpful Self-Management techniques which stress rules, systems, schedules, bottom line, consistency, logical, rational thinking.

Consider this example...If you are getting ready for a big presentation, photo shoot, date, meeting, or family gathering, you might spend from a few minutes to an hour getting ready. But if your house catches on fire, you might be smart to grab a robe and get outside fast without spending all that time getting ready. *Can you think of additional examples when it would be smart to break this rule?*

The Risky River Called Life

Once there was a professor, who met a young boy who was not doing well in school. In an attempt to motivate him, the professor took him on a weekend canoe trip. They started out on a river in the dark of night, because the professor wanted the boy to see all the stars. *"Son, look up. See all the stars? What can you tell me about the stars?"* The boy looked up at the heavens and said *"Nothing, I know nothing about the stars".* *"If you don't know about the stars",* the professor said, *"you have missed out on one third of life".* Daylight came and a branch of a tree reached out above their canoe. The professor pulled a leaf off the tree and showed the leaf to the boy. He pointed out the shape, the color and texture. Then he said, *"What do you know about trees and plants and flowers?"* The boy answered, *"Nothing sir".* *"Then you've missed out on another third of life",* the professor said. The water became shallow and the professor reached down and his hand came up with his fingers separated and on his open palm there glistened a shimmering, wet stone. He said, *"What do you know about rocks, my boy?"* The boy said, *"Nothing sir".* The professor shook his head. *"You know nothing about the stars, nothing about plants and nothing about earth and stones. You missed out on another third of life."* Just then, they heard a loud noise downstream. The boy looked at the professor and said, *"Sir what do you know about swimming?"* *"Nothing",* the professor answered. With that, the boy dove into the water and started swimming toward the shore. *"Wait!"* called the professor. *"Where are you going?"* The boy said, *"That's a waterfall downstream and you just missed out on THE REST of life!"*

Let the River Run

HOURS ARE LIKE DIAMONDS, DON'T WASTE THEM!

Motivating the Left-Brained Dominant Person

Here is how the left-brain gets fired up to take action. By starting with what feels most comfortable to them:

1. They need and want a plan.
2. They need advance information. Never surprise them.
3. They need to be updated on a regular basis.
4. They need the parameters of what is expected clearly explained.
5. They need a schedule and performance expectations of time completed projects.
6. They need a routine.
7. They need to be rewarded regularly for what they like to accomplish.

WHEN IN DOUBT DON'T THINK, JUST TRY SOMETHING, ANYTHING.

If you had 30 minutes left to live,
you would most likely be either
with people you love or calling them.
Take a minute right now and tell
someone how much you care about
them. You won't regret it. Just do it.

Let others cry over spilled milk,
...but not you.
Let others cry over small
disappointments...
but not you.
Let others leave their
future up to someone else
...but not you.

-Jim Rohn

Whoever you are, wherever you are. This can be your great day. You can be changed in the next few minutes. Your great unreleased potential can become activated. So listen, listen, listen...destiny is calling you now, this day!

3 Reactions to Suffering

1. Some are CINDERS
...They get burned-OUT!
2. Some are SINNERS
...They get burned-UP!
3. Some are SENDERS
...They just burn BRIGHTER!

"Much that you learn today won't be true five years from now; many things you haven't heard today will be important five or ten years ahead. If I teach you something supposedly 'relevant,' I'm guaranteeing irrelevance. If I teach you how to work, to have good attitudes, to take responsibility for your own ideas, to communicate and to think a problem through, no matter what subject matter I use in order to get those basic skills of mind and intellect across, then I'm giving you something you can use for a very long time. Those skills will never change."
-Prof. Jacob Neusner

Doubt sees the obstacles,
Faith sees the way.
Doubt sees the bleakest night,
Faith sees the day.
Doubt dreads to take a step,
Faith soars on high.
Doubt questions, 'Who believes?' Faith answers, 'I'.

Understanding Monochronic and Polychronic Time

Monochronic time is one-track linear: people do one thing at a time. Polychronic time is multi-track circular; it allows many things to happen simultaneously, with no particular end in sight. Monochronic time is tightly compartmentalized: schedules are almost sacred. Polychronic time is open-ended: completing the task or communication is more important than adhering to a schedule. People from polychronic and monochronic cultures have the same difficulties adjusting to one another as people from high-context and low-context cultures. In fact, polychronic time is characteristic of high-context people and monochronic time is characteristic of low-context people. Similarly, the first approach tends to characterize Southern cultures, while the second rules in the North (with some notable exceptions). Monochronic people tend to sequence communications as well as tasks. They would not be inclined, for instance, to interrupt a phone conversation in order to greet a third person. Polychronic people can carry on multiple conversations simultaneously-indeed, they would consider it rude not to do so. It is impossible to know how many millions of dollars have been lost in international business because monochronic and polychronic people do not understand each other or even realize that two such different time systems exist.

Traditionally, cultures are divided into monochronic (where time is regarded as linear, people do one thing at a time and lateness and interruptions are not tolerated) and polychronic (where time is seen as cyclical, punctuality is unimportant and interruptions are acceptable).

If there are no rules for situations, the left-brained people will probably make up rules to follow!

Polychronic Time

Polychronic time is not measurable in units but is relative to many complex factors. Time-Management is often presented as a logical series of steps but some people have a less than logical view of time. This view of time is not so easily recognized by most. It is characterized by spur of the moment decisions based upon intuition, creativity, less adherence to rigid rules. How long does it take to raise a child? Make a friend? Succeed in the business? Fall in love? What is the best design for the bedroom?

Polychronic time followers are not comfortable at repetitive tasks that are easy to define within boundaries. They benefit from the personal contact that tasks may produce. Their tasks are perhaps less easy to define and measure, for example, they work well and they benefit from people contact. They tend to be in professions where monochronic time is not so important. Jobs might be in the arts, marketing, teaching, training etc. The polychronic person will use plans but is quite happy to be flexible in their approach to achieve the desired goal. They may flit from project to project as the mood takes them gaining inspiration from one project to utilize on the other. Flexibility is a trait of the polychronic person. They can multi-task and do many things at once; are highly distractible and subject to interruptions. They consider time commitments an objective to be achieved, if possible. They already have information because they have sought it. They are loyal and very committed to people and human relationships. They change plans often and easily. They are more concerned with those who are closely related.

The right-brain thinks and works in polychronic time.
The right-brain responds to emotions and to moods.

Concentrate Your Left Brain to Get Organized

If you are married to a man who is left-brain and you are right-brain it will drive him mad that you are un-organized. Some left-brained people have a messy desk but they know exactly where everything is. Here is something that can really help. Make a ***Things To Do List***. Do you run this list or does it run you? Never put more than six items on your list. Normally this is a list that keeps on growing even though you try your best to reduce the number of items. I have been a huge list maker in my life because I don't want to forget something that is on my mind and then remem-ber it during the night. If I get it onto paper, it's out of my head.

Get a filing system. When you pay your bills, put your bills in a monthly tickler or in some order so you don't spend hours of your time looking for old receipts. That is a colossal waste of time.

Organize Your Desk

I have built a multi-million dollar business by the phi-losophy of less is more. Your desk is a reflection of your mind. I use loads of binders so I am not always seeking pieces of paper in my office. Organize and DUST your desktop. Do you know that others will respect you much more if you are organized? Did you know you will respect yourself more too? And you can get a lot more done when you are not searching everywhere for a certain piece of paper.

MBP=Management By Piles
Binder Management
Keep your desk top uncluttered

YOUR DESK IS A REFLECTION OF YOUR MIND

A What-Not-To-Do List is more important than a To-Do list!

> *"Instead of a TO-DO list, make a TA-DA list."*
> -Sarah Janell White

The cluttered desk: Look at your desktop. If you can see less than 80% of it then you are probably suf-fering from *"desk stress"*. The most effective people work from clear desk tops.

It's about time to tackle that project instead of letting papers pile up everywhere.

Monochronic Time

Monochronic time is time measurable in specific units of time like days, hours, minutes, seconds. This view of time is easily recognized by most. It is characterized by punctuality, rules, conformity and speed. Monochronics have a clear start and a well defined end point. They don't need to have a big reliance on people skills to complete them. They tend to be data orientated with results based on easily accessible precious experience. How long does it take to drive to work? Boil water? Bake a cake? Open a bottle of wine? Fly from city to city? How long does it take to get a bottle of milk? How long does it take to clean the car?

Jobs involving repetitive tasks tend to be based upon monochronic views of time, for example, accountants, train drivers, etc. If you are required to think too much or need flexibility, then the job will often falter.

Northern European countries (for example the UK, Germany) and the USA have a monochronic view of time. This can be a hindrance if a polychronic approach to tasks is not considered for those countries that favor this system. Many cultures value human contact, patience and honesty above speed, for example, Asian, Arabic, Japanese and others. Their approach to tasks will tend to conflict with yours if, like many Northern European countries and the USA, you take a monochronic view on all matters.

The monochronic person loves plans. He/she probably won't even start a project without a plan that must be adhered to. They take a logical approach to tasks which means completing activities in a stepwise manner should all go to plan provided the necessary thought has gone into it. The monochronic person's desire to follow *"rules"* may cause challenges if there is an interruption in the process flow. However, enforced flexibility can be a good thing as rethinking an issue can have benefits as for the polychronic person. Monochronic personalities like to do one thing at a time, concentrate on the job, they take time commitments (deadlines, schedules) seriously, they need statistics, details and information. They are committed to the job and adhere religiously to plans. What happens if the plans goes awry? Monochronic people are less flexible and don't like detours from plans. However, plans do go wrong and flexibility is a useful trait of the polychronic person. You may think the person would have considered a back up or contingency plan. However, a true contingency plan would have been considered already and would be awaiting a trigger to implement it. A true deviation from a plan is unforeseen. They are reluctant to modify plans unless forced to and will want to finish one task properly before beginning another. Their sense of logic will require supporting information that governs their actions. Interpersonal relationships will not hold great importance in the search for project completion.

Meetings with monochronic persons will be short and to the point. You may need to expand particular areas to fully understand the issues and possible solutions. You may need to manage the expectations of a monochronic person to expand on the exact requirements to make sure you have the correct task definition.

Renegotiate the time of individuals so that you can complete a meeting properly rather than wrapping it up prematurely. If you feel under time pressure, take some time out to recharge your thinking. Make sure you create backup plans that you may have to implement. Monochronics are concerned about not disturbing others; they follow rules of privacy and consideration.

They show great respect for private property; seldom borrow or lend. They emphasize promptness. They work well alone. They are accustomed to short-term relationships. They are normally not very empathetic.

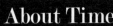
It Couldn't Be Done

"Somebody said that it couldn't be done,
but he with a chuckle replied...
that *"maybe it couldn't"*, but he would be one
who wouldn't say so till he'd tried.
So he buckled right in with the trace of a grin.
If he worried he hid it.
He started to sing as he tackled the thing
that couldn't be done and he did it.
Somebody scoffed: *"Oh, you'll never do that;
at least no one ever has done it;"*
but he took off his coat and he took off his hat,
and the first thing we knew he'd begun it.
With a lift of his chin and a bit of a grin,
without any doubting or quitting,
he started to sing as he tackled the thing
that couldn't be done and he did it.
There are thousands to tell you it cannot be
done, there are thousands to prophesy failure;
there are thousands to point out to you, one by one,
the dangers that wait to assail you.
But just buckle in with a bit of a grin,
just take off your coat and go to it;
just start to sing as you tackle the thing
that *"cannot be done"* and you'll do it."
-Edgar Guest

(Can you pick out the right/left brain words?)

Giving Directions

A good illustration of left/right-brain thinking is to listen to people give directions. The left-brain person will say something like *"From here, go west three blocks and turn north on Vine Street. Go three or four miles and then turn east onto Broad Street"*. The right-brain person will sound something like this: *"Turn right (pointing right), by the church over there (pointing again). Then you will pass a McDonalds and a Wal-mart. At the next light, turn right toward the BP station and take a left at the third mailbox which is yellow"*.

THE LEFT-BRAIN THINKS AND WORKS IN MONOCHRONIC TIME.

No one stays solely in one side of their brain for very long. Everyone uses both sides of their brain constantly. But it is critical to understand your personal brain dominance and how to motivate yourself and manage it most effectively. If you are a trainer, a teacher, a parent, a spouse or in relationships or you are interested in teaching others to learn how to...

MANAGE THEIR TIME,

it is helpful to know what works for you won't work for those with the opposite brain dominance. Right-brain people are motivated to teach others what works for them. When the right-brain person teaches this helps that person to get organized and analyze what works best for them. Soon the right-brains are gathering that marvelous

MOMENTUM

that comes from being WHOLE BRAINED. Why? Because the high energy, creativity and passion of the right-brained dominant person combined with structure, organization and critical thinking of the left-brain creates momentum. But be clear...these left-brained thinking skills become

Flexible Toys

for the right-brain dominated person.

> *"If trying harder doesn't work, try softer."*
> -Lily Tomlin

The Chinese Process of Time

The Chinese with over 5,000 years of cultural heritage have a different perspective on time. When Mao Tse Tung was asked what he thought of the French Revolution, he replied (only half-joking), *"It is too soon to tell"*. Producing a satisfactory agreement in as short a time as possible may be one of the least concerns of the Chinese. The Chinese generally believe that a considerable amount of time should be invested in establishing a general climate of understanding, trust and willingness to help, in matters quite apart from the issues brought to the table. They do not view time as a constraint or as a set of limits in which a particular task must he completed. For the Chinese, since time is cyclical, deadlines are not understood and not restrictive. Chinese see the negotiating process as an opportunity to elicit as much information as possible, particularly that of a technical nature. This tendency may be associated with the issue of face and their reluctance to display ignorance. They tend to understand in terms of wholes and total systems and their appreciation of technology may be limited until they have grasped how the diverse elements fit into the system. The Chinese approach is rather a negotiating process to establish a human relationship, often essentially dependent in nature and therefore, their prime goal to create the bonding of *"friendship"*.

SPEND TIME WISELY

Take Time

Take time to think-*It is the source of all power.*
Take time to read-*It is the fountain of wisdom.*
Take time to play-*It is the source of perpetual youth.*
Take time to be quiet-*It is the
opportunity to seek God.*
Take time to be aware-
It is the opportunity to help others.
Take time to love and be loved-
It is God's greatest gift.
Take time to laugh-*It is the music of the soul.*
Take time to be friendly-*It is the road to happiness.*
Take time to dream-*It is what the future is made of.*
Take time to pray-*It is the greatest power on earth.*
Take time to give-*It is too short a day to be selfish.*
Take time to work-*It is the price of success.*
Take time to dream-
dreams show you what is possible.
Take time to do your work well-*pride in your
work nourishes the mind and the spirit.*
Take time to show appreciation-
it's the frosting on the cake of life.
Take time to laugh- *it is the music of the soul.*

As far as we know, the *"Take Time"*
poem is based on an old English prayer
and the original author of this version is unknown.

*"Seize this very minute: what you can do or dream,
you can do, begin it; Boldness has genius,
power and magic in it. Only engage and
then the mind grows heated; Begin and
then the work will be completed."*
-Goethe

There will be time enough
to do it all. But not all at once.

Turn, Turn, Turn

"To everything-turn, turn, turn; there is a season-
turn, turn, turn and a time for every purpose
under heaven. A time to be born, a time to die.
A time to plant, a time to reap. A time to kill,
a time to heal. A time to laugh, a time to weep
And a time for every purpose under heaven
A time to build up, a time to break down.
A time to dance, a time to mourn. A time to
cast away stones. A time to gather stones together
And a time for every purpose under heaven
A time of war, a time of peace. A time of love,
a time of hate. A time you may embrace.
A time to refrain from embracing
And a time for every purpose under heaven
A time to gain, a time to lose. A time to rend,
a time to sew. A time to love, a time to hate.
A time of peace, I swear it's not too late!"
-The Byrds

"It doesn't matter what happened in the past
Because what we have, it gonna last
You make me smile; Your worth my while
You let me know how you feel...
Which lets me know you're the real deal
You let me see, what you mean to me...
Without you, who knows where I'd be?
When I'm not with you, I feel blue
Whoever knew, our love would be true?
In so little time, I made you mine
And we're gonna last, til the end of time!"
-Unknown

"Unless you are brief your complete plan
of thought will seldom be grasped. Before you
reach the conclusion, the reader or listener has
forgotten the beginning and the middle."
-Horace

Take time to feed your faith
and doubt will starve to death

No Need to Be Frazzled

Most right-brain people spend their time like this: You are choosing to be so busy with so much outside interests that soon you are going to feel like you are torn apart. No need to feel frazzled. Just stop trying to accomplish so much and focus on that which you truly want to accomplish in life. Spending your time frazzled drives the left-brained people mad. They know that if you would get organized that you would not be so frazzled. Ask for their help, not their criticism. And then let them help you. It will be a great relief to you to know that there are others who CAN help you get organized.

Highways, Tributaries and Bunny Trails

All sound decisions are the combined result of three similar, yet widely divergent phenomena — highways, tributaries and bunny trails. Each is a path from here to there, yet each has its own elemental uniqueness that, when taken into with the other two, helps form the basis of lucid strategy and tactical selection.

Highways provide the straight and narrow—the most logical and efficient way of getting from point A to point B. The thoroughfare is well-paved and well-engineered, the route is tested and proven and the guidelines are historic and easy to follow. There are signs to guide the way, there are rest stops and roadside points of interest and they are plotted on maps. Like highways, every decision that we make starts out at the beginning - with basic research, careful thought and the setting of goals and objectives. *"We are here and this is where we want to go."* We know the direction, the difficulties ahead and how much time and resources are required. We can gauge our speed and we know what and who we have to pick up along the way. Our basic course, our movement from point A to point B, is set.

Tributaries are feeders that originate at sources far from the main river. They pick up material along the way and add them to the stream. Tributaries contribute to the efficacy and power of the flow and what they bring in volume and material will help determine the potency and often the direction, of the onrush. They are directly responsible for growth. They, too, are plotted on maps (up to a point, for the smaller ones are usually ignored). Our plans can never be concrete because we don't know everything there is to know. We require the assistance of tributaries. From all sides comes a flow of new information and resources that we can use to make our journey more efficient in the long run. Some of these tributaries move into our sphere of influence through our own efforts — it is vital to initiate inquiries that pay off in strategic data and the delivery of funding for our campaign. Other tributaries just happen; they find us and enrich us with unexpected help.

Bunny trails cause our forward progress to head off in different directions. You know how bunnies are; they constantly make right-angle turns, poking their noses here and there, often reversing their direction. Whether foraging or fleeing, they make it difficult to predict where they are heading next. And yet, they always seem to make it back to the warren (their point B) safely. Planned bunny trails are important. Occasionally, we need to examine the flowers and the people who live out of the mainstream. We need to measure what will elicit the behavior that will define our campaign and whether or not new direction is indicated. So we take the side roads and trust to serendipity. Decision making will be enriched by contributions both solicited and unsolicited. If you keep your eyes and ears open — if you truly see and listen — then your arrival at point B will have more meaning. It will affect more people positively and it will facilitate more-than-satisfactory end results. There is an easy lesson to be learned by all of this: Plan your highway well, welcome the tributaries and be a bunny once in a while in your lifetime.

If I Had My Life To Live Over

I'd dare to make more mistakes next time.
I'd relax, I would limber up.
I would be sillier than I have been this trip.
I would take fewer things seriously.
I would take more chances. I would climb
more mountains and swim more rivers.
I would eat more ice cream and less beans.
I would perhaps have more actual troubles,
but I'd have fewer imaginary ones.
You see, I'm one of those people who live
sensibly and sanely hour after hour,
day after day. Oh, I've had my moments,
And if I had it to do over again,
I'd have more of them.
In fact, I'd try to have nothing else.
Just moments, one after another,
instead of living so many years ahead of each day.
I've been one of those people who never goes anywhere
without a thermometer, a hot water bottle,
a raincoat and a parachute.
If 1 had to do it again,
I would travel lighter than I have.
If I had my life to live over,
I would start barefoot earlier in the spring
and stay that way later in the fall.
I would go to more dances.
I would ride more merry-go-rounds.
I would pick more daisies.

-Nadine Stair, written when she was 85 years old.

chapter

3

In this Chapter you will learn about:

Chapter Three

"A musician must make music, an artist must paint, a poet must write, if he is to be at peace with himself. What a man can be, he must be. This is the need we may call self-actualization... It refers to man's desire for fulfillment, namely to the tendency for him to become actually in what he is potentially: to become everything that one is capable of becoming...
-Dr. Abraham Maslow

Characteristics of
Self-Actualizing People
-Dr. Abraham Maslow

Realistic

Realistically oriented, a self-actualizing (SA) person has a more efficient perception of reality and has comfortable relations with it. This is extended to all areas of life. A self-actualizing person is unthreatened and unfrightened by the unknown. He has a superior ability to reason, to see the truth and is logical and efficient.

Self-Acceptance

The SA person accepts himself, others and the natural world the way they are. He sees human nature as is, has a lack of crippling guilt or shame, enjoys himself without regret or apology and has no unnecessary inhibitions.

Spontaneity, Simplicity, Naturalness

The SA person is spontaneous in his inner life. Thoughts and impulses are unhampered by convention. His ethics are autonomous and SA individuals are motivated to continual growth.

Focus of Challenge Centering

The SA person focuses on challenges and people outside of himself. He has a mission in life requiring much energy, as it is his sole reason for existence. He is serene, characterized by a lack of worry and is devoted to duty.

Detachment and the Need for Privacy

The SA person can be alone and not be lonely, is unflappable and retains dignity amid confusion and personal misfortunes, all the while remaining objective. He is a self-starter, is responsible for himself and owns his behavior.

Creativity

The SA person enjoys an inborn uniqueness that caries over into everything he does, is original, inventive, uninhibited and he sees the real and true more easily.

Philosophical, Unhostile
Sense of Humor

Jokes to the SA person are teaching metaphors, intrinsic to the situation and are spontaneous. He can laugh at himself, but he never makes jokes that hurt others.

Resistance to Enculturation

SA people have an inner detachment from culture. Working for long term culture improvement, indignation with injustice, inner autonomy, outer acceptance and the ability to transcend the environment rather than just cope are intrinsic to SA people.

Imperfections

SA people are painfully aware of their own imperfections and joyfully aware of their own growth process. They are impatient with themselves when stuck and feel real life pain as a result.

Resolution of Dichotomies

To the SA person work becomes play and desires are in excellent accord with reason. The SA person retains his childlike qualities yet is very wise.

Que sera, sera? Whatever will be will be...the future's not for us to see, que sera sera??...it's simply not true, take charge of your life!

Two Processes Necessary for Self-Actualization

1. **Self-exploration:** The deeper the self exploration, the closer one comes to self-actualization.
2. **Action:** Use of effective affirmations can create the new behaviors of Self-Actualization.

KNOWLEDGE IS NOT POWER...ONLY PUTTING WHAT YOU KNOW INTO ACTION IS.

Constant Questions: Ask yourself constantly, every day of the week...*Is what I am doing now getting me closer to achieving my goal? What is the highest and best use of my time right now?*

"Finish each day and be done with it, you have done what you could; some blunders and absurdities no doubt crept in; forget them as soon as you can. Tomorrow is a new day; you shall begin it well and serenely."
-Ralph Waldo Emerson

stop wasting time

What future are you willing to accept?

The price of time and money... I can get more money but not more time.

keep your word

Don't say you are going to do something unless you are intent on doing it. The power of intention is worthless. Be a person who takes the time to follow up on your intentions. If you say you will be someplace on time, leave early, don't ever, ever blame the traffic. If you say you are going to call someone at a certain time, call them. If you invite someone on a date at a certain time, be there on time. Don't play games with other people's time. If you set an appointment, make it on time. How much time is spent waiting to see doctors? Doctors, if you can't see your patients on time, that is something about your Time-Management that needs to change. Your patients' time is valuable too. Airlines don't wait for you to get to them on your time. You must be responsible to get yourself where you need to be on time. Teachers can't teach if everyone in the class is late. Seminar leaders want to start their seminars on time. Don't be late. Be early, sit in the front row. Be ready to learn. Keep your word!

All My Life's A Circle

"All my life's a circle, sunrise and sundown
The moon rolls through the nighttime
Till daybreak comes around, all my life's a circle
Still I wonder why, seasons spinning 'round again
Years keep rolling by. Seems like I've been here
before...can't remember when, I got this funny
feeling that we'll all be together again
No straight lines make up my life
All my roads have bends, no clear cut
beginnings and so far no dead ends."
-Harry Chapin

Are you always a few minutes behind schedule? Just get up earlier and get focused on what you need to do to be where you need to be on time.

Be on Time

When you set an appointment with anyone and are given a time to be there, strive to be there a few minutes early. Always call ahead to make sure the appointment is a go. Do not spend valuable time traveling to an appointment to find out that something has changed. Doctors seem to be the worst. They over schedule and are most of the time running late as if to say that their time is more valuable than the patients. Don't over book if you can't see your patients on time. I have a rule that I will not wait more than 15 minutes for an appointment. They may reschedule their appointment with me if they are that busy or perhaps I will find someone who values my business more than those who are chronically late. You want to be aware of being punctual. The traffic is not an excuse. Leave early, get to where you need to be early. There is nothing worse than someone arriving late and you got there on time and you navigated through what you had to do to be on time and they didn't.

The Touch of the Master's Hand

"Twas battered and scarred and the auctioneer thought it scarcely worth his while to waste much time on the old violin, but held it with a smile; *'What am I bidden, good folks'*, he cried, *'Who'll start the bidding for me?' 'A dollar, a dollar'*; then, *'Two!' 'Only two?' 'Two dollars and who'll make it three?' 'Three dollars, once, three dollars, twice; Going for three--'*, but No! From the back of the room, a gray-haired man came forward and picked up the bow; Then, wiping the dust from the old violin and tightening the loose strings, he played a melody pure and sweet as a caroling angel sings. The music ceased and the auctioneer, with a voice that was quite and low, said: *'What am I bid for the old violin?'* And then held it up with the bow. *'A thousand dollars and who'll make it two? Two thousand! And who'll make it three? Three thousand, once, three thousand, twice and going and gone'*, said he. The people cheered, but some of them cried, *'We do not quite understand, what changed it's worth?'* Swift came the reply; *'The touch of the master's hand'*. And many a man with life out of tune and battered and scarred with sin, is auctioned cheap to the thoughtless crowd, much like the old violin. A mess of pottage, a glass of wine, a game and he travels on. He is *going* once and *going* twice, he's *going and almost gone*. But the Master comes and the foolish crowd, *'Never can quite understand, the worth of a soul and the change that's wrought by the touch of the Master's hand'*."

-Myra Brooks Welch

If

"If you can keep your head when all about you
Are losing theirs and blaming it on you,
If you can trust yourself when all men doubt you,
But make allowance for their doubting too;
If you can wait and not be tired by waiting,
Or being lied about, don't deal in lies,
Or being hated, don't give way to hating,
And yet don't look too good, nor talk too wise:
If you can dream - and not make dreams your master,
If you can think - and not make thoughts your aim;
If you can meet with Triumph and Disaster,
And treat those two impostors just the same;
If you can bear to hear the truth you've spoken
Twisted by knaves to make a trap for fools,
Or watch the things you gave your life to, broken,
And stoop and build 'em up with worn-out tools:
If you can make one heap of all your winnings
And risk it all on one turn of pitch-and-toss,
And lose and start again at your beginnings
And never breath a word about your loss;
If you can force your heart and nerve and sinew
To serve your turn long after they are gone,
And so hold on when there is nothing in you
Except the Will which says to them: 'Hold on!'
If you can talk with crowds and keep your virtue,
Or walk with kings - nor lose the common touch,
If neither foes nor loving friends can hurt you,
If all men count with you, but none too much;
If you can fill the unforgiving minute
With sixty seconds' worth of distance run,
Yours is the Earth and everything that's in it,
And - which is more - you'll be a Man, my son!"
-Rudyard Kipling (1865-1936)

Learn to say no. It is so easy to be pulled everywhere with social obligations and soon you find your calendar so overloaded that it eats up all of your time.

Desiderata

"Go placidly amid the noise and haste and remember what peace there may be in silence. As far as possible, without surrender, be on good terms with all persons. Speak your truth quietly and clearly; and listen to others, even to the dull and the ignorant, they too have their story. Avoid loud and aggressive persons, they are vexations to the spirit. If you compare yourself with others, you may become vain and bitter; for always there will be greater and lesser persons than yourself. Enjoy your achievements as well as your plans. Keep interested in your own career, however humble; it is a real possession in the changing fortunes of time. Exercise caution in your business affairs, for the world is full of trickery. But let this not blind you to what virtue there is; many persons strive for high ideals and everywhere life is full of heroism. Be yourself. Especially, do not feign affection. Neither be cynical about love, for in the face of all aridity and disenchantment it is perennial as the grass. Take kindly to the counsel of the years, gracefully surrendering the things of youth. Nurture strength of spirit to shield you in sudden misfortune. But do not distress yourself with imaginings. Many fears are born of fatigue and loneliness. Beyond a wholesome discipline, be gentle with yourself. You are a child of the universe, no less than the trees and the stars; you have a right to be here. And whether or not it is clear to you, no doubt the universe is unfolding as it should. Therefore be at peace with God, whatever you conceive Him to be and whatever your labors and aspirations, in the noisy confusion of life, keep peace in your soul. With all its sham, drudgery and broken dreams, it is still a beautiful world Be cheerful. Strive to be happy."
-Max Ehrmann

Don't Quit

"When things go wrong, as they sometimes will,
When the road you're trudging seems all up hill,
When the funds are low and the debts are high,
And you want to smile, but you have to sigh,
When care is pressing you down a bit,
Rest! if you must; but don't you quit.
Life is queer with its twists and turns,
As everyone of us sometimes learns,
And many a failure turns about
When he might have won had he stuck it out;
Don't give up, though the pace seems slow;
You might succeed with another blow.
Often the goal is nearer than
It seems to a faint and faltering man,
Often the struggler has given up
When he might have captured the victor's cup.
And he learned too late, when the night slipped down,
How close he was to the golden crown.
Success is failure turned inside out;
The silver tint of the clouds of doubt;
And you never can tell how close you are,
It may be near when it seems afar;
So stick to the fight when you're hardest hit;
It's when things seem worst that you mustn't quit."
-C.W. Longenecker

Don't just
do something.
Sit there.

"Tomorrow is not promised, nor is today.
So I choose to celebrate every day I am alive by
being present in it. Living in the present means
letting go of the past and not waiting for the future."
-Oprah Winfrey

Stop doing and start being. Today,
see how long you can do nothing.

It's about time you go for your dreams!

"Dost thou love life? Then do not squander
time, for that is the stuff life is made of."
-Benjamin Franklin

"Periunt et imputantur, - the hours
perish and are laid to our charge."
-Inscription on a dial at Oxford

"I wasted time and now doth time waste me."
-Shakespeare

"Every hour in a man's life has its own
special work possible for it and for no other
hour within the allotted span of years and
once gone it will not return."
-Noel Paton

"Believe me when I tell you that thrift of time will
repay you in after life, with a usury of profit beyond
your most sanguine dreams and that waste of it will
make you dwindle alike in intellectual and moral
stature, beyond your darkest reckoning."
-Gladstone

"And the plea that this or that man has no
time for culture will vanish as soon as we desire
culture so much that we begin to examine
seriously into our present use of time. "
-Matthew Arnold

"This is the choosing up point, kiddo, from here on. I had no idea that life was as short as it is. That concept comes very late in any human life, I think I thought life was immeasurable, extensive to the horizon and beyond. But I did know that my capacities were not unlimited. I had only so much to spend and let's do it in a big way."
-James Michener
Pulitzer Prize-Winning Novelist

The World is Your Oyster

You can have, be and do whatever you wish in life. Success is simply a matter of how you chose to spend your time in life.

Promote or Expose Yourself

What you do today will manifest itself in 3-5 years. Your activity will either promote you or expose you. Breathe out the old you and breathe in the new you, who starts on a new path today. We should leave this life when that time comes without an ounce of talent left. We should use up everything we have been given. We can't take it with us. The greatest disease of these times is the fear of life. People talk about the cost of living but what about the rising cost of not living? Why be afraid of the future? It can only come one day at a time.

Put your time in to be the best you can be, the world will place value on that time invested.

The days come to us like friends in disguise, bringing priceless gifts from an unseen hand; but it we do not use them, they are born silently away, never to return. Each successive morning new gifts are brought bet if we fail to accept those that were brought yesterday and the day before, we become less and less able to turn them to account, until the ability to appreciate and utilize them is exhausted. Lost wealth may be regained by industry and economy, lost knowledge by study, lost health by temperance and medicine, but time lost is gone forever.

"This is the Beginning of a New Day. I Can Waste It...or Use It For Good, But What I Do Today is Important, Because I am Exchanging a Day of My Life For It. When Tomorrow Comes, This Day Will Be Gone Forever, Leaving in Its Place Something That I Have Traded For It. I Want It to Be Gain and Not Loss, Good and Not Evil, Success and Not Failure, in Order That I Not Regret the Price I Have Paid For It. I Will Give 100% of Myself Just For Today, For You Never Fail Until You Stop Trying. I Will Be the Kind of Person I have Always Wanted To Be...I Have Been Given This Day to Use as I Will."
-Unknown

Every obstacle is to learn to grow, to be corrected or protected from making mistakes

*Every step is an end and
every step is a fresh beginning.*

*—— A journey of a thousand miles ——
—— begins with a first step. ——*

The 3-C Time Cycle

Wouldn't it be rewarding to know that you have made a difference to others by helping them become more competent, confident or committed? You can do exactly that as you use the 3-C Time Cycle. You can generate an ever-increasing cycle of Competence - Confidence - Commitment, each contributing in turn to the growth and energy of the other. Where do you start? You can immediately begin applying the 3-C Cycle by replacing any negative elements with positive ones. For example, train to increase Competence, praise to increase Confidence and inspire to increase Commitment.

- Competent people feel more confident about themselves.
- Confident people are more willing to take risks to increase their competence.
- Competent, confident people are more likely to be committed.
- Commitment to a person or cause is essential for confidence and competence building.

One of the most effective ways to begin is to provide the fuel for the 3-C Energy Cycle is by answering the following questions that those you are investing your time in are thinking:

WHO WILL I BECOME AS I GROW AND CHANGE?

Fear of change is a natural and valuable part of life. It alerts us to potential challenges and increases our awareness of opportunities. Change can be frightening. People fear losing their identities. *"I could never do that"* or *"That's just not for me"*. Listen for the message behind those words and offer encouragement, not criticism. Confirm your belief that others will still be the same person, only stronger and better.

*The only thing you can
count on in life is change.*

WHAT WILL BECOME?

Help them to see what is possible by painting a vivid, positive picture of their future as they grow and expand. Describe how they will feel, how others will respond to them and the benefits of their growth and new skills.

HOW WILL I REACH MY GOALS?

Offer a road map, outlining steps and stages for their journey. Those who are easily overwhelmed will need to be led in small steps. Perpetuate the 3-C energy cycle. Competence -Confidence-Commitment. You'll secure the loyalty, trust and enthusiasm of those you are seeking to lead or empower. At the end of each day you'll know that you are a person who truly makes a difference.

NO MORE ALIBIS.

SOMEDAY IS NOT A DAY OF THE WEEK.

Obsession is important

ONE CAN NEVER CREEP WHEN ONE FEELS AN IMPULSE TO SOAR.

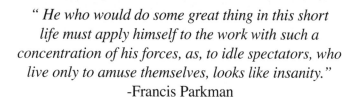

" He who would do some great thing in this short life must apply himself to the work with such a concentration of his forces, as, to idle spectators, who live only to amuse themselves, looks like insanity."
-Francis Parkman

Don't Tell Me What To Do With My Time!

Who is in charge of your *time?* You are and only you! If someone tries to coerce or force you into Self-management or criticizes your Self-Management what shows up? (See more on page 99).

Procrastination, white lies, rationalization, foot dragging, self-defeating behavior... less than stellar use of time

Rule #1: Suggest ideas to improve Self-Management. Force does not work. **Rule #2:** Get yourself exactly where you need to be, look like, weight control and get yourself totally in control before you criticize someone else. Profit from learning from your own experiences and mistakes as well. as your successes.

"That night, I could not sleep and I went out on an airstrip on Tontutta. I walked along the airstrip and that's when the war hit me and that's when I said, **'When this is over, I'm not going to be the same guy. 1 am going to live as if I were a great man.'** *I never said I was going to be a great man before because I had no idea what my capacities were. I had no great confidence; nothing in my background gave me a reason to think so. But I was not forestalled from acting as if I were."*
-James Michner, Pulitzer Prize-Winning Novelist

"I knew that if I failed, I wouldn't regret that, but I knew the one thing I might regret was not trying."
-Jeff Bezos, Founder of Amazon. com

"I felt myself very much like someone in the eve of a hurricane, because all this swirling was going on around me. It was at that moment that everything changed. Edward Murrow, the journalist and newscaster, said to me that evening, **'Young man, a great tragedy has just befallen you.'** *I said,* **'What's that, Ed?'** *He said,* **'You've just lost your anonymity.'**
-Jonas Salk, Developer of Polio Vaccine

TAKE TIME TO MAKE FRIENDS BEFORE YOU NEED THEM

Doing the same thing over and over again expecting different results is the definition of insanity.

"The longer I live, the more deeply am I convinced that which makes the difference between one man and another-between the weak and powerful, the great and insignificant, is energy-invincible determination - a purpose once formed and then death or victory."
-Fowell Buxton

"The winds of grace are blowing all of the time and it's up to us to raise our sails."
-Father Thomas Keating

You can forgive even if you can't forget. You can also forgive, forget and forge ahead. Your choice!

Common Time Stealers

In order for a Self-Management process to work, it is important to know what aspects of your personal management need to be improved. Below you will find some of the most frequent reasons for reducing effectiveness in the workplace. Check off the ones which are causing the major obstacles to your own Self-Management. Fortunately there are strategies you can use to manage your time, be more in control and reduce stress, but you can analyze your time and see how you may be both the cause and the solution to your time challenges.

- Analyses paralysis.
- Interruptions-telephone.
- Interruptions-personal visitors.
- Meetings.
- Tasks you could have delegated.
- Procrastination and indecision.
- Acting with incomplete information.
- Dealing with team members.
- Crisis management (fire fighting).
- Unclear communication.
- Inadequate technical knowledge.
- Unclear objectives and priorities.
- Lack of planning.
- Stress and fatigue.
- Inability to say *"No"*.
- Desk management and personal disorganization.
- Disappointment.
- Disasters.
- Family Challenges.
- Illness.
- Anger, staying upset and mad.
- Misunderstandings.
- Worry.

"What we wish to accomplish we must impress on the subconscious mind."
-Orison Swett Marden

Can't Sleep? Count Sheep

When you visualize sheep jumping one by one over a white picket fence, you use your imagination as a sleep enhancing ally. Focusing on a repetitive image leaves little mental brain space for worries that keep you awake. During the night, if you have sad and or negative thoughts, learn to say **CANCEL CANCEL** and replace those thoughts with something positive. Say to yourself: *I cannot change that old memory...I have moved on*...have that conversation with your brain.

Pop the cork and let yourself bubble like champagne. Become your own Chief Enthusiasm Officer!

What is your plan...
Write down the answers to these 5 questions:
What do I want to accomplish?
Who do I want to be with me?
Where do I want to end up?
When do I want this to happen?
How am I going to make it happen?

There is Plenty of Time to Do Everything You Want to Do

1. Choose your battles, don't get upset about everything.
2. Declutter your house so that things don't go missing and there is not so much to dust and polish.
3. Get a good washer and dryer, the best you can afford, don't scrimp here. Get industrial size if you can.
4. Get all matching socks, do not take time to match socks.
5. Get comforters on all beds and make making up the beds fast.
6. Use paper plates when you are super busy and toss them.
7. Clean out a cabinet in your kitchen and put family games in it and loads of art work for your children to experiment with.
8. Put cups where children can get their own drinks easily.
9. Set time for computer and sitting in front of the TV. Don't let your children be brought up by violence that they see on TV daily.
10. Make Sunday a family afternoon. Picnics, boating, etc.
11. Get your children active. Get them into sports, soccer, tennis, ice hockey, swimming, jogging, baseball, football, dance, music lessons, language lessons. Don't get them into too many activities where they don't have time to be children and that there is no family time.
12. Limit buying cookies, candy, cakes and rich desserts except on special occasions.
13. Be neighborly, do something nice and unexpected for your neighbors.
14. Don't do your children's homework for them.
15. Don't spend a lot of time at the teacher/parent conference.
16. Make sure your children get plenty of time to play in water, in swimming pools, in bathtub. Play time in water is so important. Get your children the best toys to play with in the bathtub. Keep a plastic crate in the bathtub for easy clean up.
17. Give your children an ocean liner of love. Tell them often and show them tenderness.
18. No yelling at your children. Get in control of yourself.
19. Do not interrupt your child.
20. As children get older, demand that you know where they are and that there are consequences if they do not let you know exactly where they are.
21. Fill your home with laughter and music. Keep an upbeat feeling in your home.
22. Make orange juice ice cubes and drop them in ginger ale for children. Add a cherry...yum!
23. Let them have two popsicles.
24. Limit telephone time for you and them. Don't have a phone to your head the entire time you are with your children.
25. Turn your car into a classroom. Don't waste time listening to junk music that has no value. Instead, get a book on CD, a CD with another language, a how to CD and feed your mind while in the traffic.
26. Have special days with your children called LUCKY DAYS. This is when you take them to the dentist, a movie, out to lunch, to get a new coat or dress or school books.
27. Spend one on one time with your children forever. Sometimes they act up because they want you to themselves.
28. Give your children well days off from school instead of sick days.
29. Never make your children feel ignorant or stupid.

"I don't know what your destiny will be, but one thing I know: the only ones among you who will be really happy are those who will have sought and found how to serve."
-Dr. Albert Schweitzer

A Thousand Marbles

"Well, Tom, it sure sounds like you're busy with your job. I'm sure they pay you well but it's a shame you have to be away from home and your family so much. Hard to believe a young fellow should have to work sixty or seventy hours a week to make ends meet. Too bad you missed your daughter's dance recital." He continued, *"Let me tell you something Tom, something that has helped me keep a good perspective on my own priorities"*. And that's when he began to explain his theory of a *thousand marbles*. *"You see, I sat down one day and did a little arithmetic. The average person lives about seventy-five years. I know, some live more and some live less, but on average, folks live about seventy-five years. Now then, I multiplied 75 times 52 and I came up with 3,900 which is the number of Saturdays that the average person has in their entire lifetime. Now stick with me Tom, I'm getting to the important part. It took me until I was 55 years old to think about all this in any detail"*, he went on, *"and by that time I had lived through over twenty-eight hundred Saturdays. I got to thinking that if I lived to be 75, I only had about a thousand of them left to enjoy. So I went to a toy store and bought every single marble they had. I ended up having to visit three toy stores to round-up 1,000 marbles. I took them home and put them inside of a large, clear plastic container. Every Saturday since then, I have taken one marble out and thrown it away. I found that by watching the marbles diminish, I focused more on the really important things in life. There is nothing like watching your time here on this earth run out to help get your priorities straight. Now let me tell you one last thing before I sign-off with you and take my lovely wife out for breakfast. This morning, I took the very last marble out of the container. I figure if I make it until next Saturday then 1 have been given a little extra time. And the one thing we can all use is a little more time".*

"It was nice to meet you Tom, I hope you spend more time with your family and I hope to meet you again here on the band. 75 year Old Man, this is K9NZQ, clear and going QRT, good morning!"

You could have heard a pin drop on the band when this fellow signed off. I guess he gave us all a lot to think about. I had planned to work on the antenna that morning and then I was going to meet up with a few hams to work on the next club newsletter. Instead, I went upstairs and woke my wife up with a kiss. *"C'mon honey, I'm taking you and the children to breakfast."*

"What brought this on?" she asked with a smile. *"Oh, nothing special, it's just been a long time since we spent a Saturday together with the children. Hey, can we stop at a toy store while we're out? I need to buy some marbles."*

Make Your Home a Safe Place to Spend Time

Make living in your home a safe place to spend time, to experiment and to have opinions to think creatively. Have loads of art projects your children can enjoy. Put a big drop cloth under your kitchen table and bring out a box of paper, glitter, glue, paints, crayons, chalk, rhinestones, spices and sit down with your children and enjoy an hour together doing something creative. Do not criticize them. Take your children to a park and swing with them and go down the slides with them. Take them to theme parks and ride rides with them. Take them to play golf, to the zoo, to the museums. Run in the rain, build a snowman in the winter. Find that child within you and enjoy playing again.

····· Play educational games with ·····
your children, its the best
····· investment you will ever make.·····

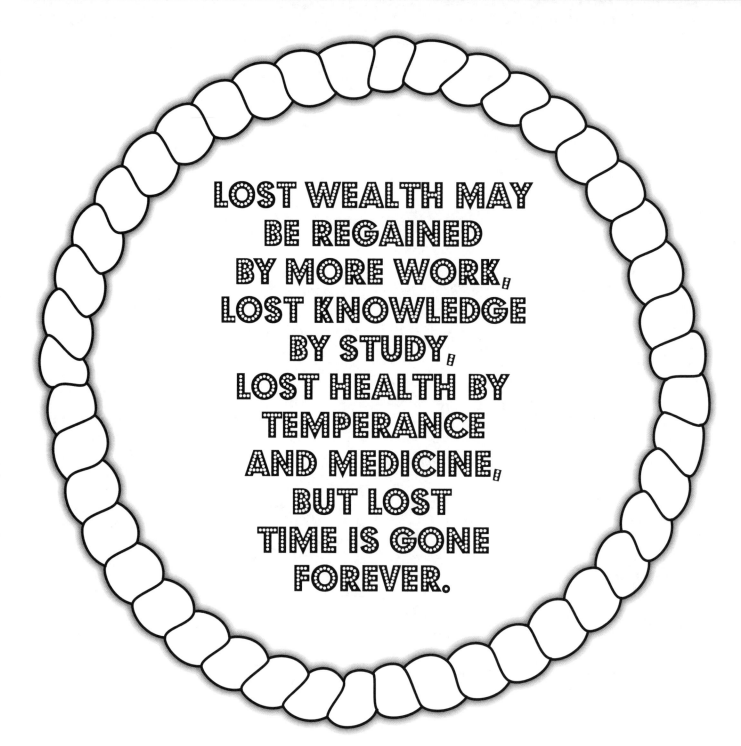

LOST WEALTH MAY
BE REGAINED
BY MORE WORK,
LOST KNOWLEDGE
BY STUDY,
LOST HEALTH BY
TEMPERANCE
AND MEDICINE,
BUT LOST
TIME IS GONE
FOREVER.

chapter 4

Chapter Four

What is it that you plan to do with your one wild and precious life?

Time Is Not Waiting For You

Time is slipping through your fingers. It is not waiting on you. It is not going to let you have overs. It is not going to care if you procrastinate or not. The clock is ticking. The time is now for you to go for your dreams. Now. Right now. No more putting it off. No more excuses, no more playing the victim. Nope, time to take action is now.

The Time is...

N⊙W

Time is up!

Is it about time you reach your goals?

NOW'S THE TIME

For YOU to stop waiting and decide to decide to go for your dreams!

"When you get what you want in your struggle for self and the world makes you king for a day, Just go to the mirror and look at yourself And see what that man has to say. For it isn't your father or mother or wife Whose judgment upon you must pass. The fellow whose verdict counts most in your life is the one staring back from the glass. You may be like Jack Horner and chisel a plum And think you're a wonderful guy. But the man in the glass says you're only a bum If you can't look him straight in the eye. He's the fellow to please - never mind all the rest, For he's with you clear to the end. And you've passed your most dangerous, difficult test if the man in the glass is your friend. You may fool the whole world down the pathway of years and get pats on the back as you pass. But your final reward will be heartache and tears If you've cheated the man in the glass."
-Unknown

You don't get paid for the day; you get paid for the value you bring to the day.

"Reputation is what you are perceived to be. Character is what you are."
-Coach John Wooden

BE MINDFUL OF HOW YOU APPROACH TIME. WATCHING THE CLOCK IS NOT THE SAME AS WATCHING THE SUN RISE.

Time

Stand before me on the sign of infinity all you who fear.
With the granting of the law of provenation comes the application
of change. I will give you the key and with this knowledge please realize comes the responsibility of sharing it. I will show you the way, *sense it?*
Throughout the universe there is order, in the movement of the planets, in nature
and in the functioning of the human mind. A mind that is in its natural state of order
is in harmony with the universe and such a mind is timeless. Your life is an expression
of your mind! You are the creator of your own universe, for as a human being you are free
to will whatever state of being you desire through the use of your thoughts and words. Ah!
There is great power there, can be a blessing or a curse it's entirely up to you for the quality
of your life is brought about by the quality of your thinking, think about that. Thoughts
produce actions; look at WHAT you are thinking, see the pettiness and the envy and the
greed and the fear and all the other attitudes that cause you pain and discomfort; realize that
the one thing you have absolute control over is your attitude; see the effect that it has on
those around you, for each life is linked to all life and your words carry with chain-reactions
like a stone that is thrown into a pond, if your thinking is in order your words
will flow directly from the heart creating ripples of love, if you truly want
to change your world my friends, you must change your thinking.
Reason is your greatest tool; it creates an atmosphere of understanding
which leads to caring which is love. Choose your words with care.

Go forth with love...
Performed by - Sir Lawrence Olivier

Take Time to Visualize

When you want something badly enough, you can't help visualizing your dream all the time. I pictured myself paying off the six figures in debt that I had accrued, moving to the Rocky Mountains, traveling the world, marrying the man of my dreams, being able to be with my children when they were grown, helping my children through their ups and downs in life and enjoying life to the fullest. These visualization techniques worked extremely well for me and they will work for you!

*"Whatever your mind can conceive
and believe, it can achieve."*
-Napoleon Hill

• • • • • • • • • • • • • • • • •

If you continue to do what you have always done, you are going to continue to get what you have always gotten.

The real big question now is...

is it enough?

• • • • • • • • • • • • • • • • •

Lost Items

Losing things, such as glasses, tickets, keys, credit cards, cell phones, blackberries, iPods, makeup bag, wastes a lot of time. Have a place for everything and put everything back in it's place. Establish a bowl at your front door for your keys and glasses.

SWEAT THE SMALL STUFF

Don't loan out books, you will most likely not get them back. Back up your computer. Never put your laptop in your luggage. Don't be a collector of your own business cards and don't pack them when you travel. Send greeting cards online. Keep a good supply of stamps on hand.

Label all of your CD's and DVD's with a black marker. Use wine charms on your wine glasses. Photo copy your credit cards and your passports, health insurance cards and your photo ID. Leave one at home when you travel so that if you lose everything you can quickly report them lost. Don't carry your Social Security card with you. You don't need it and it can cost you a lot of time if it falls in the wrong hands. Have your favorite phone numbers stored someplace in addition to your cell phone in case you lose it.

IDENTIFY WHY YOU AREN'T ENTHUSIASTIC AND TAKE A CHECK UP FROM THE NECK UP. CHANGE YOUR ATTITUDE.

Get a spine, get a backbone, not a wishbone.

If you are still alive, your work on earth is not done.

Have Faith That the Time You are Putting Forth is Worth It

The size of your success is determined by the size of your belief. I've learned, along several of my own journeys, the importance of having an uncompromising faith in myself which has been a critical component in accomplishing my goals.

Discipline and Focus

Discipline is a key component required to achieve your goals and dreams. When working toward your dream think of discipline as having the ability to flick the annoying doubting person off your shoulder who says *"Can you really do this?"* You need to have the *"I can do it!"* attitude. Holding the vision or experience that inspired you in the forefront of your mind will help you stay disciplined. Remember - self doubt destroys! With every disciplined effort there is a multiple reward.

Gratitude Time

One of the most important qualities you can have on your journey to obtaining a dream is *"an attitude of gratitude"*. Every morning make a habit of spending a minimum of five minutes reflecting on the many things you are truly grateful for in your life. When you are grateful for life's gifts, you are truly rich.

Achieve Success by giving Time To Achieve Success

Expect Success to Show Up

When you plan and prepare carefully, you can expect to have success in your time efforts. When you develop the winning qualities that you were born with, the winner you were born to be emerges. When you plan and prepare to make a sale, you can legitimately expect to make a sale. Although not all your expectations are going to come to pass, you give yourself an infinitely better chance of succeeding by taking the proper steps. Regardless of your goal...losing weight, making more sales, furthering your education, earning a promotion, saving money for a new home or an exotic vacation...you can expect to achieve your goal if you plan and prepare for it and put in time to get it.

Save Time Shopping

Shopping can be a great way to spend time. Other times, it can be a huge time waster. Think about the time it takes to leave your home and go shopping. Is it a good use of your time? Think through where you need to go so that you can park near where the store is and to get the heaviest items last. Wear easy-to-put on clothes so you can save time in the dressing room. Go early in the day when the stores are not crowded. For a couple of small items it might be faster to go to a boutique instead of a giant shopping mall. Get to know one sales person in the store and let them help you with your purchases instead of whipping out your credit card at many different locations in the store. Shop online when you can to save time. Use the computer, phone, not the car. Call ahead and make sure the store has what you want before getting there to find out it is sold out, or is closed.

The surest way to be late is to have plenty of time.

Group Your Errands

Stop at the grocery store, bank, gasoline station and any other places you need to go. Don't go home then leave again. If you have teenagers just starting to drive, let them run your errands for you.

Stop! You Don't Need It!

Just because you find a *"bargain"* or it's cheap or free you don't need it. It's something else to dust or polish or store.

Put it Away

When you get home, put everything you buy away soon after you arrive.

WHILE WE ARE POSTPONING, LIFE SPEEDS BY.

You may delay, but time will not.

You will never "find" time for anything. If you want time, you must make it.

Don't say you don't have enough time. You have exactly the same number of hours per day that were given to Helen Keller, Pasteur, Michelangelo, Leonardo da Vinci, Thomas Jefferson and Albert Einstein.

Cell Phone Time

Don't let your cell phone rule your life and ruin the lives of those around you. Don't use your cell phone while you are eating at a restaurant letting everyone hear your business. Focus on the people you are with, not who is calling you. Don't engage in a long phone conversation while driving. Invest in a headset.

The bad news is time flies. The good news is you're the pilot.

Take the Day Off

Remember your joy when school was closed due to bad weather? Don't wait for a storm or a bad cold to take a break. Reward yourself with a Mental Health Day. Cancel all your plans. And don't spend your time trying to catch up. Instead luxuriate in winding down.

Take Responsibility

"Only you are responsible for the course you take from here. You cannot say, 'I went through this', or 'I have this in my background, therefore I have a right to be unsuccessful, or a right to fail'. If you want to, fine, do that. But no matter what went on, you do have responsibility for the direction of your own life. The way you remember the past depends upon your hope for the future. And if you have the courage to grab the reins and take hold of your current life, then the past really becomes a rather nice place, no matter what went on."
-Storey Musgrave, Dean of American Astronauts. Both of his parents committed suicide, when he was only three years old.

THERE IS NO TRAFFIC JAM ON THE EXTRA MILE.

Stephen Covey's 7 Habits of Highly Effective People

Habit 1: Be proactive. Control your environment, rather than have it control you. Have a self determination, choice and the power to decide response to stimulus, conditions and circumstances.

Habit 2: Begin with the end in mind. Get a habit of personal leadership-leading yourself, towards what you consider your aims. Develop the habit of concentrating on relevant activities and you will build a platform to avoid distractions and become more productive and successful.

Habit 3: Put first things first. 1. Personal-management is about organizing and implementing activities in line with the aims established in habit. **2.** Habit 2 is the first, or mental creation; habit 3 is the second, or physical creation.

Habit 4: Think win-win. Interpersonal leadership is necessary because achievements are largely dependent on cooperative efforts with others. A win-win is based on the assumption that there is plenty for everyone and that success follows a cooperative approach more naturally than the confrontation of win-or-lose.

Habit 5: Seek first to understand and then to be understood. *Diagnose before you prescribe.*

Habit 6: Synergize. Creative cooperation-the principle that the whole is greater than the sum of its parts, which implicitly lays down the challenge to see the good and potential in the other person's contribution.

Habit 7: Sharpen the saw. Self-renewal surrounds all the other habits, enabling and encouraging them to happen and grow. Divide the self into four parts: the spiritual, mental, physical and the social/emotional, which all need feeding and developing.

THIS ABOVE ALL: TO THINE OWN SELF BE TRUE.

Affirmation Time

Taking the time to having the courage of your convictions will help you boldly meet your challenges. Believing in your physical, emotional, intellectual and spiritual standards and values enables you to apply your resources and creative energy when faced with challenges and choices. Eleanor Roosevelt said, *"You must do the thing you cannot do"*, General Patton said that courage is *"Fear holding on another minute"*. Examining your time and making changes as you grow in life is the example that enables others to have the courage to follow. As you review these ten affirmations ask yourself, *"Where do I need to put my time to change, grow and stretch to reach my full capacity?"*

1. **The time to seek the truth.** I am willing to seek out unpleasant truths, even when they may conflict with things I have a great investment in, or when the truth may threaten my physical, intellectual, or emotional security. I recognize that my personal freedom depends on my ability to seek and find truth.

2. **The time to lead an ethical life.** I realize that it takes courage to be ethical. I resist the temptation to be less than ethical, even when everyone is doing it. I regard honest people as heroes, not fools.

3. **The time to be involved.** Apathy and indifference can be more devastating than any natural or man-made disasters. Despite occasional compassion fatigue, I remain committed to making a difference and getting others involved. I refuse to look the other way.

4. **The time to reject cynicism.** Cynicism is a comforting and protective refuge, but one I resist vigilantly. I know that trust and optimism, essential to a productive life, are impossible if I give in to the cowardice of cynicism.

5. **The time to assume responsibility.** I alone am responsible for my actions, whether they lead to success or failure. I refuse to waste time on making excuses, harboring unrealistic hopes, or placing blame. I am willing to share responsibility and accountability with others and back them up 100% if things go wrong.

6. **The time to lead at home.** I know that my home and family are my most powerful legacy for the future. I mentor my children, giving them equal love and discipline. I'm there 100% for my partner. I honor my parents and older relatives, even if advanced age, ill health, or different values make communication seem difficult and unrewarding. I live each day with my family and won't think, *Tomorrow I'll have more time.*

7. **The time to persist.** I have the courage to delay gratification, to endure the long haul and to make sacrifices when necessary. I frequently visualize the next few years and anticipate the results of my actions. I summon the inner resources to stay on track by keeping my eye on this big picture.

8. **The time to serve.** In an ego-driven, success-driven society, I have the courage to put myself second. I realize that the loftiest leader is the one who serves others best. My job, no matter what the description or title, is to provide satisfaction, solve challenges, fill needs and find answers in a way that enhances and empowers those around me.

9. **The time to lead.** Few people are willing to stand for something, or even to clarify what they would stand for if they could. Others criticize without offering solutions, but I concentrate on what I stand for, on solutions and goals and on how I can motivate others to action. I'm not content to wait for someone else to take charge and point a direction.

10. **The time to follow.** Unlike leaders of image, a leader of substance knows when and how to follow willingly. I have learned the benefits of being a good follower, of welcoming the ideas and contributions of others without feeling that my position or integrity has been challenged. By sharing power, I increase my own personal and professional power and make myself aware of the challenges that others face every day.

All That I Have Accomplished

All that I have accomplished, or expect, or hope to accomplish has been and will be by that plodding, patient, non-stop, focus, determination, vision, study, personal growth, action and persevering process of accretion which builds the ant-heap particle by particle, thought by thought, fact by fact.

"The person who seeks one thing in life and but one,
May hope to achieve it before life be done;
But he who seeks all things, wherever he goes,
Only reaps from the hopes which around him he
sows, a harvest of barren regrets.
Those who make the worse use of their time
are the first to complain of its shortness."
-Jean De La Bruyere

Lessons from John Wooden

"Four things a man must learn to do
If he would make his life more true:
To think without confusion clearly,
To love his fellow man sincerely,
To act from honest motives purely,
To trust in God and heaven securely."

Be true to yourself, help others, make friend-
ship a fine art, drink deeply from good books, make
each day your masterpiece, build a shelter against a
rainy day by the life you live and give thanks
for your blessings and pray for guidance every day.

The great dividing line between success
and failure can be expressed in five words:
"I did not have time."

---

a stonecutter had butterflies for a hobby and when he died, he had one of the best collections in the world.

When others were at play, I was always at work. I built a business while a single mother and paid back six figures in debt by economizing the minutes in the day. I educated myself and did much of my best work during my spare moments. I seldom lost a moment. I studied sales and outlined books late into the night when my children were in bed and whenever I could get a spare minute. I have accomplished a lot in my life even though it has been subject to interruptions which would have discouraged most women from attempting anything outside their regular family duties. Harriet Beecher Stowe wrote her great masterpiece, *Uncle Toms Cabin*, in the midst of pressing household cares. Beecher read Froude's *England*, a little each day that he had to wait for dinner. Longfellow translated the *Inferno* by snatches of ten minutes a day, while waiting for his coffee to boil, persisting for years until the work was done. Many a great person has snatched his reputation from odd bits of time which others, who wonder at their failure to get on, throw away.

Don't Create a Time Monster

Are you trying to do too much? Are you always trying to multi-task and doing every single thing that pops into your mind? Don't lock up your imagination because you are trying to do too much.

The Fine Art of Saying

no!

YOU DON'T HAVE TO SAY YES TO EVERYTHING EVERYONE ASKS YOU TO DO!

You don't have to be the scout leader, the home room mother, the Sunday School teacher, the coach, the Field Trip parent, the Book Club leader, the Bible Study leader or any other volunteer position. You will have plenty of time later in life to volunteer. Use the first thirty years of your life time setting up the rest of your life.

The World is at Your Door

You can have anything you want in life if you want it badly enough and are willing to work to get it. Those of you in gangs, you are wasting your time. You are going to pass away from this earth and you most likely will be forgotten very quickly and will have done nothing to improve the world. Those of you on or peddling drugs, you are wasting your time. You are going to pass away from this earth and you most likely will be forgotten very quickly and will have done nothing to improve the world. Those of you stealing, lying, conniving, killing others, going to jail and not doing what is right in the human civilization, you are wasting your time. You are going to pass away from this earth and you most likely will be forgotten very quickly and will have done nothing to improve the world. Those of you hurting young children or battering your wives, shame on you. Stop what you are doing this very minute, get help. Those of you trying to control everyone in your life, stop, you are not in control of the lives of others. Those of you criticizing every politician, every theology, every teacher and everyone who has any opinion, you are wasting your time. There are no statues erected to remember the critics. You are going to pass away from this earth and you most likely will be forgotten very quickly and will have done nothing to improve the world. Those of you cheating on your spouse, you are only going to hurt your partner for the rest of their lives. Maybe generations. Those of you who are wasting your time, you might as well be in the graveyard right now. You are just taking up space on earth for those who do want to enjoy this life. Why not stop all of your foolishness and value your time? Even if you have messed up big time, there is always today to start over. Stop being a jerk to everyone. It is your choice to change you. If you are a terrorist, stop, don't be so stupid to believe mean people and instead consider that life *is* meaningful.

The Calf Path

One day, through the primeval wood,
A calf walked home, as good calves should;
But made a trail all bent askew,
A crooked trail, as all calves do.
Since then three hundred years have fled,
And, I infer, the calf is dead.
But still he left behind his trail,
And thereby hangs my moral tale.
The trail was taken up next day
By a lone dog that passed that way;
And then a wise bellwether sheep
Pursued the trail o'er vale and steep,
And drew the flock behind him, too,
As good bellwethers always do.
And from that day, o'er hill and glade,
Through those old woods a path was made,
And many men wound in and out,
And dodged and turned and bent about,
And uttered words of righteous wrath
Because 'twas such a crooked path;
But still they followed - do not laugh -
The first migrations of that calf,
And through this winding wood-way stalked
Because he wobbled when he walked.
This forest path became a lane,
That bent, and turned and turned again.
This crooked lane became a road,
Where many a poor horse with his load
Toiled on beneath the burning sun,
And traveled some three miles in one.
And thus a century and a half
They trod the footsteps of that calf.
The years passed on in swiftness fleet.
The road became a village street,

And this, before men were aware,
A city's crowded thoroughfare,
And soon the central street was this
Of a renowned metropolis;
And men two centuries and a half
Trod in the footsteps of that calf.
Each day a hundred thousand rout
Followed that zigzag calf about,
And o'er his crooked journey went
The traffic of a continent.
A hundred thousand men were led
By one calf near three centuries dead.
They follow still his crooked way,
And lose one hundred years a day,
For thus such reverence is lent
To well-established precedent.
A moral lesson this might teach
Were I ordained and called to preach;
For men are prone to go it blind
Along the calf-paths of the mind,
And work away from sun to sun
To do what other men have done.
They follow in the beaten track,
And out and in, and forth and back,
And still their devious course pursue,
To keep the path that others do.
They keep the path a sacred groove,
Along which all their lives they move;
But how the wise old wood-gods laugh,
Who saw the first primeval calf!
Ah, many things this tale might teach -
But I am not ordained to preach.
- Sam Walter Foss (1895)

How to Get More Work Done in a Day

How do you achieve financial security in a world where there is no employment security? Do you consider yourself to be honest and at least reasonably intelligent? As an honest, intelligent person, do you, as a general rule, get about twice as much work done on the day before you go on vacation as you normally get done? If you can figure out why and learn how and repeat it every day without working any longer or any harder, does it make sense that you will be more valuable to yourself, your company, your family and your community? The answer is *"Yes"*. Now on the night before the day before vacation, do you get your laptop or a sheet of paper out and plan, *"Now tomorrow I've got to do this and this...."* We call that goal setting. So, you set your goals. Then get them organized in the order of their importance. Get the disagreeable and difficult things out of the way first. Free your mind so you can concentrate on what else you have got to do. Get organized, accept responsibility and you make the commitments. Now commitment is important, whether it is to get your education, make one more call, keep the marriage together or whatever. Commitment is important because when you hit the wall-not IF, but WHEN you hit the wall-if you have made a commitment your first thought is, *"How do I solve the challenge?"* If you haven't made the commitment your first thought is, *"How do I get out of this situation?"* And you find literally what you are looking for. When you make that commitment, things happen. It shows that you really care about the other people in your life. It demonstrates that you are dependable. Even though you're leaving town, you're not going to leave an unfinished task for others to do. Your integrity comes through. Have you ever participated in organized team sports? Did you ever go home one night and say to your parents something like, *"Mom, Dad, you won't believe the game plan the*

coach has worked out. It is incredible. We 're going to kill those suckers tomorrow. You can take that to the bank". You were optimistic simply because you had a plan of action and likewise you are optimistic that tomorrow you are going to be able to get all of the things done that need to be done before you can go on that vacation. Now some people are born optimistic and some are born pessimistic. The 1828 Noah Webster Dictionary does not have the word pessimist in it. But it has the word optimist. Now I am a natural born optimist. The good news is if you are a natural born pessimist, you definitely, emphatically, positively can change. You are a pessimist by choice because you are what you are and where you are because of what's gone into your mind so far in life. You can change what you are; you can change where you are, by changing what goes into your mind. On the day before you go on vacation you not only get to work on time, you are a little early and you immediately get started. You don't stand around and say, *"Well, I wonder what I ought to do now"*. You can't wait to get after it. You want to do the right thing so you get started in a big hurry. You are enthusiastic about it. You are highly motivated. You decisively move from one task to another. Have you noticed that as a general rule people who have nothing to do want to do it with you? Now, on this day before vacation, when you finish one task you move with purpose to finish the next objective on your list.

> Rivers can't be forced to flow uphill; nor should you try to work against your inner nature.

"If you want to make good use of your time, you've got to know what's most important and then give it all you've got."
-Lee Iacocca

One Hour a Day

Oh, what wonders have been performed in *"one hour a day!"* One hour a day withdrawn from frivolous pursuits and profitably employed, would enable any person of ordinary capacity to master a complete science. One hour a day would make an ignorant person a well informed person in ten years. One hour a day in study can earn you a fortune. In an hour a day, you could read twenty pages thoughtfully - over seven thousand pages, or eighteen large volumes in a year. An hour a day might make all the difference between bare existence and useful, happy living. An hour a day might make - has made - an unknown person a famous one, a useless person a benefactor to his race. Consider, then, the mighty possibilities of two, four, yes, six hours a day that are, on the average, thrown away by young people in the restless desire for fun and diversion! Everyone should have a hobby to occupy their leisure hours, something useful to which you can turn with delight, whenever you have leisure time. It might be in line with your work or otherwise, only your heart must be in it.

Gossip is a Colossal Waste of Time

Don't let people block you for a two-minute gossip session or four-minute or five-minute or six-minute chat. The listener has more to do with gossiping than the speaker does, because if you don't listen nobody is going to gossip to you. They just won't. When you move with purpose, people will step aside and let you go. I will absolutely guarantee that you will save a minimum of an hour a day in two three, five-minute spurts of time. An hour a day day is five hours per week is 250 hours per year. That is six weeks of your life that you've wasted and six weeks of combined time that you have wasted with people who have been gossiping with you. What could you do with six extra weeks every year?

Make Work Fun

Introducing a bit of fun into your work will make the day easier for you and your customers. If possible, flip your morning and afternoon schedules for a change of pace.

80/20 Rule

Use the 80-20 Rule originally stated by the Italian economist Vilfredo Pareto who noted that 80% of the reward comes from 20% of the effort. The trick to prioritizing is to isolate and identify that valuable 20%. Once identified, prioritize time to concentrate your work on those items with the greatest reward. Did you know you wear 80% of your clothes 20% of the time? Did you know you use 20% of your towels 80% of the time? 20% of your efforts generate 80% of your results.

Waste your time and waste of your life, or master your time and master your life.

Don't be fooled by the calendar. There are only as many days in the year of which you make use. One person gets only a week's value out of a year while another person gets a full year's value out of a week.

THE KEY IS IN NOT SPENDING TIME, BUT IN INVESTING IT.

Ordinary people think merely of spending time. Great people think of using it.

"Determine never to be idle. No person will have occasion to complain of the want of time who never loses any. It is wonderful how much can be done if we are always doing."
-Thomas Jefferson

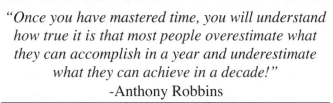

"Once you have mastered time, you will understand how true it is that most people overestimate what they can accomplish in a year and underestimate what they can achieve in a decade!"
-Anthony Robbins

Never let yesterday use up today

"I don't think of the past. The only thing that matters is the everlasting present."
-Somerset Maugham

"You cannot do a kindness too soon, for you never know how soon it will be too late."
-Ralph Waldo Emerson

"Whether it's the best of times or the worst of times, it's the only time we've got."
-Art Buchwald

ONE THING YOU CAN'T RECYCLE IS WASTED TIME

TIME IS THE MOST VALUABLE THING A MAN CAN SPEND.

"Until you value yourself you will not value your time. Until you value your time, you will not do anything with it."
-M. Scott Peck

"Time is at once the most valuable and the most perishable of all our possessions."
-John Randolph

Never leave 'till tomorrow which you can do today.

"Time is really the only capital that any human being has and the only thing he can't afford to lose."
-Thomas Edison

"Until we can manage time, we can manage nothing else."
-Peter F. Drucker

"When you are inspired by some great purpose, some extraordinary project, all your thoughts break their bonds; your mind transcends limitations, your consciousness expands in every direction and you find yourself in a new, great and wonderful world. Dormant focus, faculties and talents become alive and you discover yourself to be a greater person by far than you ever dreamed yourself to be."
-Patenjali

Never believe in never

"You cannot kill time without injuring eternity."
-Henry David Thoreau

What may be done at any time will be done at no time.

A wise person does at once, what a fool does at last. Both do the same thing; only at different times.

A year from now you will wish you had started today. Twenty years from now you will wish you had started today.

Three people were laying brick.
The first was asked, *"What are you doing?"*
He answered, *"Laying some brick"*.
The second person was asked.
"What are you working for?"
He answered, *"Fifty dollars a day"*.
The third person was asked,
"What are you doing?"
She answered,
"I am helping to build a great beautiful Cathedral".
Which person are you?

Holiday Time-Management

The number one rule for surviving the holidays is remembering that you can always say *"No"* and you can always do things more simply, even if that isn't the way it's always been done in the past.

If you're worried about getting the perfect gift for that special someone, but the thought of battling through all the holiday traffic, spending hours finding a parking place, then walking miles through a crowded mall seems too overwhelming for you, then remember that sometimes the best gift is a simple one.

You can buy almost anything online from the comfort of your own home. Shop from your seat not your feet! Gift cards are also an easy way to go, whether you want to spend a few dollars on a video rental gift card, or a lot on a gift card for a fancy restaurant.

Returning Gift Items

Don't call when you are enraged and upset. Don't attack. When you get someone on the phone, ask for their name and extension so if you get cut off you can get back in touch with the person who knows your situation. Stay kind. For example you can say, *Would it be possible for you to return this for me?*

If the thought of a party, family gathering, or other *mandatory* social event leaves you knotted up with anxiety, plan ahead for some *escape time* for yourself. No matter where you are, if you are suddenly feeling overwhelmed with anxiety, claustrophobia, or simply more emotion than you feel safe showing in public, seek out the nearest restroom or take a walk. Do not return to the party or gathering until you have mentally gathered yourself together. The bathroom is a simple solution that is always available. It gives you privacy to take a few deep breaths, try to calm down and mentally reevaluate your situation enough to decide if you think you really can calm down, or if you really need to tell the host or leader of the party or social event that you are not feeling well and need to go home.

Do you ever find yourself thinking, *"I need a vacation! Not days spent with those people!"* If the family or friends that you are spending the holidays with are going to or already are causing you more stress than you can handle, then reconsider whether spending time with them is really the best choice you could make right now. Most people are afraid to spend the holidays alone, but as opposed to being around people who invalidate you, with everything from guilt-tripping to actual abuse, you might want to consider which situation you would really prefer.

Get Plenty of Sleep

Whether you are spending the holidays rushing around doing all of your usual things or planning ahead for what to do with your alone time, sleep is essential. Schedule in your sleep time first when you plan out your day. If you are too tired to think straight, you cannot get anything done efficiently and perhaps not even done at all.

Spending Holidays Alone

How do you spend time by yourself without getting depressed? Well, here are a few tips. Stay busy. If you think there is nothing you need to do, take a closer look at your house. If you look hard enough, it's pretty easy to come up with a list of things to do.

Whatever your reason may be for being alone: forget those centuries-old traditions and create some new traditions of your own. Instead of staying up to the wee hours of the morning cooking and baking and cleaning, stay up late watching a favorite movie and sleep as late as you want to the next day.

Eat Healthy

Make sure you eat enough to keep yourself going and eat as healthfully as you can. When you are under a lot of stress, it is easy to just keep going on manic energy alone. When you are running on manic energy, your body burns calories at a much higher rate than normal, so when your body tells you that it is hungry, listen to it and eat something as soon as possible. To help keep off those infamous holiday pounds despite all the scrumptious goodies around you, buy some fruit or vegetables and eat them first before you eat anything else at mealtime or for snacks. Fresh fruit is especially good for you because it is filling and very nutritious.

Things rarely go according to a prearranged agenda. That means a lot of time falling through the cracks chasing down appointments, unreturned phone calls and other items that simply aren't going to happen. Don't try to plan on doing too many things. Assume that only 50% of the things you plan on doing during the holidays will actually get done. If you don't, you'll just waste valuable time trying to find out why things didn't happen.

Don't Stress Out

Don't stress out — and waste time in the process — by obsessing over every second of time. Do what you can and enjoy whatever time you spend more pleasantly or productively. Be grateful for what goes right and learn from your mistakes. Act as if they were scenes in a movie that you get to retake.

Entertainment Time

Throw a potluck party. Ask everyone to bring a dish or a bottle of wine. You can get appetizers already prepared. Cook what you can ahead of time. Start a party file with the invitation list and RSVP E-mails so you can keep track of how many people will be attending.

A laugh a day keeps the "blah" humbugs away!

Time to Start Over

It is really tough to start over in life when you have been through a tragedy, a death of a loved one, a breakup of a relationship, a divorce, a major disappointment, getting fired from a job, an argument, abuse or negative input constantly coming your way. Many times you want to be by yourself or to run away or to not be with people because you are fragile.

Staying in grief is personal to how long it takes you to work through it. I have found that losing a loved one in death is something I have never gotten over. I think about my loved ones on a regular basis and feel the planet earth is empty of their spirits. I miss many people so much; I don't think that will ever go away. So you press onward. Let the living live.

If you are in a time in your life where your heart is broken for whatever reason remember that this time will pass. You will get better and you will heal from a heartbreak. There will be another love. Pick yourself up and get ready for someone to come into your life who will love and cherish you.

A New Year does not have to begin with January 1st. Everyday can be the first day of the new year for you. Every day is the first day of the rest of your life.

Think about how you are treating those you love. Stop the bickering, stop the arguing, stop yourself from being nasty or mean. Just stop it now.

Make new resolutions. Resolve to change, to grow, to be better and to do more, be more and have more in the rest of your life.

HAPPY NEW YEAR!

COUNT YOUR BLESSINGS ~ IT IS THE REASON FOR THE SEASON.

MAKE EVERYDAY JANUARY THE 1ST

Make FUN resolutions from now on.
Become resolute to follow through
for at least 3 minutes

I fully intend to improve the rest of my life time. I am not just going to acquire things, but I am going to plan a lifestyle that nurtures, reinforces and lets me be the best I can be.

NEW YEAR'S RESOLUTIONS

Resolve that no one will ever
get out of this world alive.
Resolve, therefore to maintain a sense of values.
Resolve to be trusted, to be committed to
going for greatness and to care about others.
Resolve to take care of yourself. Good health
is everyone's major source of wealth.
Resolve to be cheerful and helpful.
People will repay you in kindness.
Resolve to listen more and to talk less.
No one ever learns anything by talking.
Resolve to be wary of giving advice.
Wise men don't need it and fools won't heed it.
Resolve to be tender with the young,
compassionate with the aged, sympathetic with the
striving and tolerant of the weak and the wrong.
Sometime in your life you
will have been all of these.
Resolve to tear up that letter or
email written at a time of anger.
Resolve to quit being so impatient,
annoyed and angry at others and with yourself.
Resolve to be true to yourself and let others
be true to their own dreams and desires.
Resolve that nothing ever stays the same for long.
Resolve to do what you fear the
most and overcome your fear.
Resolve to live your life to the fullest,
this isn't a dress rehearsal.
Resolve to be a student instead of the teacher.
Resolve to be dependable.
Resolve to improve your relationship
with your partner, spouse or lover.
Resolve to be the very best you can be,
to do all you can and be all you can be.
Resolve to take massive action
on your visions and dreams.
Resolve that no one is responsible for
your success or failure in life but yourself.
Resolve to throw out old ideas
and welcome new ideas.
Resolve to get out of the way of who you are
blocking and go around those who are blocking you.

Resolve to forgive those who have hurt you.
Resolve to make this year your
springboard for your happy future!
Resolve to go for greatness,
zip yourself up in a positive attitude bag.
Resolve to life with abundance
and prosperity and wealth thoughts.
Resolve to quit being average and to
throw off the chains of debt, worry and defeat.
Resolve to redecorate your home.
Resolve to Reach your Peak.
Resolve that no longer will you hang out
with people who tear down your precious dreams.
Resolve to attend more seminars and
to read more personal growth books.
Resolve to see more of the world so
you will become more interesting.
Resolve to work on your
Presentation and Leadership Skills.
Resolve to listen with great care for ideas
and inspiration that can empower you.
Resolve to increase your own self-esteem.
Resolve to quit trying to break down relationships
instead of building them up....foolish choice to
burn bridges of friendship. We all need each other.
Friendships are priceless.
Resolve to get honest with yourself.
Resolve to not be needy of someone else's approval.
Resolve to improve yourself.
Resolve to make the first quarter of the year massive.
Resolve to follow those who are
living the lifestyle you wish to follow.
Resolve to smile more, to spread happiness
out into the world. Don't worry, be happy.
Resolve to cherish the people
you love and appreciate.
Resolve to enjoy life to the fullest, every day,
every way. Every minute is ticking. Tick Tock.
Resolve to make your dreams come true
and to make your life a masterpiece.
Resolve to quit wasting time.

chapter 5

In this Chapter you will learn about:

- Grief
- Guilt and Shame
- Harvest Each Day
- Eliminate Clutter
- Technology
- Irish Blessings
- Father Time
- Cats in the Cradle
- The Request

Chapter Five

Grieving Takes Time

Part of life is saying goodbye to precious, cherished friendships and family. There is nothing easy about death or divorce. There is nothing easy about going through the death process with someone you dearly love. There is nothing quite so alarming and sad than to find out that someone you adore, love and want to live, is going to leave this world. No one gets out of this life alive. At the end of the day, it is one of the saddest times in life. There is grief time in life. If you don't handle it, it will never go away.

Never let the things that matter most be ignored.

Tough times never last but tough people do.

If God brings you to it-He will see you through it!

Here are the emotional behaviors that I believe we may certainly experience when saying goodbye forever to those we love; there is no script for grief; we cannot expect to feel any of our emotions in a particular set pattern. And acceptance is probably the last emotion felt. Grief, like so many other things in our complex lives, can't be reduced to a neat list with absolute definitions, time lines, strategies, goals and completion dates. Would that it were so easy? Grief is as individual as those of us who feel it and as varied as the circumstances of death which occur.

Denial Time: *This isn't happening to me!*
Anger Time: *Why is this happening to me?*
Bargaining Time: *I promise I'll be a better person if...*
Depression Time: *I don't care anymore.*
Acceptance Time: *I'm ready for whatever comes.*

The loss of a loved one is never finished.
The pain lives with you forever.
You just have to press onward in life.

Never say to someone in their time of grief...*It was his or her time...or it will get better over time. You don't know that or chin up, things will be better, or at least they are out of pain now.* Instead ask...*What can I do for you during this time of grief?*

There are three particular types of behavior exhibited by those suffering from grief and loss. They are:
Numbness Time: mechanical functioning and social insulation.
Disorganization Time: intensely painful feelings of loss.
Reorganization: re-entry into a more 'normal' social life.

There will be emotions of grief and loss but they might be more for what we will miss. If a young life is cut short unexpectedly, there may well be feelings of denial, anger, bargaining, depression and in some cases acceptance. Just as we have different emotional reactions to anything that happens in our lives, so too, will we experience grief and loss in different ways. The important thing to remember is that there is a wide range of emotions that may be experienced; to expect to feel some of them and to know that we cannot completely control the process. Be there for others when they are grieving. Be understanding. We are all in this together.

"We are only dancing on this earth for such a short time."
-Cat Stevens

When Will I Be Through Grieving?

Grieving used to be much more ritualistic than it is today. In generations past there were set periods of time when certain customs must be observed: Widows wore all black clothing for one year and drab colors forever after. Mourners could not attend social gatherings for months. Laughter and gaiety were discouraged for weeks or months. Today we are unfettered by these restrictions and might even be confused about when we should be done grieving. From my experience, we'll probably never be done. We will never forget the person we grieve for. Our feelings may be tempered more with good memories than sadness as time passes, but that isn't to say that waves of raw emotion won't overcome us way after we think we should be done. Feelings will occur, there will be times in your sleep that you will remember your loved one, there will be times you will see someone who looks like the person you have lost in your life and that time that you see them will bring memories flooding back. The best thing to do is to keep them in perspective, try to understand why you feel a certain way and if there are any unresolved issues that cause particular emotional pain, forgive yourself and others and if necessary talk with someone about it.

There is no completion date to grieving...let your emotions flow through the stages of grief.

If you need to, get a grief counselor. Time will continue to tick while you are grieving. You cannot put your life on hold for years to grieve and hope that will make everything better. What I have found is that it is important to let the living go on living. Others in life need you to get on with life and it is so painful for them to go on and on indefinitely with your grief.

WHEN THE PAIN OUTWEIGHS A HEALTHY MENTAL STATE, IT'S TIME TO GET HELP. SEEK GRIEF COUNSELING.

I Did Not Die

"Do not stand at my grave
and forever weep.
I am not there; I do not sleep.
I am a thousand winds that blow.
I am the diamond glints on snow.
I am the sunlight on ripened grain.
I am the gentle autumn's rain.
When you awaken in the morning's
hush I am the swift uplifting rush
of quiet birds in circled flight.
I am the soft stars that shine
at night. Do not stand at my
grave and forever cry.
I am not there. I did not die."

-American Indian Proverb

The Rose

"Some say love, it is a river that drowns the tender reed. Some say love, it is a razor that leaves your soul to bleed. Some say love, it is a hunger, an endless aching need. I say love, it is a flower, and you its only seed. It's the heart afraid of breaking that never learns to dance. It's the dream afraid of waking that never takes the chance. It's the one who won't be taken, who cannot seem to give, and the soul afraid of dyin' that never learns to live. When the night has been too lonely and the road has been to long, and you think that love is only for the lucky and the strong, just remember in the winter far beneath the bitter snows lies the seed that with the sun's love in the spring becomes the rose."

-Bette Midler

5 Steps to Overcoming Guilt and Shame

1. **Assess the seriousness of the action:** Frequently guilt and shame means that you are living your life in a way that violates your principles or that you are judging too many small actions as serious. Questions for you to consider: *Do other people consider this to be as serious as I do? Do some people consider it less serious? Why? How serious would I consider the experience if my best friend or spouse or partner was responsible instead of me? How important will this experience seem in one month? One year? Five years? How serious would I consider this to be if someone had done this to me? Did I know ahead of time the meaning or consequences of my actions (or thoughts)? Can the damage be corrected? How long will this take? Was there an even worse action I considered and avoided?*

2. **Weigh your personal responsibility:** *How much of the violation was your sole personal responsibility?* List all the people and aspects of a situation that contributed to an event about which you feel guilty or ashamed. Include yourself last.

3. **Break the silence:** When secretiveness surrounds shame, it may be important to talk to a trusted person about what occurred. This is so important because once you get it out in the open, you can better deal with it. The need to keep silent is often based on the anticipation that revealing the secret will result in condemnation, criticism or rejection by others. Often the fear of how people will react is much different from how people really react and can force reassessment of the situation. Make sure you choose someone you trust and allow yourself enough time to say everything you need to and receive feedback.

4. **Self-forgiveness:** Being a good person does not mean that you will never do any bad things. Part of being human is making mistakes. Self-forgiveness may involve changing your thought from, *"I made this mistake and I am an awful person"*, to *"I made this mistake during an awful time in my life when I didn't care if I behaved this way"* or from *"I was abused because I deserved it"* to *"I was abused because my parents were out-of-control"*. Or *"My parents raised me to the best of their ability. They did not realize that I have a different personality or that I digest information differently. They showed me their love by working so hard even though I wanted to hear that they loved me. I must let it go and be a better parent myself."* Self-forgiveness involves recognizing your imperfections, mistakes, choices and accepting yourself, shortcomings.

5. **Making reparations or retribution:** If you have injured another person, it is important to make amends for your actions. This involves recognizing your transgression, being courageous enough to face the person you have hurt, ask for forgiveness and determining what you can do to repair the hurt you have caused and to avoid such difficulties in the future.

Lots of precious time gets lost through guilt. Guilt helps you very little in life. Guilt is a warning that you are out of bounds or off limits or that you are out of line. *How often do you feel guilty because you can't do everything you want? How often do you feel guilty because you are not working your business because of wanting to spend that time with your children? How often do you feel guilty that you are taking some family or vacation time and you need to be working? How often do you feel guilty because you cannot be all things to all the people in your life? How often do you try to behave like others want you to behave? How often do you hold back going for greatness because you are afraid of ridicule or criticism?*

> Say to yourself that you did what you thought was best at the time.

Guilt and Shame

Guilt and shame are closely connected emotions, we tend to feel guilty when we have violated rules or not lived up to expectations and standards that we set for ourselves or others have set for us. Guilt and shame can rob you of precious life time. You can't change what happened five minutes ago. Say to yourself, *"I did what I thought was best for me at the time"*. If we believe that we *"should"* have behaved differently or we *"ought"* to have done better, we likely feel guilty.

> Don't 'should' on yourself.

Shame involves the sense that we have done something wrong that means we are *flawed, no good, inadequate* or *bad* and is usually connected to the reactions of others. Anytime you catch yourself thinking *if they knew _____ then they would not like me or would think less of me,* you are feeling shameful. Shame can involve family secrets involving other family members as well as around issues like alcoholism, abuse, abortion, bankruptcy, poor business decisions, stealing, unemployment, etc. Overcoming guilt and shame does not mean not caring about your actions. Because clearly you need to care about your actions. It involves taking responsibility for what you did and coming to terms with it.

Recharge Your Batteries

To recharge your batteries or adrenal glands you must take time out to spend with family and friends. A change of scenery can provide a breathing space from troubles and can be good for your soul. Even a short break away can be beneficial. Taking time off should not make you feel guilty. Even a few minutes break from what you are doing can be rejuvenating.

Don't go to bed angry!

The Formula for Delivering Bad News

The formula for delivering bad news is easy, even if the execution is usually painful. Do all you can to NEVER deliver bad news but if you have to here's the formula: **Tell it first. Tell it straight. Tell it all. Tell it first:** You save time in the long run being first to disclose a bad situation. Playing catch-up is risky. When you are the first to disclose the bad news, you set the context. You can not only talk about the challenge but also how and why it happened and what you are going to do about it. **Tell it straight:** That means no spinning. If someone makes a decision that's dumb-don't mince words and call the action *inappropriate.* If it's dumb, say so. **Tell it all:** That means don't leave anything out. If it's relevant to the situation, disclose it. If you don't, someone else certainly will and your whole message will be undermined.

Spending Quiet Time

Everyone needs time for themselves. Take the time to collect your thoughts, decide on priorities and concentrate on difficult situations. Do not feel guilty about shutting yourself off from your family or co-workers for this special time for yourself. Explain that you would appreciate no interruptions and distractions. This is particularly important if you are going through a chaotic time in your life.

> Don't beat yourself up. Deal with what you have to deal with and get on with living your life.

> *"I can" is a power sentence. "I can."*
> -Og Mandino

Don't be afraid of high hopes...

"Don't be afraid of high hopes or plans that seem to be out of reach. Life is meant to be experienced and every situation allows for learning and growth. Motivation is a positive starting point and action places you on a forward path. A dream is a blueprint of a goal not yet achieved; the only difference between the two is the effort involved in attaining what you hope to accomplish. Let your mind and heart urge you on; allow the power of your will to lead you to your destination. Don't count the steps ahead; just add up the total steps already covered and multiply it by faith, confidence and endurance. Always remember that for those who persist, today's dreams are transformed into tomorrow's successes."
-Unknown

You only have now and the rest of your life to charge forward.

Observe how others spend their time...how many people are wasting valuable hours playing computer games and acting like they are busy. It's what many people do. One of the keys to success is to observe what unsuccessful people do and don't do it.

"If I could turn back time, I'd give it all to you."
-Cher

READ, TAKE ACTION, IT'S ABOUT TIME

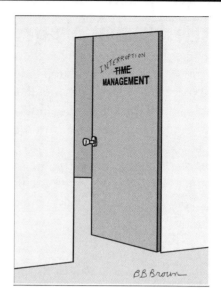

Don't let anyone kill your dreams! When one door closes, another door opens.

"Something will have gone out of us as a people if we ever let the remaining wilderness be destroyed; if we permit the last virgin forests to be turned into comic books and plastic cigarette cases; if we drive the few remaining members of the wild species into zoos or to extinction; if we pollute the last clear air and dirty the last clean streams and push our paved roads through the last of the silence, so that never again will people be free in their own country from the noise, the exhausts, the stinks of human and automotive waste. And so that never again can we have the chance to see ourselves single, separate, vertical and individual in the world, part of the environment of trees and rocks and soil, brother to the other animals, part of the natural world and competent to belong in it. We simply need that wild country available to us, even if we never do more than drive to its edge and look in. For it can be a means of reassuring ourselves of our sanity as creatures, us part of the geography of hope."
-Wallace Stegner

HARVEST EACH DAY

Everything I do is a valuable learning experience. What can I learn from today? I can reflect on my successes and my not so great accomplishments for the day without guilt. I will practice but I will save time for better things tomorrow including greater enjoyment of my life time.

Put loads of positive emphasis on what you do well with your time. Believe in your overall potential and what is probable for you to achieve. Expect the very best from yourself and take mistakes in stride. Know that mistakes are human, everyone makes them. Focus on one area at a time to strengthen you rather than overwhelming yourself with too much to do. Keep a positive, fired up spirit and attitude every day. You are capable of doing more. Half-hearted efforts are not acceptable anymore in your life. You are capable of excellence. You can have more, be more and do more if you will just do more, be more to have more. Improve daily, strive always to be the best you can be.

Average is just as close to the bottom as it is to the top

Focus on your daily achievements rather than on your weaknesses.

SHED YOUR SCARLET LETTER LETTING GO OF AN OLD REGRET OR SHAMEFUL MEMORY IS LIBERATING. WHAT COULD HELP YOU HEAL? HOW CAN YOU GET RID OF THE WEIGHT OF REGRET OR A PAST TRANSGRESSION? WRITE ABOUT IT IN A PERSONAL JOURNAL OR FIND SOMEONE YOU TRUST AND TALK ABOUT IT. GET OVER IT.

REMEMBER

Remember pleasant memories. Save those precious cards your children made for you to reread while sipping a cup of tea.

THE PLEASURE IS HOURS.

Harvest the lessons you learn from each experience or choice that ends up differently than you had expected. Don't invest your lifetime being eaten up by guilt.

Well hi there!
I have decided to give up guilt! I just don't choose to live with the bad memories of what all could have and should have been. My time on earth is so short and I am choosing to live every minute of it in the present and future.

Forget the past...it's over. I am going to hang on tight to my wonderful memories. I am going to be more patient, loving and forgiving. I am going forth in life a new happier, healthier man!

The most difficult thing is to admit the tragedy, to accept it. It is something in your life over which you had no control and God's plan for us, as we all know, is more than we can fathom. It's part of the pattern of life...life and death. Having once admitted and accepted the deep, deep pain of the wound, then you begin to realize that you have expanded your own capability of loving and caring for others. Until you are hurt, you can never truly understand the hurts of others. Until you have failed, you cannot truly achieve success. People facing tragedy suddenly take a new look at their whole life. Their perspective changes. Some of the things that they had thought were so precious don't seem to mean much anymore. Some of the treasure they valued so highly don't seem as valuable. Their value system changes and when your value system changes, your heart changes, your mood changes, your mind changes. How you use your time changes. Family becomes more important. Relationships become more precious and life itself more important than any day-to-day occupation or any material possession. When people mourn they are truly comforted. Believe it or not, they are happy.

Stress is a signal that you need to change what you are doing...suffering is when you don't make the change.

x x x x x x x x

A spotless house is the sign of a misspent life

x x x x x x x x

OUT OF CONTROL? START BY CONTROLLING WHAT YOU CAN.

Ignorance on fire out-produces knowledge on ice.

Sometimes its risky not to take a risk.

Isn't it about time to get over that broken heart? If someone mistreats you it's a GOOD thing that it is over. You don't need the grief. You want to look for someone who will cherish and adore you. Good riddance to the person who is now out of your life. Don't waste five years sulking over a broken heart. Get on with living. Learn from the relationship but move on.

Don't make a decision that you will be sorry about when you are upset.

My father asked my mother to marry him five minutes after he met her on a dance floor in Dallas, Texas. She said YES! They were married for 55 years.

Eliminate Clutter

Eliminating clutter and the chaos it causes will give you a gift of 240 to 288 hours every year. Here are a few specific organizational ideas:

- Use color coding. Visually, you identify things faster.
- Streamline processes. Look at everything you do and determine whether it's as efficient as it can be.
- Do things when the time is right. It's not likely you'll be calling people at 10 p.m. for work. Use conventional work hours for tasks that can only be done then. Earmark off-hours for less time-specific responsibilities such as filing, accounting and other jobs.
- Staple papers together, don't clip them together.
- Don't make piles.
- Organize everything in files or in binders.

Conquer the Clutter

Schedule 10 to 15 minutes each week to clear your work area of junk mail, old papers and other accumulated clutter. Change habits that lead to messes. Keep cleaning supplies handy so you can take advantage of the odd free moment to clean your work space.

The days come to us like friends in disguise, bringing priceless gifts from an unseen hand; but, if we do not use them, they are borne silently away, never to return. Each successive morning new gifts are brought, but if we failed to accept those that were brought yesterday and the day before, we become less and less able to turn them to account, until the ability to appreciate and utilize them is exhausted.

"You always pass failure on the way to success."
-Mickey Rooney

Learn to Use Technology

Although personal habits and practices can do wonders for Self-Management, don't overlook technology as yet another weapon to make the most effective use of your workday. For instance, software lets you organize a wide array of customer and product particulars, allowing quick and easy access. Sticky notes are one of the worst things in the world. Go wireless. Get a spam filter so that you are not spending so much time deleting junk mail. Organize your E-mails on a system so you don't have to sort through thousands of E-mails to find a certain one you are looking for. Avoid copying E-mails to others, be brief and to the point. Don't put anything in an E-mail that you might regret. If you don't want it read, don't print it. If you are mailing to a big list, make sure you put those E-mails onto bcc so that all those E-mails don't go out to people who will spam them. Stay updated with technology.

Defuse Distractions

Short distractions can add up to a major drain on productivity. If you're spending too much time on the phone, keep a timer at your desk and hold calls to a reasonable limit. Learn how to terminate calls politely. If co-workers often drop in to chat, close your door. If you're constantly walking around obstacles, consider a change of floor plan. Take steps to reduce distracting noise.

Eliminate Redundancy

Analyze every process you use to determine if any steps can be eliminated. Common challenges include multiple signatures for approval, extra steps designed to circumvent systems or correct challenges that could be addressed more directly and generating multiple copies that are no longer required.

You're writing the story of your life one moment at a time.

"Take care of the minutes and the hours will take care of themselves."
-Lord Chesterfield

It's a beautiful world. Clean up your act and get busy spending time enjoying our fabulous planet.

The world doesn't owe you a living.

Group and Separate

Tedious or redundant tasks can be grouped for increased efficiency: file all at once, bill all at once, order all at once. Large, multifaceted tasks, on the other hand, may be best tackled in small pieces. Sort that large stack of paperwork on Monday, process some on Tuesday, some on Wednesday and so forth until it's done. Using this approach, even the most daunting tasks become manageable.

Share the Burden

As any quilter knows, many hands make light work. Performance of dreaded chores like the annual inventory can take on a party atmosphere when many are involved and frequent breaks are scheduled.

Emulate Others

Don't try to reinvent the wheel. If someone else always seems to be ahead of the game, watch and learn. If someone else has a faster way of doing something, copy it. If you're having trouble getting specific jobs done, ask others how they organize and execute the task; perhaps you've overlooked some short cuts.

I am Only One

"I am only one, but still I am one. I cannot do everything, but still I can do something; and because I cannot do everything, I will not refuse to do something I can do."
-Helen Keller

"We don't need more money, we don't need greater success or fame, we don't need the perfect body or even the perfect mate. Right now, at this very moment, we have a mind, which is all the basic equipment we need to achieve complete happiness."
-Unknown

Oh so what that there are dirty dishes occasionally in the sink...it's not the end of the world! They will still be there in the morning!

Each day is a priceless opportunity to share laughter and love.

IRISH BLESSINGS

May your troubles be less
And your blessings be more.
And nothing but happiness
Come through your door.
May you be poor in misfortune,
rich in blessings,
slow to make enemies
and quick to make friends.
But rich or poor, quick or slow,
May you know nothing but happiness
from this day forward.

May the luck of the Irish be always at hand,
And good friends always near you.
May each and every coming day,
Bring some special joy to cheer you.
May the saints protect ye-
An' sorrow neglects ye,
An' bad luck to the one
That doesn't respect ye!
T'all that belong to ye,
An long life t' yer honor-
That's the end of my song t'ye!

May the leprechauns be near you,
To spread luck along your way.
And may all the Irish angels
Smile on you St. Patrick's Day.

May those who love us, love us.
And those who don't love us,
May God turn their hearts.
And if he doesn't turn their hearts,
May he turn their ankles,
So we may know them by their limping.

May you have all the happiness
And luck that life can hold-
And on the end of all your rainbows
May you find a pot of gold.

May your thoughts be as glad
As the shamrocks.
May your heart be as light as a song.
May each day bring you bright happy hours,
That stay with you all year long.
For each petal on the shamrock
This brings a wish your way-
Good health, good luck and happiness
For today and every day.
May your blessings outnumber
The Shamrocks that grow
And may trouble avoid you wherever you go.
May you always have these blessings...
A soft breeze when summer comes,
A warm fireside in winter,
And always the warm, soft smile of a friend.
May there always be work for your hands to do.
May your neighbors respect you,
Trouble neglect you, the angels protect you
And heaven accept you.
May your home be filled with laughter,
May your pockets be filled with gold,
And may you have all the happiness,
your Irish heart can hold.

May the good saints protect you
And bless you today
And may troubles ignore you
Each step of the way
Lucky stars above you,
Sunshine on your way,
Many friends to love you,
Joy in work and play,
Laughter to outweigh each care,
In your heart a song,
And gladness waiting everywhere
All your whole life long!

May the lilt of Irish laughter
Lighten every load,
May the mist of Irish magic shorten every road,
May you taste the sweetest pleasures
That fortune e're bestowed,
And may all your friends remember
All the favors you are owed.

A man that can't laugh at himself
should be given a mirror.

The light heart lives long.

Let your anger set with the sun
and not rise again with it.

It is as foolish to let a fool kiss you
as it is to let a kiss fool you.

She didn't know it couldn't be done,
so she went ahead and did it.

May your pockets be heavy and your heart be light;
may good luck pursue you morning and night.

May the saddest day of your future be no
worse than the happiest day of your past.

Time

"Ticking away the moments that make up a dull day. You fritter and waste the hours in an offhand way. Kicking around on a piece of ground in your home town. Waiting for someone or something to show you the way. Tired of lying in the sunshine staying home to watch the rain. You are young and life is long and there is time to kill today. And then one day you find ten years have got behind you. No one told you when to run, you missed the starting gun. So you run and you run to catch up with the sun but it's sinking. Racing around to come up behind you again. The sun is the same in a relative way but you're older, shorter of breath and one day closer to death. Every year is getting shorter never seem to find the time. Plans that either come to naught or half a page of scribbled lines. Hanging on in quiet desperation is the English way. The time is gone, the song is over, thought I'd something more to say."
-Pink Floyd, Dark Side of the Moon

Luck is spelled WORK. It's not easy to find a four leaf clover but they can be found if you look hard enough.

"Most of us think ourselves as standing wearily and helplessly at the center of a circle bristling with tasks, burdens, challenges, annoyance and responsibilities which are rushing in upon us. At every moment we have a dozen different things to do, a dozen challenges to solve, a dozen strains to endure. We see ourselves as overdriven, overburdened, overtired. This is a common mental picture and it is totally false. No one of us, however crowded his life, has such an existence. What is the true picture of your life? Imagine that there is an hour glass on your desk. Connecting the bowl at the top with the bowl at the bottom is a tube so thin that only one grain of sand can pass through it at a time. That is the true picture of your life, even on a super busy day, the crowded hours come to you always one moment at a time. That is the only way they can come. The day may bring many tasks, many challenges, strains, but invariably they come in single file. You want to gain emotional poise? Remember the hourglass, the grains of sand dropping one by one."
-James Gordon Gilkey

The Journey Begins WithIN.

Don't let other people tell you what you want.

"You must first act. God says to us, 'If you don't move, I don't move.' He said, If you sow, you can reap—but you must sow first.' And 'Unless you change what you are, you will always have what you've got.'"
-Jim Rohn

CHASE YOUR PASSION, NOT YOUR PENSION

There is no time like the present.

"We get to think of life as an inexhaustible well. Yet everything happens only a certain number of times and a very small number, really. How many more times will you remember a certain afternoon of your childhood, some afternoon that's so deeply a part of your being that you can't even conceive of your life without it? Perhaps four or five times more. Perhaps not even that. How many more times will you watch the full moon rise? Perhaps twenty. And yet it all seems limitless."
-Paul Bowles

Half our life is spent trying to find something to do with the time we have rushed through life trying to save.

TIME IS FREE, BUT IT'S PRICELESS. YOU CAN'T OWN IT, BUT YOU CAN USE IT. YOU CAN'T KEEP IT, BUT YOU CAN SPEND IT. ONCE YOU'VE LOST IT YOU CAN NEVER GET IT BACK.

"Take time to deliberate; but when the time for action arrives, stop thinking and go in."
-Napoleon Bonaparte

Life is all about timing... the unreachable becomes reachable, the unavailable become available, the unattainable...attainable. Have the patience, wait it out, it's all about timing.

IN GOOD TIMES AND BAD TIMES, I'LL BE ON YOUR SIDE FOR EVER MORE... THAT'S WHAT FRIENDS ARE FOR.

Don't count every hour in the day, make every hour in the day count.

COMPRESS DECADES INTO DAYS.

Begin doing what you want to do now. We are not living in eternity. We have only this moment, sparkling like a star in our hand and melting like a snowflake.

A stray, unthought of five minutes may contain the event of a life. And this all important moment who can tell when it will be upon you?

Program the goal, take the necessary actions, create the reality... seize the day and get to the top!

I'm working to improve my methods and every hour I save is an hour added to my life.

Time goes by so fast, people go in and out of your life. You must never miss the opportunity to tell these people how much they mean to you.

We all have our time machines. Some take us back, they're called memories. Some take us forward, they're called dreams.

"In everyone's life, at some time, our inner fire goes out. It is then burst into flame by an encounter with another human being. We should all be thankful for those people who rekindle the inner spirit."
-Albert Sweitzer

Time is the cruelest teacher; first she gives the test, then teaches the lesson.

IF YOU WAIT, ALL THAT HAPPENS IS THAT YOU GET OLDER.

Time is ticking by...how long do you want to stay upset, exhausted, overweight, tired, bored, mean, unhappy, unfulfilled...isn't it about time that you change what you are doing in life?

Keep Your Fork

There was a woman with a terminal illness and had been given three months to live. So she contacted her pastor and had him come to her house to discuss certain aspects of her final wishes. She told him which songs she wanted sung at the service, what scriptures she would like read and what she wanted to be buried wearing. Everything was in order and the pastor was preparing to leave when the woman remembered something very important to her. *"I want to be buried with a fork in my right hand."* The pastor stood looking at the woman, not knowing what to say. *"That surprises you, doesn't it?"* she asked. *"Well, too I'm puzzled by the request,"* said the pastor. The woman explained. *"In all my years of attending church socials and potluck dinners I always remember that when the dishes were cleared, someone would inevitably lean over and say, Keep your fork. It was my favorite part because I knew that something better was coming... like velvety chocolate cake or deep-dish apple pie. So I just want people to see me there in that casket with a fork in my hand and I want them to wonder, 'What's with the fork?'"* Then I want you to tell them: *'Keep your fork...the best is yet to come.'* He sadly hugged the woman goodbye. But he also knew that the woman had a better grasp of heaven that he did. She knew that something better was coming. At the funeral people were walking by the woman's casket and they saw the fork placed in her right hand. The pastor heard the question, *"What's with the fork?"* Over and over he smiled. During his message, the pastor told the people of the conversation he had with the woman shortly before she died. He also told them about the fork and what it symbolized to her. The pastor told the people how he could not stop thinking about the fork and told them that they probably would not be able to stop thinking about it either. He was right. So the next time you reach down for your fork, let it remind you oh so gently, that the *best is yet to come.*

The Request

A man came home from work late again, tired and irritated, to find his five year old son waiting for him at the door. *"Daddy, may I ask you a question?" "Yeah, sure, what is it, son?"* replied the father. *"Daddy, how much money do you make an hour?" "That's none of your business! What makes you ask such a thing?"* the father said. *"I just want to know. Please tell me, how much do you make an hour?"* pleaded the little boy. *"If you must know, son, I make $20.00 an hour."*

"Oh", the little boy replied, head bowed. Looking up, he said, *"Daddy, may I borrow $10.00 please?"* The father was furious and said, *"If the only reason you wanted to know how much money I make is just so you can borrow some to buy a silly toy or some other nonsense, then you march yourself straight to your room and go to bed. Think about why you're being so selfish. I work long, hard hours everyday and don't have time for such childish games"*.

The little boy quietly went to his room and shut the door. The father sat down and started to get even madder about the little boy's questioning. How dare he ask such questions only to get some money? After an hour or so, the father had calmed down and started to think he may have been a little hard on his son. Maybe there was something he really needed to buy with that $10.00 and he really didn't ask for money very often. The father went to the door of the little boy's room and opened the door. *"Are you asleep son?"* he asked. *"No daddy, I'm awake"*, replied the boy. *"I've been thinking, maybe I was too hard on you earlier"*, said the father. *"It's been a long day and I took my aggravation out on you. Here's that $10.00 you asked for."* The little boy sat straight up, beaming. *"Oh, thank you daddy!"* he yelled. Then, reaching under his pillow, he pulled out some more crumpled up bills. The father, seeing that the boy already had money, started to get angry again. The little boy slowly counted out his money, then looked up at the father. *"Why did you want more money if you already had some?"* the father grumbled. *"Because I didn't have enough, but now I do"*, the little boy replied. *"Daddy, I have $20.00 now. Can I buy an hour of your time?"*

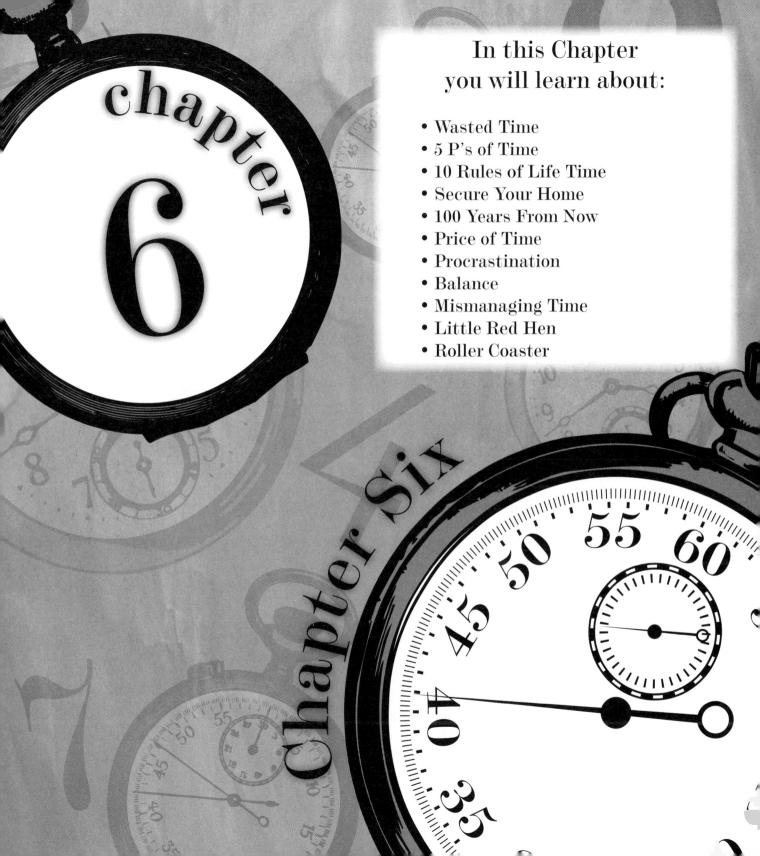

chapter

6

In this Chapter you will learn about:

- Wasted Time
- 5 P's of Time
- 10 Rules of Life Time
- Secure Your Home
- 100 Years From Now
- Price of Time
- Procrastination
- Balance
- Mismanaging Time
- Little Red Hen
- Roller Coaster

Chapter Six

Where Does the Time Go

Consider the following dismal scenario for the average life lived in the United States. Research shows that the average 70 year old will have spent his life in this manner:

- 24 years in sleep.
- 14 years in work.
- 8 years in amusement.
- 7 years in the bathroom.
- 6 years in education.
- 6 years eating.
- 5 years waiting in line.
- 5 years in transportation.
- 4 years in conversation.
- 3 years in reading.
- 3 years in meetings.
- 2 years playing telephone tag.
- 8 months opening junk mail.
- 8 months in church and prayer.
- 6 months sitting at red lights.
- No telling how much time looking for things.

You will get interrupted 73 times a day, take an hour of work home, read less than five minutes, talk to your spouse for four minutes, exercise less than three minutes and play with your child for two minutes.

Time To Make Changes

You can make huge changes. You could quit your job, leave your family, move to a cabin in the Rockies and paint mountainscapes. You could but you probably won't. You can make small changes, without needing anybody's help or permission. You can, for example, learn to take five mini-breaks a day. You can explore the possibilities for some mid-size changes, involving the cooperation of other people in your life. Could you, for example: take your next raise in time rather than money or advancement? Work at least part of the time at home? Substitute barter and skills- swapping for cash for some of what you need?

Add life to my years, not years to my life.

Wasted Days and Wasted Nights

Many claim their days are never wasted. *I'm very organized"* they say *"I know where 1 am going and what I'm going to do".* If you truly feel that way, then you are in the minority. Most people become frustrated with a day that is unproductive. We would all like to get more done in a day. How many times have you looked outside and find that it is dark and thought... how can it be the end of the day? I haven't gotten anything accomplished...oh well, there is always tomorrow!

You get what you focus your time and thinking on... nothing less, nothing more.

The real question in life *is...are you determined?*

To get all there is out of living, we must employ our time wisely, never being in too much of a hurry to stop and sip life, but never losing our sense of the enormous value of a minute.

Spend your time determined to achieve your goal

Work first... then reward yourself!

Cherish things while you still have them, before they're gone and you realize how precious they really are.

Life can only be understood backwards, but it must be lived forwards. Everything in life is temporary. So if things are going good, enjoy it because it won't last forever. And if things are going bad, don't worry because it won't last forever either.

"Moving toward an inwardly simple life is not about deprivation or denying ourselves the things we want. It's about getting rid of the things that no longer contribute to the fullness of our lives. It's about creating balance between our inner and outer lives."
-Elaine St. James

Professionals built the Titanic, amateurs built the Ark.

Sorry is between slump and sympathy in the dictionary.

When you collect unnecessary guilt, you lose energy and positive momentum and waste a lot of time just feeling horrible about yourself. That is simply a choice. Get back in the game. Do not be denied a fabulous future because you are riddled with guilt. What is, is. You can not change the past.

A WORD TO THE WISE IS INFURIATING.

The 5 P's of Time
Pride

Pride in what you do and who you are makes you unafraid, totally confident and unstoppable. It is what you have chosen to become and have put your heart, soul and time into. No matter what your business is, nor what your life is like, if you are proud of it and live with pride and confidence, you're already a winner.

Passion

Passion fuels the courage it takes to be who you need to be and want to be and to stand up against conventional wisdom. When you're passionate about creating the results you want to achieve, it gives you the courage to be different and avails you with the power to overcome your fears and use those emotions to your advantage.

Purpose

Purpose is what gets you out of bed each morning, what fuels your passion, your pride and your sense of profits. Knowing why you do what you do brings into the open your life's purpose and your driving force.

Profit

Profit is your given right to create a bottom line that provides you with the lifestyle you want for yourself, your family and those you care about. Profit supports your business plans, your vision, your mission and your dreams.

Perception

Perception is what puts all of the above into the lens of your own truth. You must develop the ability to change perception. You understand that you can change your perceptions, create change within yourself and change situations to continually serve your business and your life's purpose. You become a Master of Meaning and perception becomes power.

The 10 Rules of Life Time

Rule #1-You will receive a body. Whether you love it or hate it, it's yours for life, so accept it. What counts is what's inside.

Rule #2-You will be presented with lessons. Life is a constant learning experience, which every day provides opportunities for you to learn more. These lessons are specific to you and learning them is the key to discovering and fulfilling the meaning and relevance of your own life.

Rule #3-There are no mistakes, only lessons. Your development towards wisdom is a process of experimentation, trial and error, so it's inevitable things will not always go to plan or turn out how you'd want. Compassion is the remedy for harsh judgement - of ourselves and others. Forgiveness is not only divine - it's also *the act of erasing an emotional debt*. Behaving ethically, with integrity and with humour - especially the ability to laugh at yourself and your own mishaps - are central to the perspective that *mistakes are simply lessons we must learn*.

Rule #4-The lesson is repeated until learned. Lessons repeat until learned. What manifest as challenges, irritations and frustrations are more lessons - they will repeat until you see them as such and learn from them. Your own awareness and your ability to change are requisites of executing this rule. Also fundamental is the acceptance that you are not a victim of fate or circumstance - "causality" must be acknowledged; things happen to you because of how you are and what you do. To blame anyone or in anything else for your misfortunes is an escape and a denial; you yourself are responsible for you and what happens to you. Patience is required - change doesn't happen overnight, so give change time to happen.

Rule #5- Learning does not end. While you are alive there are always lessons to be learned. Surrender to the *rhythm of life*, don't struggle against it. Commit to the process of constant learning and change - be humble enough to always acknowledge your own weaknesses and be flexible enough to adapt from what you may be accustomed to, because rigidity will deny you the freedom of new possibilities.

Rule #6-"There" is no better than "here". The other side of the hill may be greener than your own, but being there is not the key to endless happiness. Be grateful for and enjoy what you have and where you are on your journey. Appreciate the abundance of what's good in your life, rather than measure and amass things that do not actually lead to happiness. Living in the present helps you attain peace.

Rule #7-Others are only mirrors of you. You love or hate something about another person according to what you love or hate about yourself. Be tolerant; accept others as they are and strive for clarity of self-awareness; strive to truly understand and have an objective perception of your own self, your thoughts and feelings. Negative experiences are opportunities to heal the wounds that you carry. Support others and by doing so you support yourself. Where you are unable to support others it is a sign that you are not adequately attending to your own needs.

Rule #8-What you make of your life is up to you. You have all the tools and resources you need. What you do with them is up to you. Take responsibility for yourself. Learn to let go when you cannot change things. Don't get angry about things - bitter memories clutter your mind. Courage resides in all of us - use it when you need to do what's right for you. We all possess a strong natural power and adventurous spirit, which you should draw on to embrace what lies ahead.

Rule #9-Your answers lie inside of you. Trust your instincts and your innermost feelings, whether you hear them as a little voice or a flash of inspiration. Listen to feelings as well as sounds. Look, listen and trust. Draw on your natural inspiration.

Rule #10-You will forget all this at birth. We are all born with all of these capabilities - our early experiences lead us into a physical world, away from our spiritual selves, so that we become doubtful, cynical and lacking belief and confidence. The Ten Rules are not commandments, they are universal truths that apply to us all. When you lose your way, call upon them. Have faith in the strength of your spirit. Aspire to be wise - wisdom is the ultimate path of your life and it knows no limits other than those you impose on yourself.

Make What You Are Doing With Your Time important

Be unstoppable, get up earlier, stay up later and achieve your goal. Don't just be busy being busy, wasting time. Be busy living your dreams from today on. Take one day a week and give 100% of yourself just for that day. Desire success not failure, not loss but gain, not evil but good; because when tomorrow comes yesterday is gone forever. Leave in yesterdays place something that you have traded for. The only way in life to not succeed is to quit trying. Put today to good use. What you are doing is important because what you do with your day is that for which you are exchanging your lifetime. Follow your real goals and persist until you succeed.

the grass may be greener on the other side but it still has to be mowed and watered

Help each other to be happy.
Never mind if help be small.
Giving a little is far better
than giving not at all.

Don Ruiz's Code for Life
Agreement 1

Be impeccable with your word - speak with integrity. Say only what you mean. Avoid using your words to speak against yourself or to gossip about others. Use the power of your words in the direction of truth and love.

Agreement 2

Don't take anything personally - nothing others do is because of you. What others say and do is a projection of their own reality, their own dream. When you are immune to the opinions and actions of others, you won't be the victim of needless suffering.

Agreement 3

Don't make assumptions - find the courage to ask questions and to express what you really want. Communicate with others as clearly as you can to avoid misunderstandings, sadness and drama. With just this one agreement, you can completely transform your life.

Agreement 4

Always do your best - your best is going to change from moment to moment; it will be different when you are healthy as opposed to sick. Under any circumstance, simply do your best and you will avoid self-judgment, self-abuse and regret.

"I'm gonna do it until..."

NO MATTER HOW WONDERFUL OR WRETCHED THINGS ARE, YOU DECIDE IF YOU ARE HAPPY. HAPPINESS IS AN INSIDE JOB.

Take Time To Secure Your Home

While my youngest child, Ashley was playing in a soccer game years ago a child was kidnapped from a nearby playground. No one saw it happen. All the parents were focused on the game. This one child wandered off to the playground and was gone in an instant. She was later found dead. I also remember seeing an exposé on TV where a youngster was riding his bike and a van pulled over, the predator threw a blanket over the child and snatched the child. That child was found dead several days later. Then there were people who would come in during the night through open doors and windows and snatch children. At that time, we lived on a very busy street at the end. As a single mother of three young children, I was frantic to provide security for my children. Not only for them, but for me. So, I invested in a security system. We all slept on the same side of the house and I invested in a bolt lock for the hallway door so that if someone did get into the main room of our home, they could not get into the bedroom part of our home. I also sold all of my children's bikes. As the years rolled by and the day of garage openers came to be, as women were getting out of their cars in their garages, men would be there to snatch them or snatch their handbags, many wielding guns. So, I had additional flood lights put onto my back lawn so that at least that might be a deterrent to someone thinking of coming into our garage at the rear of our home. Be smart. Be safe. Take time to secure your home.

Become a Student

I was not a born salesperson. When I began my career, I did not know anything about sales. So, I realized it would be extremely critically important to become a student of sales. I checked out from the local library and outlined over 300 books to teach myself the art of sales. Once I took the time to become a student of sales, I became an independent woman.

Be a go giver as well as a go getter.

What Will You Do With the Time You Have Left?

What you will do with the time you have left on earth? How many more Christmas Days do you have to look forward to? More than 40? More than 30? More than 20? More than 10? How about less than 10? Approximately when do you want to live the lifestyle that you have dreamed of? It's going to go so fast! Technology is going to be out of control. What you have right now will be old and obsolete. You want to spend your time wisely NOW, take urgent action so that you will be able to enjoy what is coining to our civilization in the future years. You want to have the money to enjoy life. Get busy, the clock is ticking...tick tock! The secret of getting things done is: DO IT NOW!

> *"Waste no more time arguing what a good man should be, be one."*
> -Marcus Aurelius

100 Years From Now

*"One hundred years from now
It will not matter
What kind of car I drove,
What kind of house I lived in,
How much I had in my bank
Nor what my clothes looked like.
One hundred years from now
It will not matter
What kind of school I attended,
What kind of computer I used,
How large or small my church,
But the world may be...
a little better because...
I was important in the life of a child."*
-Unknown

Don't hate yourself for missing out

What is the Price of Time?

"What is the price of that book?" at length asked a man who had been dawdling for an hour in the front store of Benjamin Franklin's newspaper establishment. *"One dollar"*, replied the clerk. *"One dollar"*, echoed the lounger; *"Can't you take less than that?"* *"One dollar is the price"*, was the answer. The would-be purchaser looked over the books on sale awhile longer and then inquired: *"Is Mr. Franklin in?"* *"Yes"*, said the clerk, *"He is very busy in the press room"*. *"Well, I want to see him"*, persisted the man. The proprietor was called and the stranger asked *"What is the lowest, Mr. Franklin, that you can take for that book?"* *"One dollar and a quarter"*, was the prompt rejoinder. *"One dollar and a quarter! Why, your clerk asked me only a dollar just now."* *"True"*, said Franklin, *"and I could have better afforded to take a dollar than to leave my work"*. The man seemed surprised; but, wishing to end a parley of his own seeking, he demanded: *"Well, come now, tell me your lowest price for this book."* *"One dollar and a half"*, replied Franklin. *"A dollar and a half! Why, you offered it yourself for a dollar and a quarter."* *"Yes"*, said Franklin coolly, *"and I could better have taken that price then than a dollar and a half now"*. The man silently laid the money on the counter, took his book and left the store, having received a salutary lesson from a master in the art of transmuting time, at will, into either wealth or wisdom.

Give yourself permission to leave some low priority things you want to get done undone

The Biggest Thief of Time

Procrastination is the biggest thief of time; not decision making but decision avoidance. By reducing the amount of procrastinating you do you can substantially increase the amount of active time available to you. Doing things at the last minute is much more expensive than just before the last minute. Deadlines are really important: establish them yourself! If you've found yourself putting off important tasks over and over again, you're not alone. In fact, many people procrastinate to some degree - but some are so chronically affected by procrastination that it stops them achieving things they're capable of and disrupts their careers. Is this you? Are you always finding a way to fill up your minutes, hours, days, weeks, months and years and now you are looking back at all the wasted time in your life? Did you make excuses over the last year or years of why you didn't get anything accomplished? Why did others, with the same time, get something accomplished that you could have and you did not?

The key to controlling and ultimately combating this destructive habit called procrastination is to recognize when you start procrastinating, understand why it happens and take active steps to better manage your time and outcomes.

Why do You Procrastinate?

You procrastinate when you put off things that you should be focusing on right now, usually in favor of doing something that is more enjoyable or that you're more comfortable doing. Or you don't value your time or the time of those who you say you love.

Overcoming Procrastination

Whatever the reason behind procrastination, it must be recognized, dealt with and controlled before you miss opportunities or your career is derailed and lifetime slips through your fingers.

Step 1: Recognize that you are procrastinating. If you are honest with yourself, you probably know when you are procrastinating. First you need to make sure you know your priorities. Putting off an unimportant task is not necessarily procrastination, it's probably good prioritization. Here is what the average do:

- Fill their day with low priority tasks from their To-Do List.
- Read an E-mail or request that you have noted in your notebook or on your To-Do List more than once, without starting work on it or deciding when you're going to start work on it.
- Waste way too much time watching TV or playing computer games.
- Sitting down to start a high-priority task and almost immediately going off to make a cup of coffee or check your E-mails.
- Waiting to be reminded.
- Can't find their To-Do List.
- Cluttered desk. Can't find anything.
- Leaving messages with people to call back without leaving what the purpose of the call is so that you now take time to play phone tag.
- Telling people you will do it that day with no intention of getting to it.
- Leaving an item on your To-Do List for a long time, even though you know it's important. Regularly saying *"Yes"* to unimportant tasks that others ask you to do and filling your time with these instead of getting on with the important tasks already on your list.

Step 2: Figure out WHY you're procrastinating. Why you procrastinate can depend on both you and the task.

The 2 Common Causes of Procrastination

1. You find the task unpleasant; or
2. You find the task overwhelming.

Step 3: Get over it!

If you are putting something off because you just don't want to do it and you really can't delegate the work to someone else, you need to find ways of motivating yourself to get moving. Or tell whomever is counting on you that you don't intend to do it. Don't keep promising that you will do something. That will tear up your relationships faster than anything else. Be accountable. The following approaches can be helpful here:

- Make up your own rewards.
- Ask someone else to check up on you. Peer pressure works.
- Identify the unpleasant consequences of NOT doing the task. Attach fear to not doing the task.
- Work out the cost of your time to your employer. As your employers are paying you to do the things that they think are important, you're not delivering value for money if you're not doing those things. Shame yourself into getting going!

"Look up and not down. Look forward and not back. Look out and not in."
-Edward Everett Hale

If you are a person who chooses to go with the flow rather than make and take the time to achieve your dreams, think of fish. The successful fish overcome all obstacles to swim where they need to swim, upstream. The ones that go with the flow downstream are dead.

And in the end it's not the years in your life that count. It's the life in your years.

Investing Your Time Improperly

Procrastinators work as many hours in the day as other people and often work longer hours, but they invest their time in the wrong tasks. Sometimes this is simply because they don't prioritize by deciding on urgent tasks and important tasks and instead jump straight into getting on with urgent tasks that aren't actually important. They fuss and fume over the unimportant duties or schedule or lack of planning and never can get around to doing what is important.

They may feel that they are doing the right thing by reacting fast or taking some kind of action. Or they may not even think about their approach and simply be driven by the person whose demands are loudest. Either way, by doing this, you have little or no time left for the important tasks, despite the unpleasant outcomes this may bring about for you and your future.

Feeling Overwhelmed

You may not know where to begin. Or you may doubt that you have the skills or resources you think you need. So you seek comfort in doing tasks you know you're capable of completing. Unfortunately, the big task isn't going to go away - truly important tasks rarely do.

Other causes of procrastination include:
- Waiting for the *"right"* mood or the *"right"* time to tackle the important task at hand.
- A fear of failure or success.
- Underdeveloped decision making skills.
- Poor organizational skills.
- Perfectionism: *"I don't have the right skills or resources to do this perfectly now, so I won't do it at all."*

How To Balance Your Time

Most adults are so busy chasing the money from paycheck to paycheck, being workaholics, or making excuses for getting laid off, or making excuses why they can't *"get it together"*. If you are a workaholic, it's time to loosen up and appreciate how important it is to take some time out to do something you enjoy. Loads of people talk about how fun they are but do you ever see them having fun? Many talk about play but can't play unless they totally beat themselves up with guilt. They give, give, give, give to others and in a just a few years they are old and tired and worn out. Look at most adults faces. You are responsible for your own face by the time you turn forty!

Change is not easy, but change is always good. Try doing this...alternate your work time with play time. Work some, play some. Use your left-brain then your right brain. Try this...alter your breathing tempo. Instead of breathing in, out, in, out and in again...try breathing in, in, in, in, in, in. What happens when you do that? All of a sudden you can't take any more air in because you haven't exhaled. Now do this...exhale, exhale, exhale, exhale. Now what happened? You are now out of rhythm totally with your regular breathing. Now go back to your regular breathing and you can continue indefinitely. The same is true in work and play. If you work, work, work, work you ultimately will burn out. If you play, play, play, play you will ultimately find that you miss having some kind of meaningful work or service to others.

Are you balancing work and play? Maybe it's time to start thinking about that in your life. All work and no play makes Jack a dull, dull boy, much less man!

IN ALL ACTIVITY, PRACTICE CALMNESS. TO REMAIN CALM AMIDST THE CHAOS OF LIFE REQUIRES A TREMENDOUS AMOUNT OF FOCUSED ENERGY. BE CALMLY ACTIVE AND ACTIVELY CALM.

ONE KEY WORD CAN SAVE YOU A LOT OF TIME WHEN YOU ARE UPSET...CALMNESS. WHEN OTHERS ARE SAYING "DO SOMETHING!" YOU WANT TO BE THE ONE WHO STAYS CALM.

Questions to Ponder for the Use of Your Time

1. *Have I set a personal goals for the future?*
2. *How much am I sticking to them?*
3. *Do I apply myself to the necessary tasks to accomplish my goals?*
4. *Am I improving my performance day to day?*
5. *Do I attempt to get along with others?*
6. *Do I refuse to bow to frustration and use it to motivate me?*
7. *Am I patient in waiting for others to recognize my attributes?*
8. *When I am greeted with a new idea, do I always examine it without prejudice?*
9. *Do I look at challenges from every point of view?*
10. *Do I recognize others' needs and attempt to fulfill them?*
11. *Am I doing everything that I can to ensure my personal advancement?*
12. *Am I satisfied with my rate of advancement?*
13. *If money were not a challenge and I had free time, what would I do?*
14. *What have I always wanted to do but never had the money or time to do it?*
15. *Where do I see myself in five years from now?*
16. *If I really get busy the next two months what would my life look like?*
17. *If I really get committed more than I am right now for the next six months, what would my life be like in 5-10 years?*
18. *If I don't take massive action, what will my life be like in 5-10 years?*
19. *If there is one area of my life I am dissatisfied with, what would that be?*
20. *What do I like least about what I am doing?*
21. *What do I enjoy most about what I am doing?*
22. *What do I have to do to change, to grow?*
23. *What are the reasons I am never going to give up?*
24. *What are the things that will help me face my fears?*
25. *What do I have to do to change?*
26. *Have I made a conscious effort to know myself?*
27. *Do I know my life's goals?*
28. *Have I established a plan for achieving them?*
29. *Do I make an effort to be pleasant to my friends and acquaintances?*
30. *Am I sarcastic?*
31. *Do I attempt to understand the difficulties of others?*
32. *Do I praise others when they achieve their goals?*
33. *Do people want to be around me?*
34. *Do I restrain myself from making needless criticism?*

Pace Your Day

Listen to the rhythmic clack-clack of a train and the whistle marking its approach. You cannot hurry the train. Just notice it and breathe slowly until its music fades away. For those of you who are overly busy, pace yourself for a peaceful day once a week. Be aware of the time of day when you have the most energy and go after the most difficult tasks then. But allot some languid time to just live.

Travel Light

Struggling with heavy and bulky luggage is stressful and slows you down. Instead make sure you pack a small rolling bag and a matching carry-on bag.

No Nagging Allowed

Don't you hate it when someone starts nagging you? Nagging doesn't work. It simply is a waste of time. You want to be a person who takes responsibility so that others don't nag you. Everyone knows how to look busy when they aren't. Everyone knows how to conveniently forget to do what you were supposed to do. If you choose to mismanage your time in life, no one, no amount of nagging, will improve the situation. Parents can limit privileges until children can demonstrate they are ready for them through showing that they are responsible for their own Self-Management. In business, the bottom line does not lie. If you produce, you get paid, if you do not, you are let go. It's as simple as that. For those of you unfortunately married to a nag, just say... *YES DEAR* with a smile on your face and try your best to get done what you have promised to get done. If someone doesn't respond in 48 hours, they'll probably never respond. (True for phone as well as e-mail and personal projects).

If you are not good at doing something, get someone else to take care of it instead of delaying and excuse making all the time and trying to do it yourself.

Designate today as your personal

TASTE day.

Let go of bitterness and strife by stretching your sense of taste.
Ask yourself these 3 questions...
Which flavors delight me?
Which flavors relax me?
What might I taste new today?

THIS TOO SHALL PASS...

"Life does not listen to your logic, it goes on its own way undisturbed. You have to listen to life; life will not listen to your logic, it does not bother about your logic."
-Osho

Take Time

"For what's important to you
　　For what makes
　　　　you happiest....
Take time to be with
　　Those you love
　　　　And share your deepest wish
　　　　　　Most secret dream,
　　　　　　　　Your favorite fantasy....
Take time to look around
　　At all the gladness
　　　　The world can offer....
All of it is yours
　　If only you
　　　　Take the time."
　　　　　　-Larry Chengges

The Rewards of Mismanaging Time

You can mismanage a good deal of your time even though you read most of the Time-Management books and attend seminars on the subject of Self-Management. You are getting something you want or need when you mismanage time.

IF YOU ARE MISMANAGING YOUR TIME, THE CHALLENGE IS NOT HAVING ENOUGH TIME, BUT HOW YOU USE THE TIME YOU HAVE. BE SMART.

FILL YOUR TIME WITH POSITIVE OUTCOMES

The things that are important in life can be written on the top of an emerald.

TAKE THIS EASY SELF-TEST:

1. Do you get ready to leave your home and can't find your car keys?
   Often _____ Sometimes _____ Never _____

2. Do you discover you are out of gas on the way to where you are going with no time to stop, no money or no gas station in sight?
   Often _____ Sometimes _____ Never _____

3. Do you schedule yourself to be in two places at the same time by forgetting to write down your schedule?
   Often _____ Sometimes _____ Never _____

4. Do you procrastinate doing what you need to do and then race against time to complete the task?
   Often _____ Sometimes _____ Never _____

5. Do you arrive at the airport at the very last minute, find long security lines and barely make your flight?
   Often _____ Sometimes _____ Never _____

SELF-TEST FOR STUDENTS:

1. Do you forget about doing your homework and leave your assignments at school? Then you try calling everyone to get the assignments?
   Often _____ Sometimes _____ Never _____

2. Do you misplace your lunch, wallet, glasses or jacket and get all tense trying to find them while your ride honks impatiently for you to hurry up and get into the car?
   Often _____ Sometimes _____ Never _____

3. Do you put off studying for big tests or projects and then have to stay up all night or get the entire family involved trying to help you make your deadline?
   Often _____ Sometimes _____ Never _____

4. Do you wake up from over sleeping, grab your clothes and race to get to school?
   Often _____ Sometimes _____ Never _____

5. Do you put off chores while playing computer games and then your parents get upset with you?
   Often _____ Sometimes _____ Never _____

IF YOU CHECKED 2 OR MORE OFF YOU ARE MISMANAGING YOUR TIME

The Little Red Hen

Once there was a Little Red Hen who lived in a barnyard. One day the Little Red Hen found some grains of wheat. *"Look look!"* she clucked. *"Who will help me plant this wheat?"* *"Not I"*, quaked the duck. *"Not I"*, oinked the pig. *"Not I"* meowed the cat. *"Then I will plant it myself"*, said the Little Red Hen. And she did. When the wheat was tall and golden, the Little Red Hen knew it was ready to be cut. *"Who will help me cut the wheat?"* she asked. *"Not I"*, said the duck. *"Not I"*, said the pig. *"Not I"*, said the cat. *"Then I will cut this wheat myself,"* And she did. *"Now"*, said the Little Red Hen, *"it is time to take the wheat to the miller so he can grind it into flour. Who will help me?"* *"Not I"*, said the duck. *"Not I"*, said the pig. *"Not I"*, said the cat. *"Then I will take the wheat to the miller myself"*, said the Little Red Hen. And she did. The miller ground the wheat into fine white flour and put it into a sack for the Little Red Hen. When she returned to the barnyard, the Little Red Hen asked, *"Who will help me make this flour into dough?"* *"Not I"*, said the duck, the pig and the cat all at once. *"Then I will make the dough myself"*, said the Little Red Hen. And she did. When the dough was ready to go into the oven, the Little Red Hen asked, *"Who will help me bake the bread?"* Not I"*, said the duck, the pig and the cat again all at once. *"Then I will bake it myself"*, said the Little Red Hen. And she did. Soon the bread was ready. As she took it from the oven, the Little Red Hen asked, *"Well who will help me eat this warm, fresh bread?"* *"I will"*, said the duck. *"I will"*, said the pig. *"I will"*, said the cat. *"No you won't"*, said the Little Red Hen. *"You wouldn't help me plant the seeds, cut the wheat, go to the miller, make the dough or bake the bread. Now, my three chicks and I will eat this bread ourselves!"* And that's just what they did. And the moral of this story is...Don't expect anyone to help you. They will wait until there is no work to be done and no risk to be taken. They will step up and expect you to share with them as if they helped you.

Roller Coaster Time

Does your enthusiasm for taking the time to get done what you need to get done stay high or low? If you go up and down, wasting time, making excuses and not getting on with doing what you need to do, your life will be like a roller coaster. Procrastinating, rationalizing, excuse making, lying, negativity and putting off, wastes precious time.

Right when you think everything is going great, boom, something happens to distract you, disturb you, make you question what is happening, or stops you from moving forward in life. This is part of the human experience. It is not just happening to you. Many people make choices to be busy. Begin today by setting aside some time to look at your calendar and see where it's lacking in what's important and where it's too full of what's simply pressing. It may mean that you have to eliminate some things. It may mean that you choose only one sport or planned activity for your children instead of three, or that you choose to join only one special interest group instead of many, or that you don't attend every social event your church hosts.

Twists and Bumps

The path from where you are to where you want to be is not always smooth and straight. The reason for the twists and bumps is simple and it has nothing to do with you. It has more to do with the fact that not everyone is as interested in your success as you are. Some people may accidentally hinder your efforts; others who are in competition with you and have little or no integrity may try to sabotage your efforts. Keep in mind, though, that when you hit those roadblocks your character, commitment and attitude are the determining factors in your success...Carefully review your plan of action, seek wise counsel and be particularly careful to feed your mind empowering information.

Enjoy the ups and downs of life...it's all part of the cycle of life!

From The Desk of

This is what I really want to spend my time doing:

Be like an art gallery that attracts amateurs, collectors and dealers. Be like your own art museum. Feature your works that you are proud of.

"Make no needless plans."
-General Robert E. Lee

Just A Reminder

It is your life after all!

chapter 7

Chapter Seven

Today Sure Went by Fast

How many times have your said to yourself *"today sure went by fast"*. It seems that our lives are so complex and so full of things to do that we forget to feel the moments that together make up a day. Moments are lost amid the clutter of everyday and they become blurred by the activities we invent. It seems like activity is more important than the moments in which they occur. Moments come and go as we do our *"important"* tasks of the day. Our focus seems to be on what needs to be done instead of on what we can do with the moments we are given. Quantity becomes more important than quality and quality moments slip by one by one into the shadows of our life. They become forgotten, lost, or not important.

Seize the moment of excited curiosity on any subject to solve your doubts for if you let it pass, the desire may never return and you may remain in ignorance.

I want to be needed! Need me! call me! come see me! E-mail me! visit me! Invite me! I am SO LONELY! make me feel special! Appreciate me! I have loads of time for you! But I might be too busy!

Seize the Moments

In seizing the moments of your life, you extend their value and allow each to create magic. You see each as a miracle and know that within them lies the importance of life. Life is not full of quantity time but full of quality time. It is up to each of us to recognize the quality within each moment and to allow it to shine throughout our day. Stop all your activity and be thankful for each moment by recognizing its importance to your life. Celebrate the fact that you are alive and can see the wonder contained within each moment of your life. Stop all your excuses. Become aware. Seek the beauty of each event and allow the majesty of your life to be known. Each moment is the seed of your future and as such gives power to what may seem like a lost second but in reality is a chrysalis waiting to be opened. It is energy waiting to be born and the gift you give to your future. Each moment is a capsule of love just eager to be seen amid the chaos of an ever noisy world.

"In the name of God, stop a moment, cease your work, look around you."
-Leo Tolstoy (1828-1910)

"Man is free at the moment he wishes to be.
-Voltaire (1694-1778)

See each moment as you would a work of art and search within them for the ideals you wish to be. It is your life to build out of the many moments you are given. Allow each moment to fashion a life of choice for within each moment is the miracle of creation.

"How wonderful it is that nobody need wait a single moment before starting to improve the world."
-Anne Frank, Diary of a Young Girl, 1952

What's Most Important in Life

It had been some time since Jack had seen the old man. Life itself got in the way. Jack moved clear across the country in pursuit of his dreams. There, in the rush of his busy life, Jack had little time to think about the past and often no time to spend with his wife and son. His mother called to tell him, *"Mr. Belser died last night. The funeral is Wednesday." "Jack, did you hear me?"* Oh, sorry, Mom. Yes, I heard you. It's been so long since I thought of him." *"Well, he didn't forget you. Every time I saw him he'd ask how you were doing. He'd reminisce about the many days you spent over 'talking with him,"* Mom told him. *"I loved that old house he lived in,"* Jack said. *"Jack, after your father died, Mr. Belser stepped in to make sure you had a man's influence in your life,"* she said. *"Mom, He spent a lot of time teaching me things he thought were important...I'll be there for the funeral,"* Jack said. Mr.. Belser's funeral was small and uneventful. He had no children of his own and most of his relatives had passed away. The night before he had to return home, Jack and his Mom stopped by to see the old house next door one more time. Standing in the doorway, Jack paused for a moment. The house was exactly as he remembered. Every step held memories. Every picture, every piece of furniture . . . Jack stopped suddenly. *"What's wrong, Jack?"* his Mom asked. *"The box is gone,"* he said. *"What box?"* Mom asked. *"There was a small gold box that he kept locked on top of his desk. I must have asked him a thousand times what was inside. All he'd ever tell me was 'the thing I value most,'"* Jack said. It was gone. *"Now I'll never know what was so valuable to him,"* Jack said. It had been about two weeks since Mr.. Belser died. Returning home from work one day Jack discovered a note in his mailbox. *"Signature required on a package. No one at home. Please stop by the main post office within the next three days,"* the note read. Early the next day Jack retrieved the package. The small box was old and looked like it had been mailed a hundred years ago. The handwriting was difficult to read, but the return address caught his attention. *"Mr. Harold Belser"* it read. Jack took the box out to his car and ripped open the package. There inside was the gold box and an envelope. Jack's hands shook as he read the note inside. *"Upon my death, please forward this box and its contents to Jack Bennett. It's the thing I valued most in my life."* A small key was taped to the letter. His heart racing, as tears filling his eyes, Jack carefully unlocked the box. There inside he found a beautiful gold pocket watch. Running his fingers slowly over the finely etched casing, he unlatched the cover. Inside he found these words engraved:

"Jack, Thanks for your time!"
-Harold Belser

"The thing he valued most was . . . my time." Jack held the watch for a few minutes, then called his office and cleared his appointments for the next two days. *"Why?"* Janet, his assistant asked. *"I need some time to spend with my son,"* he said. *"Oh, by the way, Janet, thanks for your time!"*

When you think you have no chance of getting what you want, you probably won't get it, but if you trust God to do what's best and wait on His time, sooner or later, you will get it or something better. When you make the biggest mistake ever, something good can still come from it.

**"SHOWER THE PEOPLE YOU LOVE WITH LOVE. SHOW THEM YOU REALLY CARE."
-JAMES TAYLOR**

I am busier than a one-armed paperhanger!

Everyone needs me! I have so many outside interests that I am out of energy for any time for me. How can I find time for myself without being selfish?

What about ME? What about my time?

ME, IT'S ALWAYS AND FOREVER ABOUT ME...QUIT TALKING ABOUT YOU, LET'S SPEND TIME TALKING ABOUT ME AND HOW BUSY I AM! COME ON, BE IMPRESSED... I AM SOOO BUSY!

Wow! Ten years have passed by! Where have the years gone?

I am busier than anyone you know! I just don't get anything accomplished!

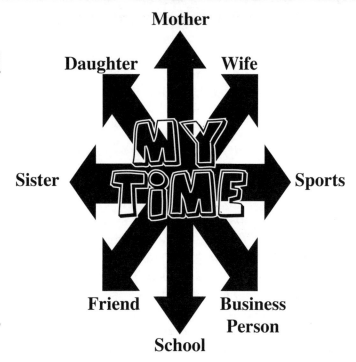

I Just Don't Have The Time To Set Goals, So What About Me?

This is where some people fail. They don't consider the amount of time available. They fly up, down, in circles and when they find 40 working years have dribbled by with no rewards, they wonder where their life has gone. It's so sad. I want greatness for you. I want you to have the lifestyle that is yours. Focus on your goals. Don't have stinkin' thinkin', Take the time. After all, it's your life.

Never Give Up

Some of the most successful people in history have become monumental failures. They have been pushed to the depths of misery and yet rose to success. They never lost sight of a gleam of light and eventually stood completely in the glowing spotlight of success. They chose to go for greatness. Success is, after all, up to you. Get back in the game. Make new goals, never ever give up.

IT'S OPENING NIGHT!

STARRING THE FANTASTIC BUSY ME!

May I have all of your attention please? I am here tonight to tell you just how busy I am! I am a wife, a mother, a daughter, a friend, a neighbor, a grand-daughter, I work out every day and I volunteer. I have no free time, I am exhausted and just am so busy being someone important to and needed by so many people. Please don't ask me to do anything else or expect me to be a big part of your life. I really have not one minute to spare but I want you to know how busy I am! Oh yes...I am very busy!

(Isn't it interesting that truly busy people do not have time to tell you how busy they are?)

If You Have A Dream

Don't wait for some distant day to come,
it may be too late before you've even begun.
Not everyone will agree with all you decide.
Be true to yourself first and foremost.
The only important thing in life is what you do
with the time you spend here on earth.
Don't be afraid to follow your desires,
they are not silly nor selfish.
Take the time and do what makes you feel alive.
Leave your fears and regrets in the past,
for this is where they belong.
Don't cloud today with things that
can't be undone. You have no more
control over yesterday or tomorrow,
than you do the raging of your passions.
Do not quiet these dreams nor quench
your desires. For if you do, your journey
is ended. You have only today to begin
anew and follow your dreams.
For in the end all we have are our memories.
When the twilight comes to us, let there be,
No excuses, no explanations, no regrets!
-Unknown

When you learn something new just say to yourself...

There I Grow Again

I AM VERY IMPORTANT!

I AM IN CHARGE OF SO MUCH . . . LOOK HOW IMPORTANT I AM! NOBODY CAN DO MY BUSINESS LIKE ME. I AM A GIANT IN MY INDUSTRY. TA-DA . . . I AM SIMPLY THE BEST. I HAVE WORKED MYSELF TO DEATH BUT NOW I AM SOMEBODY AND DON'T YOU FORGET IT.

I want to be somebody so badly!
I want to succeed! I want to be noticed!
I want to be a star!
I want to be known!

Pay attention . . .
Do you KNOW
who I am?

The Businessman and the Fisherman

A management consultant, on holiday in a fishing village, watched a small fishing boat dock at the quayside. Noting the quality of the fish, the consultant asked the fisherman how long it had taken to catch them. *"Not very long"* answered the fisherman. *"Then, why didn't you stay out longer and catch more?"* asked the consultant. The fisherman explained that his small catch was sufficient to meet his needs and those of his family. The consultant asked, *"But what do you do with the rest of your time?"* *"I sleep late, fish a little, play with my children, have an afternoon's rest under a coconut tree. In the evenings, I go into the community hall to see my friends, have a few beers, play the drums and sing a few songs...I have a full and happy life,"* replied the fisherman. The consultant ventured *"I have an MBA from Harvard and I can help you... You should start by fishing longer every day. You can then sell the extra fish you catch. With the extra revenue, you can buy a bigger boat. With the extra money the larger boat will bring, you can buy a second one and a third one and so on until you have a large fleet. Instead of selling your fish to a middleman, you can negotiate directly with the processing plants and maybe even open your own plant. You can then leave this little village and move to a city here or anywhere you wish, from where you can direct your huge enterprise."* *"How long would that take?"* asked the fisherman. *"Oh, ten, maybe twenty years,"* replied the consultant. *"And after that?"* asked the fisherman. *"After that? That's when it gets really interesting"*, answered the consultant, laughing, *"When your business gets really big, you can start selling shares in your company and make millions!"* *"Millions? Really? And after that?"* pressed the fisherman. *"After that you'll be able to retire, move out to a small village by the sea, sleep in late every day, spend time with your family, go fishing, take afternoon naps under a coconut tree and spend relaxing evenings having drinks with friends..."*

YOU HAVE TO PUT THIS TIME IN, STUDYING, PRACTICING, DRILLING, REHEARSING AND PERFECTING YOUR PRESENTATION... FOR AS LONG AS IT TAKES.

A helicopter will not take you to the top of any dream and drop you off at the top.

You must climb the stairs one at a time, the elevator to the top is out of order.

Some people spend their lifetime trying to get noticed, but the real lesson in life is to help others achieve their dreams. When you do, you will succeed and have a much richer life than you can ever imagine.

Isn't it about time that you do what you want to do with your time?

Tick tock

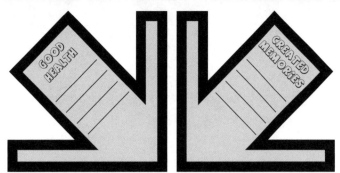

WHAT IS REALLY IMPORTANT
TO YOU AT THE END OF THE DAY?

GOOD HEALTH

CREATED MEMORIES

MADE A DIFFERENCE

LIVED WITH NO REGRETS

**Spend quality time with your pets.
Pets need love and affection just like people.**

"When I feel like giving up and I'm ready to walk away, in the stillness I can hear a voice inside me say...do something, do something. It's too late for saving face, don't just stand there takin' up space, do something. It's not over, no, it's never too late. When I feel like giving up and there's nowhere left to go, that's the time I dig down deep. It's the only thing I know, do something. Don't leave it up to someone else and don't feel sorry for yourself. Do something. It's not over, no, it's never too late. You'll sleep better knowing you tried to do something. It's too easy not to care and you're not ready for the rocking chair do something. Don't wait too long, even if its wrong, do something."
-from *Do Something* on the Eagles CD
Long Road out of Eden

If you are not living a joy filled life, take my word for it, you are wasting your precious life time. Be willing to get over what *WAS* and get on with what *IS*. Learn from the past! Yes! Keep focused on the past? No! An old movie star was turned away at the gate of the studio where he once was the dazzling super star. Indignantly he says to the guard, *"Do you realize who I was? Do you realize who I used to be?"* Bottom line? Who cares? Move on! Life is temporary. Believe those who tell us to only live for today and let the future take care of itself. You need to control your time to get the most out of life. Focus more, after reading this book on the time you have left. Live in the present, but *plan* for the future, it's about time.

"The past is a guidepost, not a hitching post."
-Thomas Holcroft

Isn't it strange that princes and kings and clowns that caper in sawdust Ring's; and common folks, like you and me, all are builders for eternity. To each is given a book of Rules, a block of stone and a bag of tools; and each must shape ere time has flown, a stumbling block or a stepping stone.

I bargained with life for a penny and life would pay no more, however I begged at evening, when I counted my scanty store. for life is a just employer, he gives you what you ask, but once you have set the wages, why you must bear the task. I worked for a menial's hire, only to learn, dismayed, that any wage I had asked for life, life would have willingly paid.

-Unknown

Don't worry, be happy!

Hakuna Matata!

What Is Really Important

1. Name the five wealthiest people in the world.
2. Name the last five Heisman trophy winners.
3. Name the last five winners of the Miss American Pageant.
4. Name ten people who have won the Nobel or Pulitzer Prize.
5. Name the last half dozen Academy Award winners for best actor or actress.
6. Name the last decade's worth of World Series winners. (Even the last two or three years winners)

Most of us don't remember the headlines of yesterday. All those people who fit into the winners of those categories were the best in their field. But after a while the applause dies. Awards tarnish. Achievements are forgotten. Accolades and certificates are buried with their owners. Here is another list of questions you might do much better answering:

1. List a few teachers who aided your journey through school.
2. Name three friends who have helped you through a difficult time.
3. Think of a few people who have made you feel appreciated and special.
4. Think of five people you enjoy spending time with.

Was that easier? I think so. The point here? The people who make a difference in your life are not the ones with the most credentials, the most money or the most awards. They are the ones that care. Your family and close associates are who really matter in your life.

when the **why** gets clear enough about what you want in life, the **how** gets easy

Realize the Value of Time

To realize the value of one year;
Ask a student who has failed a final exam.
To realize the value of one month;
ask a mother who has given
birth to a premature baby.
To realize the value of one week;
ask the editor of a weekly newspaper.
To realize the value of one hour;
Ask the lovers who are waiting to meet.
To realize the value of one minute; ask the person
who has missed the train, or bus or plane.
To realize the value of one second;
ask a person who just avoided an accident.
To realize the value of one millisecond;
Ask the person who has won
silver at the Olympics.

> # If you find out you have 6 months to live, what will you do with your time?

Isn't it about time to make some changes in your life?

> *"There will stretch out before you an ever lengthening, ever ascending, ever improving path. You know you will never get to the end of the journey. But this, far from discouraging only adds to the joy and glory of the climb."*
> -Winston Churchill

If you only have 8 decades to live and your last decade is not as productive as your other decades that leaves 7 decades of lifetime. Subtract how many decades you have lived... what is left?

Are you preparing now to live the rest of your life with prosperity and abundance? What you are doing now will make a difference in how you spend your time twenty years from now.

Love being who you are, taking care of others needs, but be sure you take time for you too!

Plan now for retirement

Your Time Bank Account

Every morning, it credits you with 86,400 seconds. Every night it writes off, as lost, whatever of this you have failed to invest to good purpose. It carries over no balance. It allows no overdraft. Each day it opens a new account for you. Each night it burns the remains of the day. If you fail to use the day's deposits, the loss is yours. There is no going back. There is no drawing against the *tomorrow*. You must live in the present on today's deposits. Invest it so as to get from it the utmost in health, happiness and success! The clock is ticking.

I AM THE MASTER OF FASTER

MOST WORK SO HARD MOST OF THEIR LIVES AND THEN AT THE END OF THEIR LIVES THEY WONDER WHERE TIME WENT.

Burn out happens when you are burning the candle at both ends. You must take time out for yourself. Get to a spa regularly. Take care of yourself. You are the only one who really will take care of you.

Hello Burnout!
I knew you would show up!
What took you so long?
I have been giving to everyone but me for so long. I can't go on doing what I am doing.
It's about time I get in control of the time I have left.

BURNOUT BEGINS QUIETLY

Think of your latest big deadline. Your heart starts beating so fast, the adrenaline starts flowing, your palms get sweaty and you clinch your teeth. The faster you work, the faster the clock ticks off those cherished moments. Life is not boring for you at all. In fact life is...very exciting! Somehow you like being so busy and living a hectic life. But burnout is going to get you...**beware!** Hard work doesn't burn people out. What burns people out is not knowing if their work makes a difference. When you are giving to everyone else, focused on building someone else's dream, a go-getter, a go-giver and are on the run all of the time, you ARE going to burnout. It's just a matter of time. If you have nothing exciting in your life to look forward to, you just drag out everything you do and make it last

Is your only REAL JOY getting your self into a frenzy, upsetting, constantly in an uproar JAM? Do you really need the negative misadventures of constantly living your life in a panic mode?

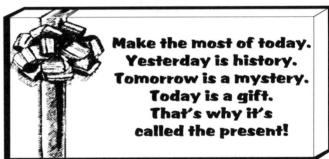

**Make the most of today.
Yesterday is history.
Tomorrow is a mystery.
Today is a gift.
That's why it's
called the present!**

The person who says it can't be done is often interrupted by the person who is doing it!

Don't Wait Until

Don't think you have to wait until you are 60 or 70 years old to take the time to be great. Handel composed two operas at age 21, Mozart composed a minuet at age 5, at age 12 his first opera and age 13 he composed concertos and sonatas. Alexander the Great became King of Macedonia at age 20. At age 21 Genghis Khan was called *Universal Ruler*. Napoleon was in his mid 30's as the Emperor of Europe.

The Empty Jug Story

Pretend that you are at the beach with 50 of your friends celebrating a promotion. Everyone is having a great time tossing frisbees and boomerangs and they all become thirsty at the same time. You are the only one with a jug of ice cold lemonade. It's your job to fill everyone's plastic cup with lemonade.

But as you pour the last lemonade from your first pitcher, only six glasses are filled. Six people drink thirstily, but now you are surrounded by everyone else with their empty glasses thrust in your direction. Realizing their great thirst, you anxiously pour into glass after glass with only drops falling out of your now empty pitcher. But! You explain, *with so many to serve, I don't have time to fill my own glass!*

The challenge that seems so obvious to those looking on goes unnoticed by you because you are anxious that every friend have a full glass as soon as possible. This is a parable about the way many people live their lives. You have a great capacity (though not an unlimited one) to give to others and a great need to do so. You have a lot of inner permission to serve others, but low awareness or inner permission of the need to take time to...refill your own glass...consider the ways to refill your jug or life with energy and the personal resources to give again: How many of these do you make time for on a REGULAR basis and how many are you just too busy to take time to do? Do you find time to have fun and feel joy several times a day or are you too busy? When you are with your children and loved ones do you turn off the worries and experience true intimacy or do you let your worries contaminate and rob you of this precious time? Unless you take time to fill your glass or your personal reservoir, you will soon hit empty. Notice how descriptive these are of the empty jug syndrome:

FUN Proper rest Good Nutrition Play
Time alone **EXERCISE** Spiritual Life Intimacy
Time to read and learn **Regular vacations**
QUALITY TIME WITH FRIENDS AND FAMILY

Come on! I am thirsty! Please fill my glass NOW!!

Many people are so resourceful that they are able to force themselves to keep going for long times on empty. If you start getting more joy into each day, you will soon discover that you have something to look forward to. Do not contaminate your joy with guilt by thinking: *"I should be working or accomplishing something!"*

Some make it a way of life to

NEVER TO MAKE TIME FOR YOURSELF

Some of you have amazing role models in your life who are all work and no play. I made my first fortune in the educational toy business because I believed a child's work was *their* play. I lived, ate, breathed and spent many years doing nothing but providing for my children because my work was my play. There was no difference between work and play for me, it was fun to work, I loved what I did, nonstop...but it also became a trap. I went years without rejuvenating and replenishing my adrenal glands. Today, I have to take much more time to rejuvenate than most people because I failed to do that early in life.

Earning a steady income from my own efforts, working at home and enjoying being the mother of three beautiful, fantastic, loving children and creating memories for the four of us was the only place I found joy for many years of my life. I did not take a vacation for ten years. Not one day off. I never looked up. All of a sudden, a decade was gone. I had plenty of joy but was burned out. Everyone has a different need for joy in their life so I can't give you a perfect formula for this. You can learn to tell when you are out of balance though by watching your feelings. Don't play too long though and lose your momentum. Don't fall into the trap of thinking...*no play til I finish this major project!* If you go too long, 12 or 24 hours without joy, you will begin to show symptoms of being joy starved.

Unless you find time to refill your jug (or your adrenal glands and personal reservoir) you will soon hit

These symptoms include:
- Loss of energy.
- Loss of motivation.
- Loss of enthusiasm.
- Oversleeping or insomnia.
- Overeating.
- A good case of the *I don't wanna* and *poor me*.
- Inability to concentrate.
- Lots of procrastination.
- Lots of rationalization.

As the years go by, most people apply the brakes to Self-Management. They succumb to a hardening of their mental arteries, doing the minimum necessary to get by. As a result, life becomes unfulfilling.

What is Burnout?

Burnout is a state of emotional and physical exhaustion caused by excessive and prolonged stress. It can occur when you feel overwhelmed and unable to meet constant demands. As the stress continues, you begin to lose the interest or motivation in what you are doing. Burnout reduces your productivity and saps your energy, leaving you feeling increasingly hopeless, powerless, cynical, exhausted and resentful. The unhappiness burnout causes can eventually threaten your job, your relationships and your health. Actually, your adrenal glands are burned out. No matter how much rest you get, you are still exhausted.

Signs and Symptoms of Burnout

Because burnout doesn't happen overnight and it's difficult to fight once you're in the middle of it, it's important to recognize the early signs of burnout and take action. Burnout usually has its roots in stress, so the earlier you recognize the symptoms of stress and address them, the better chance you have of avoiding burnout. The signs of burnout tend to be more mental than physical. They can include feelings of: loss of energy, loss of motivation, loss of enthusiasm, loss of rationalization, oversleeping or insomnia, overeating, inability to concentrate, procrastination, frustration, powerlessness, hopelessness, being drained of emotional energy, exhausted when you wake up in the morning, detachment, withdrawal, isolation, depression, being trapped, having failed at what you are doing, irritability, loss of interest, loss of motivation, sadness, cynicism, beyond caring and disappointment.

Burnout Can Take Months and Years to Surface

The symptoms of burnout — the hopelessness, the cynicism, the detachment from others — can take months to surface. If someone close to you points out changes in your attitude or behavior that are typical of burnout, listen to that person. If you're burning out and the burnout expresses itself as irritability, you might find yourself always snapping at people or making snide remarks about them. If the burnout manifests itself as depression, you might want to sleep all the time or always be *too tired* to socialize. You might turn to escapist behaviors such as drinking, drugs, partying, or shopping binges to try to escape from your negative feelings. Your relationships at work and in your personal life may begin to fall apart.

What Causes Burnout?

Most of us have days when we're bored to death with what we do at work; when our co-workers and bosses seem irremediably wrong-headed; when the dozen plates we keep spinning aren't noticed, let alone rewarded; when dragging ourselves into work requires the determination of Hercules; when caring about work seems like a waste of energy; when nothing we do appears to make a difference in a workplace full of bullying supervisors, clueless colleagues and ungrateful clients. We all have bad days at work. But when every day is a bad day, you're flirting with burnout. Most burnout has to do with the workplace and it's present in every occupation.

The 4 Stages of Burnout

1. **Physical, Mental and Emotional Exhaustion.** Maybe you are still holding it together at work (or school). For those grappling with all three of these stressors...automatically proceed to stage two, if not three.) Normally, you pride yourself on doing a thorough job, a high quality performance. Now you are looking for shortcuts, if not cutting corners. This gnaws at your self-esteem and you may even have pangs of guilt. A case of the *brain strain* is developing, accompanied by an energy shortage and feelings of exhaustion. If stress levels continue unabated, you probably are ripe for the second stage.

2. **Shame and Doubt.** You want to take on a new project...but this voice inside silently screams, *Who are you kidding!* So what's happening? You're not feeling confident about the future and you're feeling pretty lousy in the present. Not surprisingly, you may even start discounting your past accomplishments. Beware...This is not a logical process; it's a psychological one. Now you wonder if others will detect that something is wrong. While projecting a competent image has been the norm, now this voice inside is relentlessly shouting, *Impostor! Impostor!* Then you catch yourself emitting heavy, labored sighs. You begin to chronically grappling with a profound sense of vulnerability and uncertainty. No surprise then that some will *progress* to the third phase: Then next, we'll check out your *attitude* .

3. **Cynicism and Callousness.** In response to that prolonged feeling of insecurity or vulnerability, some feel there's only one thing left to do: put on the heavy armor. They develop an ATTITUDE: *Look out for #1 Cover your derriere. No one's getting to me.* In the short run, the strategy often works. You become sufficiently abrasive or obnoxious, people start avoiding you. But this hard exterior can eventually become a burdensome, self-defeating strategy. If you are in a position that pull you in all directions - compelling demands,

favors, complaints, bribes, beware! Still, what do you think is the biggest stress trap? That's right, this *good guy syndrome*. You are such a *nice guy*. What can't nice guys and nice gals do? They can't say *"No!"* Nor are they confident establishing their boundaries. They have difficulty with authority - being one or interacting with one. These nice people tend to avoid conflict; they don't want to hurt others' feelings. They are not comfortable with anger, or don't know how to express their frustration or displeasure in a focused manner. Their personal mantras are being *fair* and *accommodation* (while feeling deep rejection when other's aren't fair or accommodating). These accommodators, despite having a full workload plate, when asked to take on new work will just do it and keep their mouths shut. Being a team player doesn't mean you have to sacrifice your integrity or health. There's an option: Learn to communicate. *Sure I'll help you with this new demand and deadline. But for me to give the assignment the attention it deserves, we'll have to renegotiate my priority list and time lines.* There is a difference between urgent and important. When everything is urgent, nothing is important! Setting realistic limits is not a negative reflection on your work ethic or your ability to go the extra mile. Without boundaries, that mile often turns into many miles.

Without realizing it, you can be sucked up by the progressive burnout whirlpool. Burnout doesn't just facilitate a hardening of the psyche. When your stress starts to smolder into frustration and anger; then turns to suspicion and mistrust as you enclose yourself in embattled armor or a crusty shell...This is not just how you harden an attitude, but it's a formula for hardening the arteries, as well. Cardiovascular complications, high blood pressure, even premature heart attacks can ensue. Which is why, usually, it's better that you hit the fourth stage of burnout, than linger in the third. Of course, *Failure. Helplessness and Crisis* sounds terrible. Hitting bottom means there's no more downward spiral. And, if you can reach out, there's no where to go but up.

4. **Failure, Helplessness and Crisis.** Being caught in a familiar *Catch-22* often signals the final phase: *Damned if you do, damned if you don't. Damned if you stay, damned if you leave.* Your coping structure seems to be coming unglued. The crisis smoke signals are billowing big time. *Why is that?* Burnout is like trying to race a marathon full speed, nonstop. Even Olympic marathon runners must pace themselves. If not, the body parts will break down. With burnout, over time, the mental apparatus also wears out. One reason the fourth stage is so disorienting is that a person's psychological defenses have worn down. Cracks start appearing in the defensive armor. Painful memories and old hurts normally contained by your emotional defenses are leaking through the cracks. A slight or an emotional bump can set off an overly sensitive and personal reaction that takes you a long time to recover. Now a mate's or partner's or child's occasional, somewhat annoying behavior really irritates as it reminds you of a mannerism of your father. Or, jealousy towards a colleague reeks of sibling rivalry.

Burnout is Not for Wimps

Many reach the farther stages of burnout because of their tenacity and dedication. They have a strong sense of responsibility and don't like being deterred from reaching their goals. All noble qualities...unless compelled by rigid perfectionism and *there's only one right way* thinking. Then, pursuing their goals takes a back seat to proving others wrong and overcoming humiliation.

Take Time to Improve Your Relationships

- Nurture your closest relationships, such as those with your partner, children or friends. These relationships can help restore energy and alleviate some of the psychological effects of burnout, such as feelings of being under-appreciated. Try to put aside what's burning you out and make the time you spend with loved ones positive and enjoyable.

- Develop casual social relationships with people at your workplace. We do all kinds of things, whether it is getting together to play cards or going out to eat. It gives everyone an opportunity to relax and blow off steam. Avoid hanging out with negative-minded people who do nothing but complain.

- Connect with a cause or a community group that is personally meaningful to you. Joining a religious, social, or support group can give you a place to talk to like-minded people about how to deal with daily stress and to make new friends. If your line of work has a professional association, attend meetings and interact with others coping with the same workplace demands.

- Practice healthy communication. Express your feelings to others who will listen, understand and not judge. Burnout involves feelings that fester and grow, so be sure to let your emotions out in healthy, productive ways.

The Vital Lesson of the 4 'R's

If no matter what you say or what you do, **R**esults, **R**ewards, **R**ecognition and **R**elief are not forthcoming and you can't mean *"no"* or won't let go...trouble awaits. The groundwork is being laid for apathy, callousness and despair.

burnout is less a sign of failure and more that you gave yourself away.

EGO Driven Goals

Are you are chasing (maybe, also, being chased by) ego-driven goals? Especially in times of overload, uncertainty and major change, *driven and rigid responsibility* can quickly transform a performance benefit into a personal and professional liability. Many of these rigid people are usually not just responsible, they often are quite responsive to others. People lean on them for support. *Are you a pillar of strength for those around you all of the time? If so, will those dependent upon you be quick to notice when you are feeling shaky? That you may need a shoulder?* Most likely not, as their sense of security is contingent on your always being strong and available. Are you buying into this *superperson* role or hiding behind a heroic mask? Maybe you always had to help mom with (sometimes raise) the other children. Or you're the emotional listener in the office, frequently absorbing others' complaints. *Can you hear that screeching, scratching sound?* That's the stress knot twisting and turning tighter and tighter about your neck.

On the Edge

No wonder people start jumping out of jobs or school, out of relationships, sometimes just jumping. And for those not into jumping, they may be into swinging by the fourth stage. Mood swinging, that is, between short highs and/or prolonged depressive lows. Okay, the existential question: *Is it Miller Time or Prozac Time?* Now it's way too late for the former and a decision on the latter requires expert opinion. But that's exactly the key for transforming a danger into an opportunity. Fourth stage burnout is the crisis point, it's crunch time. *Are you ready to reach out for the help and resources you need?*

Don't Rush Through Life

Life is not a race. Allow yourself plenty of time to linger. Relaxation and satisfaction have space to grow only when we slow our pace.

> *"There is nothing worth more than this day."*
> *-Goethe*

Recover Your Strengths

1. Get proper and sufficient support; someone trained in crisis intervention and loss,
2. Confront denial, false hopes, cynicism or helplessness,
3. Grieve past and present losses while turning guilt, hurt, anxiety and aggression into focused energy; and
4. Acquire and apply skills and technology for turning new challenge-solving options into productive attitudes and actions.

FOR THE PHOENIX TO RISE FROM THE ASHES ONE MUST KNOW THE PAIN TO TRANSFORM THE FIRE INTO BURNING DESIRE.

We are only on Earth for a short while, so we should do our very best to make it pleasant. It doesn't take much, pick up some litter, repaint a fence or conserve electricity. But do something to prettify our planet today.

Take time to do each project to the best of your ability and enjoy it.

While you're usually aware of being under a lot of stress, you don't always notice burnout when it happens.

Stress vs. Burnout

Burnout may be the result of unrelenting stress, but it isn't the same as too much stress. Stress involves too many pressures that demand too much of you physically and psychologically. Stressed people can still imagine, though, that if they can just get everything under control, they'll feel better. Burnout, on the other hand, is about not enough. Being burned out means feeling empty, devoid of motivation and beyond caring. People experiencing burnout often don't see any hope of positive change in their situations. If excessive stress is like drowning in responsibilities, burnout is being all dried up.

Stress: Characterized by over engagement, emotions are over reactive, produces urgency and hyperactivity, exhausts physical energy, leads to anxiety disorders, causes disintegration, primary damage is physical, stress may kill you prematurely and you won't have enough time to finish what you started.

Burnout: You can't seem to stay focused and you just want to rest all the time. You get discouraged easily and have trouble bouncing back with great enthusiasm. Burnout may never kill you. but your life may not seem worth living.

"Perhaps the most valuable result of any education is the ability to make yourself do the thing you have to do, when it ought to be done, whether you like it or not: it is the first lesson that ought to be learned and however early a man's training begins, it is probably the last lesson he learns thoroughly."
-Thomas Henry Huxley

First you need a dream and then you have to put a gleam on your dream. Then you need a scheme to back up your dream. Then put a beam under your dream. Finally, you need a team to build the dream.

Who is Most At Risk

Those most at risk may be service professionals, who spend their work lives attending to the needs of others, especially if their work puts them in frequent contact with the dark or tragic side of human experience, or if they're underpaid. unappreciated, or criticized for matters beyond their control. Also, those who work from home with no supervision, no appreciation, not plugged into a system where they can be a part of something bigger than working on their own. Single parents are at high risk because they have the responsibility of being both the mother and father and provider and protector. There is never time for their own needs.

Drink More Water!

It's amazing how little actual water people drink these days. Instead, they guzzle soft drinks and coffee which introduces various unnecessary substances into our bodies, such as artificial colors, flavors, caffeine, stomach and bowel irritants, empty calories via high fructose corn syrup. Many people drink enough calories every day in soda to comprise an entire extra meal. Modern-day humans are often afflicted with the inability to distinguish hunger from thirst, mainly because we used to get most of our water from raw foods. If you feel hungry, drink some water first and see if that helps. As you become dehydrated, your brain shrinks and your basic body functions begin to slow down, which often causes intense fatigue. If you drink ice cold water, your metabolism will accelerate as your body rushes to warm it to body or room temperature. Drink more water. Your kidneys will thank you. Don't drink until you feel sick, but drink often, pacing your consumption throughout the day.

The match of life has been struck and too soon it will burn out. All that matters is the beauty of the flame, not the length of it's burning.

Caregiver Burnout

Outside the world of paid work, the people more prone to burnout than any other group are those who are caregivers: those who devote themselves to the unpaid care of chronically ill or disabled family members. While care giving always represents stress for the caregiver, what may be a burden to one person may be more manageable to another. When care giving goes on indefinitely, burnout — the point at which the care giving experience is not a healthy option for the caregiver or the person receiving care — is always a possibility.

The Stressors of Care Giving

The changes in the family dynamic, household disruption, financial concerns, the expectations and demands of the person being cared for, the way those being cared for treat the caregiver and the sheer amount of work involved — can be overwhelming. People today are feeling tremendous pressure to *do it all,* taking care of children and aging parents while maintaining career and home. Instead of having a sense of accomplishment, many people feel guilt when they run out of energy to handle all of the tasks.

Lack of Hope

The lack of hope for a happy outcome is difficult to live through. When you know someone you love is terminal and yet their life goes on and on at the end, often the rewards of your care giving, if they come at all, are intangible and far off. The lack of control the caregiver feels over the situation is often compounded by other factors such as lack of finances, little or no family support, lack of time for themselves, poor management and planning skills. Without support, the caregiver becomes more and more isolated and sinks further and further into frustration and despair.

Pablo Casals, the world-renowned cellist, said, *"The capacity to care is the thing that gives life its deepest significance and meaning"*. It's essential that caregivers receive enough support that they don't lose that capacity.

Can Burnout Be Prevented or Treated?

The most effective way to head off burnout is to totally quit doing what you're doing and do something else, whether that means changing jobs or changing careers. But if that isn't an option for you, there are still things you can do to improve your situation, or at least your state of mind. Because burnout is related to stress, many of the methods effective in countering stress can help prevent burnout as well. It's important to build or maintain a foundation of good physical health, so be sure to eat right, get enough sleep and make exercise part of your daily routine. Work out. Get to a gym, take a walk. Take some time for yourself. Rejuvenate and refresh often. Get to a spa. Read a good book, watch something funny. Get into water, either the ocean, a swimming pool, a home spa, shower or bath. Water helps the body to calm down. Eat dinner early. Do not eat or drink anything after 6 pm. Clarify your job description. Ask your supervisor for an updated description of your job duties and responsibilities. You may then be able to point out that some of the things you're expected to do are not part of your job description and gain leverage by showing that you've been putting in work over and above the parameters of your job. Request a transfer. If your workplace is large enough, you might be able to escape a toxic environment by transferring to another department. Talk to your supervisor. Ask for new duties. If you've been doing the exact same work for a long time, ask to try something new: a different level, a different sales territory, or a different machine.

Change Your Circumstances

Look for a new job. Update your resume and apply for jobs that are related to but different from what you do now. Make a career move. Get whatever training you need to make a big move a big move. Start a home based business. Make a career change. If you know you want to work in a different career, start taking steps toward it now. Attend seminars to learn everything you can. Or even if it's one course at a time, that will help you discover if you are on the right path. Find out what the requirements are for the job you really want and start meeting them bit by bit. Get career advice. Consult a career counselor or use the services of an agency that offers vocational services. *The best defense against all burnout is to be with other people.* Although taking time to yourself to relax is important in reducing stress, if you are approaching burnout, it's also crucial that you cultivate relationships with other people and spend time socializing with them. Poor relationships and isolation can contribute to burnout, but positive relationships can help prevent or reduce its onset.

circumstances???
Ha! I make my own
circumstances!

> *"People are always blaming their circumstances for what they are. I don't believe in circumstances. The people who get on in this world are the people who get up and look for the circumstances they want and if they can't find them, they make them."*
> -George Bernard Shaw

GOD, grant me
the serenity
to accept the things
I cannot change
Courage to change
the things I can
and the wisdom to
know the difference
Living
ONE DAY AT A TIME;
Enjoying one
moment at a time;
Accepting hardship
as the pathway
to peace.

When We Feel Threatened

An event or situation only becomes a stressor because we see it as one, because it represents a threat. Every stressor also entails an expectation of whether or not we can cope with it. If we don't think we can cope with a situation, we create expectations of not coping.

A natural reaction to particularly stressful situations is known as the *fight-or-flight* response, which is triggered by the brain rapidly activating the central nervous system: Adrenalin and other hormones are released into the blood, which boosts our heart, blood pressure and respiration rates. Blood flow is re-routed from the skin and surface areas of the body to major muscle groups, flooding them with oxygen, which enables us to prepare to *fight* or take to our heels in *flight*.

When stress is prolonged, however, a more complex response takes place in the body. *A General Adaptation Syndrome* begins, which consists of three stages: physiological, psychological and behavioral responses. The physiological response consists in turn of three stages – the Alarm Stage, the Resistance Stage and the Exhaustion Stage.

The Alarm Stage: (increased heart rate and blood flow, etc. as described above), is an appropriate reaction to a life-threatening situation. Shortly after the danger has passed, the mind and body begin to relax, entering the *Resistance Stage*. If the stressor continues, the physiological response enters the *Exhaustion Stage*, in which our bodies continue the *fight-or-flight* response, like a car motor racing, which naturally will eventually cause damage to the bodily systems, just as it would to the racing motor. It is very important to slow down when you have been through a major tragedy or have not taken care of yourself in a long time and look at what the stress is doing to your body.

The psychological response to stress consists of our feelings and emotions, which are sometimes positive, but more often negative when we become anxious, angry, fearful and tense. We may feel frustrated, hopeless, depressed. The intensity of these feelings will vary from person to person. Often the way we express the feelings we experience is the result of conditioning that goes back to our childhood. If for whatever reason we can't express those feelings, that only adds to the stress we're experiencing — our minds and bodies are interdependent, so feelings are an important factor in our overall response to stress. But don't give in just because you are exhausted. Get some well deserved rest, get to a spa, get some body treatments and rejuvenate and replenish your body.

We have behavioral responses to stress, attempts we make, mostly unconsciously, to eliminate or stop the experience of bad or negative feelings: We may turn to food, increasing consumption or, alternatively, stop eating; we may reach for the bottle to drown our feelings, smoke more heavily, take more medications, or indulge in aggressive *fight* or passive *flight* behavior by picking arguments or retreating to our rooms.

Obviously, it's impossible to escape all the stresses of life or to completely turn off our *fight-or-flight* response to them. The way to handle the challenge of stress is by involving both internal and external factors. Wherever possible, reduce the number and intensity of stressors in your life; and second, change the way you respond to unavoidable stress.

Meet Jeb

Every day when Jeb was growing up, his mother would come into his room and wake him at 5:30am, saying, *"Jeb, it's going to be a great day."* But that wasn't what the boy wanted to hear at that time in the morning. It was his job every day to go outside first thing and get coal to start the fire and heat the house. And he hated it. One day when his mother came in and said, *"It's going to be a great day,"* Jeb snapped, *"No, Mom, it's going to be a lousy day. I'm tired. The house is cold. And I don't want to get up and get the coal. It's a crummy day!"* *"Sweetheart,"* she replied, *"I didn't know you felt that way. Why don't you just go back to bed and get some more sleep?"* Jeb thought he had it made. *"Why didn't I think of this before?"* he asked himself. He woke up about two hours later. The house was warm and he could smell breakfast cooking. He rolled out of bed, put on his clothes and went out to the kitchen table. *"Boy, am I hungry,"* he said. *"I'm all rested up. Breakfast is already cooked. This is great."* *"Sweetheart,"* his mother said, *"You don't get any food today. Remember how you said it was going to be a crummy day? As your mother, I am going to do my best to make it a crummy day for you. You go back to your bedroom and stay there all day. You are not allowed to come out, and you don't get anything to eat. I'll see you tomorrow morning at 5:30."* Jeb walked dejectedly back to his room and got into bed. And he was able to go back to sleep, for about an hour. But there was only so much sleeping a person could do. He spent the day moping around his room, getting hungrier and hungrier. And when it finally got dark, he went back to bed again and tried to sleep. He woke up hours before daylight and he put on his clothes. He was sitting on the edge of the bed when his mother opened the door to his room at 5:30. Before she could say a word, Jeb jumped up and said, *"Mom, it's going to be a great day!"* What was true for Jeb is also true for you. You can change your attitude. You may not be able to change other things about yourself, but you can sure make your attitude more positive. If you try, you will soon discover that the best helping hand is at the end of your own arm.

Happiness is Something You Decide On Ahead of Time

She is 92 years old, petite, well poised and proud. She is fully dressed each morning by eight o'clock, with her hair fashionably coifed and her makeup perfectly applied, in spite of the fact she is almost blind. Today she has moved to a nursing home. Her husband of 60 years recently passed away, making this move necessary. After many hours of waiting patiently in the lobby of the nursing home, where I am employed, she smiled sweetly when told her room was ready. As she maneuvered her walker to the elevator, I provided a visual description of her tiny room, including the eyelet curtains that had been hung on her window. *"I love it,"* she stated with the enthusiasm of an eight-year old having just been presented with a new puppy. *"Mrs. Jones, you haven't seen the room...just wait,"* I said. Then she spoke these words that I will never forget: *"That does not have anything to do with it,"* she gently replied. *"Happiness is something you decide on ahead of time. Whether I like the room or not, does not depend on how the furniture is arranged. It is how I arrange my mind. I have already decided to love it. It is a decision I make every morning when I wake up. I have a choice. I can spend the day in bed recounting the difficulty I have with the parts of my body that no longer work, or I can get out of bed and be thankful for the ones that do work. Each day is a gift, and as long as my eyes open, I will focus on the new day and all of the happy memories I have stored away...just for this time in my life."*

happiness is something you decide on ahead of time

Isn't it About Time?

To forgive your parents for not
raising you as you wish they had?
To forgive yourself for poor choices
you and you alone have made?
To quit blaming others,
the government, the
weather and anyone else
for your lot in life?
To call your parents and start a new and
healthier relationship with them?
To drop the grudges you have held onto?
To bless and release those who have
mistreated you or hurt you?
To quit a job where you
are being abused?
To quit a relationship were
you are being abused?
To provide for your family, even if that
means getting a job you don't really want?
To read more and be a serious
student of that which you wish to do?
To get off drugs?
To get to the gym?
To say you are sorry?
To let go a toxic relationship?
To take an interest in others?
To ask her to marry you?
To have a baby?
To quit chasing someone you are in love
with who is not in love with you?

To realize if a relationship is over,
it's over?
To move on?
To quit lying to everyone
including yourself?
To recharge your batteries?
To clean out your closet?
To unclutter your desk?
To smile more?
To shower the people
you love with love?
To book a vacation?
To make more of an effort to
be the best you can be?
To make a difference?
To get more rest?
To drink more water?
To give others business who
give business to you?
To not keep reacting?
To be proactive?
To quit being so angry?
To get rid of clutter?
To be more polite?
To use your manners?
To be proud to be free?
To dance more?
To love more?
To quit expecting your parents
to pay for your way in life?

chapter 8

Chapter Eight

What Kind of Messages Do You Hear in Your Head?

Negative or positive? Instead of having more information but no real faith, no drive, no will, no persistence, no determination... and no achievement and more negative self talk, now you can have positive thoughts with almost no effort.

The Most Important Things...

and YOU can control them...**Anxiety and fear** self-talk strips away courage and makes great performances impossible. **Doubt self-talk** makes even the best decisions feel difficult and causes procrastination, **Anger self-talk** rips your focus away from your goals. **Frustration self-talk** can only serve to make you quit. **Guilt self-talk** makes it impossible to enjoy any successes you achieve. **Jealousy and envy self-talk** create dishonesty, hate and corruption. Your thoughts and emotions are the only things that can truly stop you.

Affirm to yourself every day that you are going to burn into your subconscious what others are saying that positively impacts their lives. Don't say it won't work for you. It will.

Say "I will do it..." not "I will try."

Today is the first day of the rest of your life.

Say to yourself right now: *I have more energy; I can handle the ups and downs of work with greater ease. My posture is improving and I am in a better frame of mind. Mental fatigue has diminished, as well and I can sleep 7-8 hours a night easily. I sleep better and get to sleep faster. I know that what I am doing makes a difference. If I choose to, I can help tens of thousands of people all over the world to feel in ways they never have and do things they've never done. I can do more than I have ever done.*

Every morning before my feet hit the floor I say to myself...*Good Morning Champion! Prosperity, abundance and better health are coming my way.* I was six figures in debt when I changed my self-talk. I made a fortune and then another fortune and then another fortune after I turned my self-talk around. Isn't it about time you try it too?

Make an *I Can* List

I can hit my ideal weight and stay there forever without feeling miserable. *I can* exercise like a maniac and LOVE it. *I can* be free of depression no matter how severe or how long I've suffered. *I can* explode my personal sales and fall in love with prospecting. *I can* get rid of my panic attacks and stop obsessive behaviors. *I can* live every single day with passion and purpose no matter what my age. *I can* have more money than I could ever need. *I can* quit bad habits for good - and not miss them one little bit. *I can* become a goal achieving machine. *I can* feel great about who you I am.

Here comes prosperity and abundance!

Don't spend time thinking negative thoughts and talking about negative things in life. Move forward.

Moment-By-Moment Thoughts

The only things that can help you to do, be and have anything you want in life are also your thoughts and emotions. Change your moment-by-moment thoughts to be like those who easily do what you want to do. You might have thought that there is no way to permanently change the voice inside your head, to change how you think, to let go of your past, to release unsupportive emotions. No *how-to* book will insert the motivation to get up after you keep beating yourself up. No lecture or seminar can implant unstoppable determination to do whatever it takes to succeed. No punishment you could endure would guarantee that you'll stop doing what you've done most of your life. No exercise equipment can force you to take the time to use it. Until now, there has been no way to predictably eliminate the mental patterns that make fear jump up and stop you and install all the qualities it takes to make a dream life.

Stop the Negative Self-Talk Now

You have to, you must, right now, stop the negative self-talk. Quit talking about all the things your parents went through to be together and to have you. Quit telling anyone who will listen all of your hurdles you have had to overcome. Quit complaining. Instead, from today on, do not let another negative word out of your mouth. What you say to others, your brain believes you like and it will bring you more negativity. Only talk about the positive and positive outcomes of what you are going through and have gone through. The reality is...no one cares about your sad times for long. Don't think you are the only one who has gone through tough or sad times. You are not. The human experience is filled with ups and downs.

IT DOESN'T HELP TO FEEL BAD ABOUT A MISTAKE YOU HAVE MADE. IT ONLY HELPS TO LOOK AT IT AS A VALUABLE LEARNING EXPERIENCE.

Champion Self-Talk

By studying self-talk of people who not only achieve consistently at high levels but who enjoy high constant personal self-esteem, you find that they consistently focus on the positive. You will lose a great deal of energy and time by constantly feeling guilty.

Positive self-talk is a proven way to improve your time. It's powerful. It's helped people who have suffered from constant panic attacks and chronic depression for decades to achieve remarkable, amazing things. Quit beating yourself up repeatedly over mistakes and enjoy your life more and more as you go on. Let the things that have bound you in the past depart from your thinking. Make conscious decisions, but don't have them become the focus of your entire life.

Your brain is constantly recording things. Your brain will give you more of what you think about and what you spend time thinking about. From today on, listen to all the negative things others say and be the one to only let positive words over your lips.

Walk away from those who are constantly tired, exhausted, making excuses, unhappy, filled with guilt and morose, sarcastic and downtrodden. Hang out with those who view life in a positive way.

Do you want to be supremely confident? Optimistic? Motivated? Enthusiastic? Appreciative? Determined? Happy? Do you want the will and drive to do what you know you should do? Positive words will change you...you will feel empowered. Your choices will be right a lot more often. Your actions will take you toward greater and greater accomplishments and your time will be filled with happiness.

NO MORE NEGATIVE SELF-TALK

"I'm no good and I don't know why I put myself through this torture so everybody else can see what I already know." Do you think that's the self-talk of millionaires? If not, then what is their self-talk? I believe as Babe Ruth steps to the plate with considerable eagerness to face the pitcher, they think to themselves, *"Okay, you got me the last time, but I've got your number this time. I've been thinking it through, watching you and I happen to know I'm one of the best athletes in the world. I've hit that ball under every circumstance known to man. I've gotten hits off tall pitchers and short pitchers, winning pitchers and losing pitchers. I've hit in close games and runaway games and this time . . I'm coming after you. This is my turn! I am the greatest".*

Regardless of what happened to you the last time you stepped up to the plate, this time it's a brand new day and at this very moment you are preparing to make it a winning one.

Your Internal Self Dialogue

Of all the time you spend communicating, none is more important than how you talk to yourself. Your internal dialogue has more to do with your success in life than any other factor. Every minute you are awake, you engage in 800 to 1,200 words of self-dialogue. In these conversations, you solve challenges or create them, make decisions or avoid them, judge, praise, disparage or motivate yourself. You can spend time dwelling on past mistakes or plan future achievements. Obviously, the more time you spend with positive self-talk, the stronger and better prepared you become to face your daily challenges.

> Life is as fleeting as a rainbow. A flash of lightning. A star at dawn. Knowing this, how can you continue to be negative?

GIGO

GIGO means *garbage in, garbage out*. Your mind works the same way. What you talk to yourself about directly affects how you live your life. Saying the right words to yourself will create a positive mental picture in your mind. That picture will encourage and motivate you to take the right actions that will lead to your personal success.

Life is a Do-it-To-Yourself Job

Five years from now, you'll be the same person you are today, except for the people you meet, the situations you've encountered, the books you have read and the thoughts you've thought. Keep your internal dialogue positive, upbeat and future-oriented.

> PAY CLOSE ATTENTION TO YOUR PERSONAL SELF-TALK

> Go the extra smile!

> A grimace or a grin, how will your day begin?

> Here we grow! Or is it here we glow?

Those Encouraging Words

Whenever you catch yourself spending your time engaging in negative self-talk, try the following:

1. **Choose one thing for which you are grateful and talk to yourself about it.** This blocks out your negative self-talk. The mind cannot hold two conflicting images at the same time. Gratitude is one of the most powerful emotions you possess to have the rich fulfilling life you deserve.

2. **Choose something you like about yourself.** Describe it. Are you smart? Are you kind? Are you creative? How does this enhance the things you do? How does it advance and enrich others? What is its impact on your family, work or community?

3. **What future event are you most looking forward to?** Describe it to yourself in vivid detail. Elaborate, expand and expound. Add technicolor and stereo. Allow yourself to daydream. All your accomplishments are first a thought, a dream or goal pulling you toward it.

5. **Keep an inspirational book or CD nearby to reinforce your positive self-talk.** Use them whenever you are feeling negative. When you are moving around, listen to a positive CD. When you are settled in one place, read positive words.

Oh give me a home . . .
where seldom is heard
a discouraging word

Give yourself a huge
lifetime happy goal

The Comfort Zone

I used to have a comfort zone where I knew
I couldn't fail, the same four walls of busy
work were really more like a jail.
I longed so much to do the things
I'd never done before, but I stayed inside
my comfort zone and paced the same old floor.
I said it didn't matter that I wasn't doing much,
I said I didn't care for things like diamonds or
furs and such. I claimed to be so busy with the
things inside my zone, but deep inside I longed
for something special of my own. I couldn't let
my life go by just watching others win, I held my
breath and stepped outside to let the change begin.
I took a step and with new strength I'd never
felt before, I kissed my comfort zone good-bye
and closed and locked the door.
If you are in a comfort zone afraid to venture
out, remember that all winners were at one
time filled with doubt. A step or two and words
of praise can make your dreams come true.
Greet your future with a smile.

SUCCESS IS THERE FOR YOU!

Identify Why You Don't Want to Get Out of Your Comfort Zone

If you are bummed out, unhappy, unwilling to take a risk and are afraid of failure or fear of embarrassment then maybe you need a checkup from the neck up and you need to get a spine. Get a backbone instead of a wishbone. Quit being a wimp in life. Quit holding back. Stop all that nonsense about being shy and that you don't want to be pushy. It's your life. What are you going to do with it?

*Isn't it about time you focus
and make something of yourself?*

Take Time Out to Find Your Personal Identity

One of the things a person holds most important is her/his *identity*. Take the time to figure out what you want your identity to be. Keep working on this until you find it.

TAKING TIME OUT

No one can make you feel inferior without your consent. No amount of water can sink a boat unless it gets on the inside of it. Just when things are at rock bottom, hold on because that is when the tide will turn.

"It is not the critic who counts; not the man who points out how the strong man stumbles or where the doer of deeds could have done better. The credit belongs to the man who is actually in the arena, whose face is marred by dust and sweat and blood, who strives valiantly, who errs and comes up short again and again, because there is no effort without error or shortcoming, but who knows the great enthusiasms, the great devotions, who spends himself a worthy cause; who, at the best, knows, in the end, the triumph of high achievement and who, at the worst, if he fails, at least he fails while daring greatly, so that his place shall never be with those cold and timid souls who knew neither victory nor defeat."
-Theodore Roosevelt

Shake off criticism... it is part of the growth that you must go to step out of mediocrity

Take a lesson from the weather. It pays no attention to criticism.

WHAT IS THE WORST THAT COULD HAPPEN?

Don't let the fear of success paralyze you with analyses paralyses.

Attach fear to not spending your life time achieving your goals and dreams.

Why not you succeed? And why not now?

WHEN IT IS NOW OR NEVER, FOCUS ON NOW.

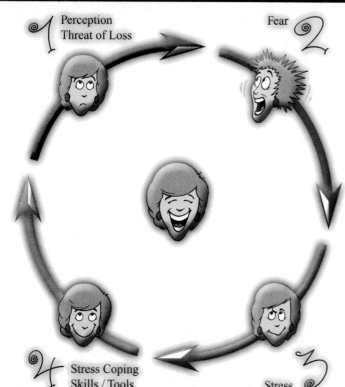

1 Perception Threat of Loss

2 Fear

3 Stress

4 Stress Coping Skills / Tools

"Your time is limited, so don't waste it living someone else's life. Don't be trapped by dogma - which is living with the results of other people's thinking. Don't let the noise of other's opinions drown out your own inner voice. And most important, have the courage to follow your heart and intuition. They somehow already know what you truly want to become. Everything else is secondary."
-Steve Jobs

Put Your Fear on a Flame

There can be no vision when we are scared and fearful. So many people continue to brood about the future and what it holds for us. Try to think of a time when there were no challenges. Wouldn't it be exciting if we could all spend at least an equal amount of thinking on the positive side of our challenges? Put your fear on a flame.

The Fear Of Success Cycle

1. Talk about your fears with someone who will listen and be neutral. Get it out, all of the facts and all of your feelings.
2. Imagine trying to overcome the fear and falling short of the goal; then figure what the worst consequences would be and what could be done about them. So if the worst does happen, you are at least prepared and if it doesn't then you are relieved and probably will be pleasantly surprised.
3. Fear of loss brings about stress. Give yourself extra chances. An illustration of this might be the team whose slogan is, *Wait till next year.* Eventually their continued effort will pay off.
4. Be ready when stress comes to realize that it's okay to take a step back and determine all the possible solutions. Don't take everything that happens to you so seriously.
5. Most important of all, take a risk, take the chance and face it. There is nothing better to reduce the fear of failure than having it happen and knowing what it can and can't do. Face it, live through it and prove to yourself that you can survive it.

"Our deepest fear is not that we are inadequate. Our deepest fear is that we are powerful beyond measure. It is our light, not our darkness that most frightens us. We ask ourselves, Who am I to be brilliant, gorgeous, talented, fabulous? Actually, who are you not to be? You are a child of God. Your playing small does not serve the world. There is nothing enlightened about shrinking so that other people won't feel insecure around you. We are all meant to shine, as children do. We were born to make manifest the glory of God that is within us. It's not just in some of us; it's in everyone. And as we let our own light shine, we unconsciously give other people permission to do the same. As we are liberated from our own fear, our presence automatically liberates others."
-from A Return to Love, by Marianne Williamson

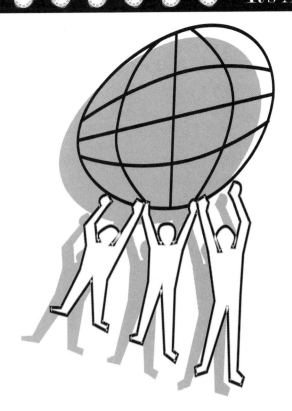

You don't have to spend your life holding the world up to save it. We are all in this together.

Harm no other beings, they are your brothers and sisters.

After all, isn't it about time?

You hold the magical key to all that you want in the universe and it is this you alone make all the choices in your life and in making these choices you determine what you become.

Have A Seat Upon A Cloud

"Have a seat upon a cloud
and make yourself at home
You are now inside my dreams,
inside a book, inside a poem.
Where anything can happen
if you only make it real.
Plunge into my waters
if you're not afraid to feel.
Take off your shoes
and close your eyes,
relax upon my sand.
Join me in my land of dreams,
reach out and take my hand.
Let me share my dreams with you
until you find your own.
I'll take you there if you believe,
take mine out on loan.
Where birds are words so gracefully
they glide across the sky.
Leave behind your worries,
here the rules do not apply.
Pick my flowers if you like
and plant a seed or two.
Paint the sky in polka dots
if you do not like it blue.
Climb my trees, face your fears;
erase them one by one.
See the world from up above
and don't stop at the sun.
When the world starts raining down
and the sun is out of sight
Let your dreams control your mind
and help you through the night.
There's a place inside my dreams
for all who care to roam
So have a seat upon a cloud
and make yourself at home."
-Danielle Rosenblatt

Don't stay too busy with trivia and be so afraid that you might fail

The trouble is that you think you have time.

In the beginner's mind there are many possibilities, in the expert's mind there are few.

Word Travels Fast So Handle Complaints Quickly

Normally one takes customer complaints in stride, but if you receive a complaint that you think fairly ridiculous and tell the customer so you are in for a great deal of discomfort. Instead of telling one or two people that they thought you were a jerk, they post it online and blog negatively about you and your business. How can you avoid this in the future without always rolling over? Answer: The fact is, for all of us, in this era of increased transparency and viral networking, the stakes have been raised. Today, there are personal websites, the so-called blogosphere, chat boards, instant polls, insta-feedback and ideas travel seemingly at the speed of light. This is especially true when it comes to complaints about you or your business. Acting like an analogue player in this digital world is a mistake that can kill your business. In the PI era (pre-Internet), reputations and brands were created far more slowly and unless yours was a national business or product that got national coverage, it was far more difficult to change people's impressions of you one way or the other. Today if you blow it, it's not a handful of people who will hear about it, but one or two hundred, or thousand, or...yep, the stakes have been raised.

FULL TIME

- Full time faith in what you are doing.
- Full time faith in others.
- Full time faith that everything will be okay.
- Full time faith that there is a higher power in charge.
- Full time faith that you are going to get well.
- Full time faith that you will pull through that operation and recover.
- Full time faith that you will stay married.
- Full time faith that you will find the love of your life.
- Full time faith that the sun will come up in the East and set in the West.
- Full time faith that the moon will rise every night.
- Full time faith that the lakes and rivers and oceans will be filled with water.
- Full time faith that the waves will keep crashing up onto the beaches of the world.
- Full time faith that you are a good person no matter what happened 5 minutes ago.
- Full time faith that you can heal from your hurts.
- Full time faith that the planet is going to keep on spinning.
- Full time faith that the sunshine will replace the rain.

chapter 9

Chapter Nine

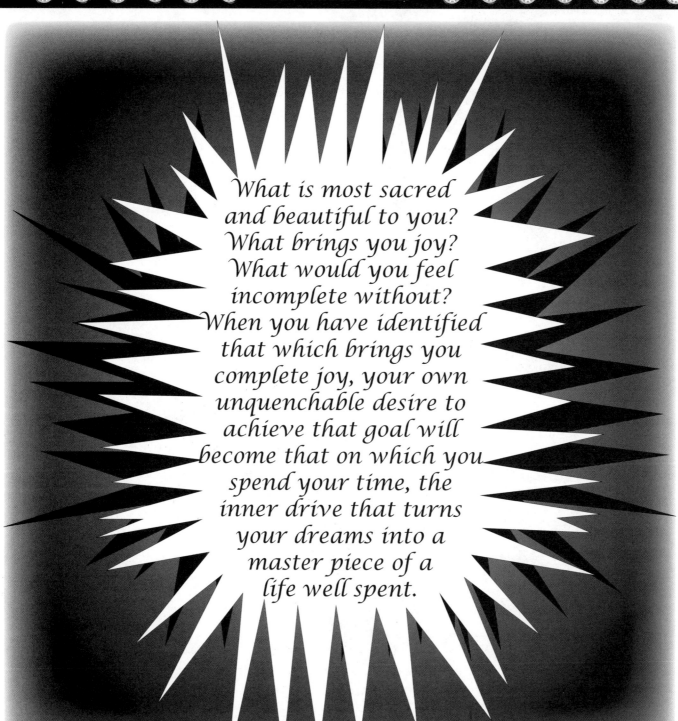

What is most sacred and beautiful to you? What brings you joy? What would you feel incomplete without? When you have identified that which brings you complete joy, your own unquenchable desire to achieve that goal will become that on which you spend your time, the inner drive that turns your dreams into a master piece of a life well spent.

A HEART STRETCHED BY A SINGLE SMILE NEVER GOES BACK TO ITS ORIGINAL DIMENSIONS.

I, _____
(your name)

Do solemnly swear from today forward to grease my laughter gears every single day and to wear a smile on my face for no reason at all. I promise to laugh often. I promise to laugh no less than fifteen times per day. I belive that frequent belly laughter cures stiffness, tightness and hardening of the attitudes. And that laughter often leads to AHA! In the power invested in me at birth I do now vow to from now on to brighten the day of everyone I meet and to enjoy the rest of my time on earth.

Laughter is healthy. Drink deep of living. Deeper yet of mirth, for there is nothing better than laughter anywhere on earth!

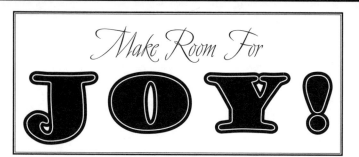

Make Room For

JOY!

When you take time to play you will increase your adrenal glands capacity to keep you going, you will rest and sleep better, you will smile more, you will have more energy, enthusiasm, zest, motivation, merriment, happiness and positive momentum.

It's so important to take time to play.

A child is not a vessel to be filled but a lamp to be lighted.

Take Time Out For Play!

There is nothing quite like a view from the top.

Do not let the years, chances and opportunities for creating joy in life slip away. Begin today to gather a wealth of experience and memories that will endure in the hearts of others long after you are gone.

Today, welcome a new baby into the world. Stop parents with newborns and ooo and ahhh over their newborn. An average of 202,176 babies are born a day worldwide. That's one new life on the planet every 25 seconds. Welcome them with a smile.

If you are not hearing from your children, you might want to consider the time you gave to them reaching THEIR goals. It's not too late to do something about it. Many times parents show their children love through financially taking care of them but what they really want is your time, being interested in them, their opinions, their hopes, dreams, desires and insecurities. Spend quality time with your children...it is the best investment you can ever make.

*"I have the simplest tastes.
I am always satisfied with the best."*
-Oscar Wilde

Worry and Then Pass the Torch

Is there a magic cut-off period when offspring become accountable for their own actions? Is there a wonderful moment when parents can become detached spectators in the lives of their children and shrug, *It's their life* and feel nothing? When I was in my twenties, I stood in a hospital corridor waiting for doctors to put a few stitches in my son's head. I asked, *When do you stop worrying?* The nurse said. *When they get out of the accident stage.* My mother just smiled faintly and said nothing. When I was in my thirties, I sat on a little chair in a classroom and heard how one of my children talked incessantly, disrupted the class and was headed for a career making license plates. As if to read my mind, a teacher said, *Don't worry, they all go through this stage and then you can sit back, relax and enjoy them.* My mother just smiled faintly and said nothing. When I was in my forties, I spent a lifetime waiting for the phone to ring, the cars to come home, the front door to open. A friend said, *They're trying to find themselves. Don't worry, in a few years, you can stop worrying. They'll be adults.* My mother just smiled faintly and said nothing. By the time I was 50, I was sick and tired of being vulnerable. I was still worrying over my children, but there was a new wrinkle, there was nothing I could do about it. My mother just smiled faintly and said nothing. I continued to anguish over their failures, be tormented by their frustrations and absorbed in their disappointments. My friends said that when my kids got married I could stop worrying and lead my own life. I wanted to believe that, but I was haunted by my mother's warm smile and her occasional, *You look pale. Are you all right? Call me the minute you get home. Are you depressed about something?* Can it be that parents are sentenced to a lifetime of worry? Is concern for one another handed down like a torch to blaze the trail of human frailties and the fears of the unknown? Is concern a curse or is it a virtue that elevates us to the highest form of life? One of my children became quite irritable recently, saying to me,

Where were you? I've been calling for 3 days and no one answered. I was worried. I smiled a warm smile. The torch has been passed.

-This *"Worry"* saying was given to Jan Ruhe when her mother, Lois Kelley, was in her 80's.

PEOPLE WHO REALLY ENJOY THEIR WORK OFTEN HAVE SO MUCH FUN AT THEIR WORK THAT THEY FORGET TO TAKE TIME TO PLAY.

Lesson 1:

When a person stays joy-starved for very long, the right-brain that needs time to play will start interfering with the left-brain work effort by pouring energy and imagination into rationalizing, procrastinating and other behaviors that drain energy from left-brain goals.

Lesson 2:

When you are joy-starved you can expect your Self-Management to be at its worst.

A study at Stanford University found that *"Twenty seconds of guffawing gives the heart the same workout as three minutes of hard rowing"*. Who needs oaring when you could be roaring...with laughter? So next your doctor prescribes some pills, think of the directions for your prescription of laughter read: *Must be taken sitting down, standing up, laying down, or while rowing Cost: $0.00. If nausea results, you are laughing so hard and burning so many calories that you may want to take with food. Refills: unlimited.* Even when you fake a smile or laugh, you get the same physiological benefits as when it's the real thing, because your mind is smart, but your body is stupid and can't tell the difference! Whether you're a parent that stays at home with the kids, or an office manager wanting to stay home (with or without the kids), we could all use a little Vitamin Hee Hee! First installment...

He Who Laughs...Lasts

Make a List of What Brings you Joy

* Reading a magazine article *
* Phoning a special friend *
* Looking through old photo albums *
* Taking a walk *
* Jumping rope *
* Skating *
* Dancing *
* Bicycling *
* Meditating *
* Watering flowers *
* Browsing through a catalog *
* Drinking wine *
* Planning a party *
* Working Sudoku *
* Going Barefoot *
* Telling a Joke *
* Recalling happy times *
* Reading poems *
* Cross country skiing *
* Having a massage *
* Planning a vacation *
* Sending sugar grams by email *

* Lighting candles *
* Playing soft music *
* Organizing my office *
* Watching the snow fall *
* Clipping flowers for vases in my home *
* Wandering the world *
* Watching the History Channel *
* Reading a powerful book *
* Spending time in my garden *
* Taking a walk with music *
* Solving a challenge *
* Laughter *
* Playing computer games *
* Playing a round of golf *
* Walking on the beach *
* Hiking *
* Watching the sunset *
* Walking on the beach *
* Spending time with our children *
* Experiencing new cultures *
* Getting emails from friends *

Plan your fun as carefully as you plan your work.

Make files of what brings you joy

Joy I can claim in	Joy I can claim in	Joy I can claim in	Joy I can claim in	Label the last section
2-5 MINUTES	5-30 MINUTES	30 MINUTES 1/2 DAY	1/2 DAY OR LONGER	DREAMS

TAKE TIME FOR FUN!

Tongue Twisters

- Double bubble gum bubbles double.
- You know New York. You need New York. You know you need unique New York.
- Sixty-six sick chicks.
- Strange strategic statistic.
- Tie twine to three tree twigs.
- Preshrunk shirts.
- Shy Sarah saw six Swiss wristwatches.
- The sixth sheikh's sixth sheep's sick.
- Truly rural.
- The seething sea ceaseth and thus seething sea sufficeth us.
- A bloke's back brake block broke.
- Does the ship stock short socks with spots?
- Three gray geese in the green grass grazing.
- Gray were the geese and green was the grazing.
- Sinful Caesar sipped his snifter, seized his knees and sneezed.

DON'T GLOWER, THERE'S POWER IN A LAUGH, IT'S AN INNER UPPER, IT'S MORE FILLING THAN A SEVEN COURSE SUPPER, SO STRETCH THOSE FOURTEEN MUSCLES AND SMILE. IF YOU DO, I'M WITH YOU, CAUSE YOU'VE GOT STYLE!

"To laugh often and much; to win the respect of intelligent people and the affection of children; to earn the appreciation of honest critics and endure the betrayal of false friends; to appreciate beauty; to find the best in others; to leave the world a bit better; whether by a healthy child, a garden patch or a redeemed social condition; to know even one life has breathed easier because you have lived. This is to have succeeded."

-Ralph Waldo Emerson

Start a Mirth-Quake

Start out in silence with a smile, just the hint of a grin, not too much now. This will crack the mental ice. Now, without making a sound, turn to someone and smile. Go ahead. I dare you to smile at someone without a peep! Good. Next, silently move as if you are laughing. That's right. *Aren't you starting to feel happier already?* Next, move into the state of silent hilariousness. Act as if you are caught in a fit of laughter. Exaggerate your body movements; tilt your head back, slap your knee, go on and do it. That's it. Now the laughter is starting to shake loose. Finally, add sound to your motions and let out a long, loud, luxurious laugh. Fake it until you make it. Go ahead, let it out. *Don't you feel a lot happier now?* A variation of this is to have two people face each other. Have one person laugh silently while the other watches stone faced. This will always bring laughter and seems to remind us of the times we couldn't stop laughing despite our good intentions to stay quiet.

AND THEY LAUGHED HAPPILY EVER AFTER.

It's your laughitude, not your aptitude that determines your attitude.

With laughter, you can face the unfaceable and erase the unerasable.

"There is only one thing that makes a dream impossible to achieve: the fear of failure. Life is really generous to those who pursue their destiny."
-The Alchemist

TGIF Thank God it's Friday...
your time is important but give your
employer a full work day. Work like no
one is watching...get your work done...

The world does not need more
sceptics! If you are a know-it-all...
STOP and learn something new!
It will be so refreshing to be around
you instead of listening to your
old opinions all of the time!

What is the worst thing that could happen
if something doesn't get done right on
time? If you have a something due in the
future, get to work on it as soon as you
can so that you are not completing
the project at the last minute.

Make what you do RIGHT
not just RIGHT on time.

It's about time to
quit being so upset.
Before flying off the
handle, zip your lip.

So many people have siblings or parents who are peak performers and high achievers. It's hard not to feel like you have to fill another's shoes, to achieve what they have achieved or to even do better. *Isn't it about time that you realize that you don't have to do that?* You can be whoever you need to be and want to be. Don't compare yourself to what someone else has achieved. Be the best YOU can be. If you are not succeeding, all that is, is a message that you need to go a new direction in life and try something different.

Take Time to Breathe

Inhale and hold your breath and count to ten. Exhale and count to ten. Do this frequently all day and during the night. When you are out of breath or having trouble catching your breath, your body believes you are in the fight or flight mode. When frozen with fear or worry breathing becomes shallow. Alleviate your anxiety by constantly altering the depth and rhythm of your breathing. Try putting one hand on your chest and the other on your abdomen. Now quietly create a wave between your chest and your abdomen and deepen your breathing.

Let Sighs Out

Go on and sigh. It's good for you and will reduce stress. An audible exhalation releases tension.

And the daily grind begins again. You say you are going to do something different with your life but yet you don't. Twenty, thirty years go by and you are still where you were long ago. *Why not take the time to improve your skills? Did you know that if you work on learning a new skill just 30 minutes each day that you can learn a new language?* You can learn to play a musical instrument, you can learn about so many subjects. *Isn't it about time you quit the daily grind and take time to live?*

nOThing VenTured,
nOThing gAined
nO pAin, nO gAin

> *"Hope is a thing with feathers that perches in the soul and sings a tune without words and never stops at all, and sweetest, in the gale, is heard; and sore must be the storm that could abash the little bird that keeps so many warm. I've heard it in the chilliest land, and on the strangest sea; Yet, never in extremity, it ask a crumb of me."*
> -Emily Dickinson

Are you always looking like you are so deep in thought about all the details you MUST get accomplished by the end of the day? Is that really living? Always worried about how you are going to pay the bills? Your customers, friends and family see this even if you don't and it shouts that you are sure serious about your business but that you are NO FUN.

Isn't it about time to STOP! Take your hard working employees out to lunch. Don't always be so serious about EVERYTHING. Take a break and take an some time during the day to entertain your staff. They will work much happier and harder for you.

Today make sure that your parents know you love them. It may seem impossible to say, but don't wait until it is too late. Pick up the phone now and call your parents and if you are blessed enough, call your Grandparents. Make time for them. It's important.

Things that matter most must never be at the mercy of things that matter least.

How well do you treat your employees, your staff, your workers? Do you know that most people do not feel appreciated enough? The people working for you are helping you build your dream. You most likely don't know how hard it is for them to navigate through their lives to get to work on time, to stay focused and to help keep the work going. How much would it cost you in money and time to set up an Employee of the Month certificate and take the time every month to give someone well deserved recognition? Instead of your business being all about you, why not take the focus off of you just once a month to make someone's time working for you mean so much more?

MAKE DEADLINES A THING OF THE PAST. INSTEAD MAKE LIFELINES MORE IMPORTANT.

It s about time to calm it down a notch. Are you the one in your circle of influence who is always looking for papers or racing around looking unorganized? Why? Isn t it about time to stay a bit later in your office to get your work under control?

IF YOU ARE SINGLE, ITS TIME TO MINGLE! EVERYONE KNOWS SOMEONE TO INTRODUCE YOU TO. GET OUT AND ABOUT...ITS ABOUT TIME!

LOOK TOWARD TOMORROW

One thing which gives radiance to everything is the hope of something better around the corner

there is never a crowd spending time on the extra mile

LOOK AT LIFE THROUGH THE WINDSHIELD, NOT THE REARVIEW MIRROR.

Advance confidently in the direction of your dreams and endeavor to spend your time like you have imagined.

In times of change, there is no incentive so great as hope for a better tomorrow.

We cannot change yesterday. We can only make the most of today and look with hope toward our time tomorrow.

Some people dream of success, while others wake up and spend their lifetime working hard at it.

MAKE IT A POINT TO DO SOMETHING EVERY DAY WITH YOUR TIME THAT YOU FIND CHALLENGING AND APPLY YOURSELF TO BE THE BEST.

"I will persist until I succeed."
-Og Mandino

If you are fired, so what? What is the worst that can happen? Press on to find something else to do to earn enough money to live on. Do not worry if you are fired, don't blame anyone, time is ticking by...get on with finding a new job.

Don't die luxuriating. Don't die hibernating. Don't die procrastinating, don't die vegetating. Instead die climbing. Don't quit when you've had your hit. When you stop dreaming you start dying. Keep climbing... there are fountains on mountains.

Don't permit anyone to make you feel small. Stand up for what you believe is right. It is time to quit being intimidated.

Don't get frustrated, get fascinated.

ACHIEVEMENT LIES IN THE HONEST ENDEAVOR TO SPEND YOUR TIME DOING YOUR BEST UNDER ALL CIRCUMSTANCES.

If you are mistreated in life you have choices. You do not have to put up with someone's abuse. Go where you are valued. Quit complaining about your day and start getting FROM the day. It's about time.

chapter 10

Chapter Ten

Today's Dreams Are Tomorrow's Successes

*"Don't be afraid of high hopes
or plans that seem to be out of reach.
Life is meant to be experienced,
and every situation allows for
learning and growth.*

*Motivation is a positive starting point
and action places you on a forward path.
A dream is a blueprint
of a goal not yet achieved;
the only difference between the two
is the effort involved in attaining
what you hope to accomplish.*

*Let your mind and heart urge you on;
allow the power of your will
to lead you to your destination.*

*Don't count the steps ahead;
just add up the total
of steps already covered,
and multiply it by faith,
confidence and endurance.*

*Always remember that
for those who persist,
today's dreams are transformed
into tomorrow's successes."*
-Unknown

The Climb

*"The small boy heard the mountain speak.
There are secrets on my highest peak.
But beware, my boy, the passing of time
Wait not too long to start the climb.
So quickly come and go the years
And young man stands below with fears
Come on, come on, the mountain cussed
Time presses on: on climb, you must.
Now he is busied in middle-age prime
And maybe tomorrow he'll take the climb
Now is too soon; it's raining today
Gone, all gone, years are eaten away.
An old man looks up, still feeling the lure
Yet he'll suffer the pain, not climb for the cure
The hair is white; the step is slow
And it's safer and warmer to stay here below.
So all too soon the secrets are buried
Along with him and regrets he carried
And it's not for loss of secrets he'd cried
But rather because he'd never tried."*
-Phyllis Trussler

*"If I feel depressed, I will sing.
If I feel sad, I will laugh.
If I feel ill, I will double my labor.
If I feel fear, 1 will plunge ahead.
If I feel poverty,
I will think of wealth to come.
If I feel incompetent,
I will remember past success.
If I feel insignificant,
I will remember my goals.
Today I will be the master of my emotions."*
-Og Mandino

Make better decisions.
Make conscious decisions.
Make incredible moments.

Make life your message not your words.

Make this year the year or your dreams.

Make the rest of your life an incredible masterpiece.

My 10 Wonderful Dreams

What are the 10 outrageous dreams for your future? They can be way out. Put this list in a file and forget about it. You will be surprised, within the next 10 years, many of them will come true. Put no limits on the possibilities. Neither age, nor sex, nor money, nor anything else can be a limiting factor. Come on... dream big! Here are some examples:

- Find the person who I want to marry.
- Buy a new home.
- Take a wonderful vacation.

1.

2.

3.

4.

5.

6.

7.

8.

9.

10

"It is a psychological law that whatever we wish to accomplish we must impress on the subjective or subconscious mind."
-Orison Swett Marden

2 Simple Steps For Achieving Your Dreams

Here are two simple steps to achieve any dream that you desire.

1. **SET GOALS YOU INTEND TO ACHIEVE:**

- You have to want something with all of your heart, sacrifice for, get up early, stay up late, focus, feed your mind, search the world for answers, invest in yourself and seek out mentors to help you.
- Be willing to do what others won't do. Help build your company to be a great company.
- Writing down your goals: Studies have shown that when you write down a goal the chances of achieving it are a thousand times greater.
- Become a reader and student of that which you wish to accomplish. Don't miss the books. Be a serious student. You can tell when someone is a student of personal growth. Just ask them what books they have read in the last six months.

2. **BE PERSISTENT:** It might take you 10 years to achieve your dream. Never waver in your goals or your ultimate dream.

> **Never tell a child his/her dreams are unlikely or outlandish. Few things are more humiliating and what a tragedy it would be if she/he believed it.**

Masterpieces take time.

An hour a day (Monday through Friday) is five hours per week is 260 hours per year. That is over six weeks of your work life. What are you doing with those precious hours?

How to Use Mind Mapping

Mind Mapping is an important technique that improves the way you take notes and supports and enhances your creative challenge solving. When you use Mind Maps, you can quickly identify and understand the structure of a subject and the way that pieces of information fit together, as well as recording the raw facts contained in normal notes. Mind Maps provide a structure which encourages creative challenge solving and they hold information in a format that your mind will find easy to remember and quick to review.

Mind Maps are also useful for:

Summarizing information; consolidating information from different research sources; thinking through complex challenges; and presenting information in a format that shows the overall structure of your subject. They are very quick to review as you can often refresh information in your mind just by glancing at one. Remembering the shape and structure of a Mind Map can give you the cues you need to remember the information within it. So, they engage much more of your brain in the process of assimilating and connecting facts visually.

What do you want to accomplish?

Be the merchant of your own dreams

Drawing Basic Mind Maps

To make notes on a subject using a Mind Map, draw it in the following way:

1. Write the title of the subject you're exploring in the center of the page and draw a circle around it.
2. As you come across major subdivisions or subheadings of the topic (or important facts that relate to the subject) draw lines out from this circle. Label these lines with these subdivisions or subheadings.
3. As you get into the subject and uncover another level of information (further subheadings, or individual facts) belonging to the subheadings above, draw these as lines linked to the subheading lines.
4. For individual facts or ideas, draw lines out from the appropriate heading line and label them.

As you come across new information, link it in to the Mind Map appropriately. A complete Mind Map may have main topic lines radiating in all directions from the center. Sub-topics and facts will branch off these, like branches and twigs from the trunk of a tree. You do not need to worry about the structure produced, as this will evolve of its own accord. Major headings radiate from the center, with lower level headings and facts branching off from the higher level headings.

Your Mind Maps are your own property: once you understand how to make notes in the Mind Map format, you can develop your own ideas to take them further. The following suggestions may help to increase their effectiveness:

- **Use single words or simple phrases for information:** Most words in normal writing are padding, as they ensure that facts are conveyed in the correct context and in a format that is pleasant to read. In your own Mind Maps, single strong words and meaningful phrases can convey the same meaning more potently. Excess words just clutter the Mind Map.
- **Print words:** Joined up or indistinct writing can be more difficult to read.
- **Use color to separate different ideas:** This will help you to separate ideas where necessary. It also helps you to visualize the Mind Map for recall. Color also helps to show the organization of the subject.
- **Use symbols and images:** Where a symbol or picture means something to you, use it. Pictures can help you to remember information more effectively than words.
- **Using cross-linkages:** Information in one part of the Mind Map may relate to another part. Here you can draw in lines to show the cross-linkages. This helps you to see how one part of the subject affects another.

Mind Mapping is an extremely effective method of taking notes. Mind Maps show not only facts, but also the overall structure of a subject and the relative importance of individual parts of it. They help you to associate ideas and make connections that you might not otherwise make.

I can confirm that you'll find mindmapping a great way of calming yourself down when you have many needs for your time, ideas buzzing round your head and objectives to meet. But it must fit your own personal style of thinking and you must set aside the time to do it!

If you have a lot going on and your time is scarce, try mind mapping, you will find it surprisingly effective!

Amateurs hope. Professionals work. Be a professional in a world of amateurs.

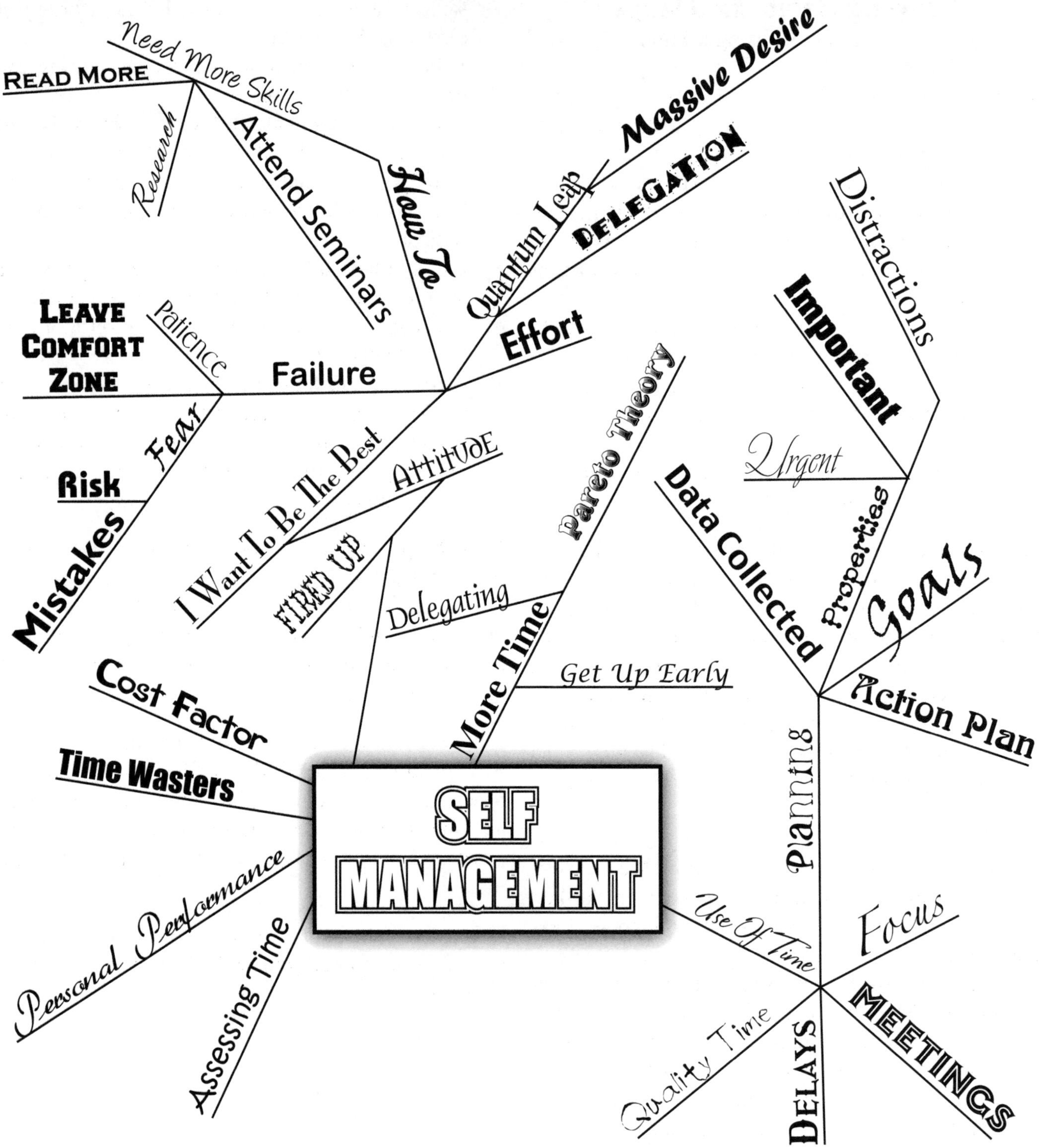

READ MORE

Need More Skills

Research

Attend Seminars

How To

Quantum Leap

Massive Desire

DELEGATION

Effort

Distractions

Important

LEAVE COMFORT ZONE

Patience

Failure

Fear

Urgent

Pareto Theory

Risk

Mistakes

I Want To Be The Best

Attitude

FIRED UP

Delegating

Properties

Goals

Data Collected

Action Plan

More Time

Get Up Early

Cost Factor

Time Wasters

Personal Performance

Assessing Time

SELF MANAGEMENT

Planning

Use Of Time

Focus

Quality Time

DELAYS

MEETINGS

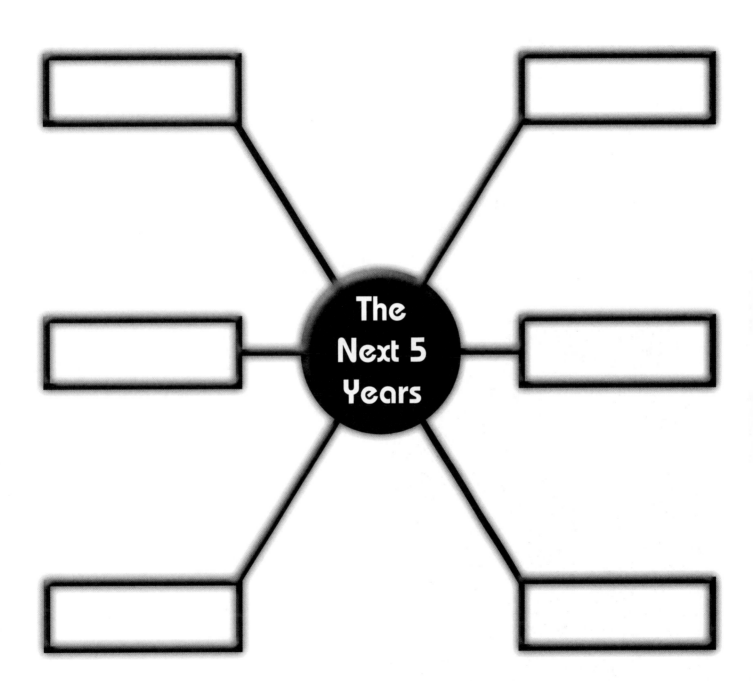

EVERY DAY IS A WEEKEND

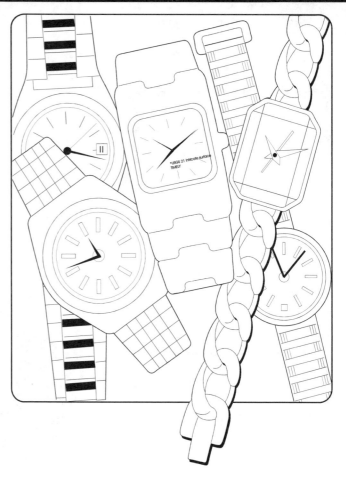

Isn't it about time to relax and take a break? All work and no play makes Suzi Creamcheese a dull woman!

S URELY
GOODNESS
AND
M ERCY
S HALL
F OLLOW
ME ALL THE
DAYS OF
MY
LIFE PSALM 23:8

"Time slips through our fingers" -Abba

"When I stand before God at the end of my life, I would hope that I would not have a single bit of talent left and could say, "I used everything you gave me." -Erma Bombeck

Stop running away from opportunities and possibilities. Run toward fulfillment, prosperity, abundance and success.

It's a Beautiful Life

"You can do what you want just seize the day
What you're doing tomorrow's
gonna come your way
Don't you ever consider giving up
Take a walk in the park when you feel down
There's so many things there that's gonna lift you up
See the nature in bloom, a laughing child
You're looking for somewhere to belong
You're standing all alone
For someone to guide you on your way
Now and forever
Such a dream, oh oh oh
It's a beautiful life, oh oh oh oh."
-Unknown

"A mother should hold her child close, so that he knows his world intimately. A father, meanwhile should take his child to the highest peak so that he knows how large the world can be."
-Mayan Proverb

Most people live their lives in quiet desperation.

If you knew how little people thought about you – you wouldn't worry about what they thought.
At 20 we worry constantly about what others think of us.
At 40 we are less concerned what others think of us.
At 60 we don't care what others think of us. At 80 we realize that they weren't thinking about us at all.

Going Too Fast Live Your Life Like the Wind

Speed up when necessary and know when to slow down. Slow down when life pushes so hard and fast, you cannot consume any more air. Slow down when you can't see where you're going or where you're coming from. Take time to stop and realize what you have right in front of you when you cannot find what you're looking for. When you cannot find what you want in someone else, look inside of yourself. Don't sweat the small things, and make the best of the big things. Cherish the experiences you've had, and use the lessons you've learned. Our lives are rubber bands, bending and stretching to fit even the most awkward situations. You can adapt to anything, regardless of its size or shape. You just have to realize and use what you have in your own hands.

Plan ahead...it wasn't raining when Noah built the ark.

Write a message to the future: Mark the envelope *DO NOT OPEN until November 13, 2020*. Begin the letter with today's date and send it To Whom It May Concern. Here are some topics: Predictions, your opinions today, your secret real goals and or something that happened in your life that you think might be of interest to those in 2020. When it arrives to you, put it in a safety deposit box at the bank. Don't open it until November 13, 2020. You will be so surprised to see how much you have changed in that time.

THERE IS NOTHING QUITE LIKE A VIEW FROM THE TOP.

Some Days Are Diamonds

"Now the face that I see in my mirror
More and more is a stranger to me
More and more I can see there's a danger
In becoming what I never thought I'd be
Some days are diamonds some days are
Stones sometimes the hard times
Won't leave me alone
Sometimes a cold wind blows
A chill in my bones."
-John Denver

Have a great time from this point on in your life. There is not a moment to waste in your life...

J. Paul Getty, acknowledged once as the richest man in America, used goals in accumulating his fortune. He would study current markets, decide what he needed to increase his value and work to attain it. Mr. Getty didn't let obstacles deter him. When Standard Oil Company of New Jersey attempted to block his purchase of Tidewater Oil, he didn't give up. Even though the largest Petroleum Company in the world tried to keep Mr.. Getty from achieving a necessary part of his business expansion, he gained control of Tidewater. If Mr. Getty had looked at the vastly greater resources and power of Standard and been intimidated into backing away from his purchase, the growth of his oil empire might have stagnated right there. But he had confidence in his ability and the soundness of his goals and Tidewater Oil became part of the Getty holdings.

Thomas Edison said about his work: *"I never did anything worth doing by accident, nor did any of my inventions come by accident."* Edison kept a map because the end point on his map was his goal. He knew where he wanted to go and he used his map to find the best possible route. Edison never began a project without first writing a description of the ultimate result he was working toward.

In 1961, President John F. Kennedy made the statement *"We shall land men on the moon by the end of the decade"*. That was a goal. Congress and the President then set about to achieve that goal. Thousands of men, thousands of minds, billions of dollars were put to work on the various projects that preceded the landing shot. On the way, the project met with some failures and challenges, but succeeded in using those failures to create further successes. With each and every person from the astronauts down to the lowest custodian in the project headquarters concentrating on that goal and working to achieve it, the project went on. In August of 1969, the statement was relayed to earth: *"One small step for man; one giant leap for mankind."*

chapter 11

Chapter Eleven

I will commit more time to my business in the coming year. I am ready to knock myself out to set up next years calendar.

> Have I been procrastinating and
> fooling around all day?
> Do I feel guilty for not working?
> Even though I haven't met my goal yet,
> do I deserve a break?
> Have I been working all day?
> Have I been working at all during the day?
> Am I just hoping this will all happen?

PDD (Personal Daily Decision)

> Am I passionate?
> Will it bring me joy?
> Will it be fun?
> Will it be satisfying?
> Is it unique to me?

When you make commitments to yourself: write them down and keep them.
Why? This cuts a path to a new level of self-determination in your life.
When you do this, it paves the way for productive action toward the more important undertakings you've recorded in your charts.

Live every act fully, as if it were your last.

Let go of your opinions

when the why gets clear enough about what you want in life, the how gets easy

It's About Time

When your ship comes in, it won't be a dinghy.

"You must learn to be still in the midst of activity and to be vibrantly alive in repose."
-Indira Gandhi

The Vision Multiplier

The common feelings of inadequacy are not rooted in our lack of ability. The potential of the human mind has never really been measured. Negative concepts stem from not having mastered ourselves. We cannot and must not accept second-rate performance, average as our best. When you begin trying again...trying to direct your life with determination...blast out of the shell of self-imposed ceilings and enter into a new environment of achievement action. A great part of achieving your goals is by being able to determine a particular move to take in a given situation and then throwing the entire weight of your energies behind that decision. Visions are the beacons for directing our lives, but it takes the strength to make a clear-cut choice for action and the perseverance to follow that decision if we are to ever arrive at the port of personal fulfillment. Get the fire of desire and use your time wisely.

Have you ever picked up a five gallon gasoline can and expected it to be full...but it wasn't? The can goes sailing over your head because you had mentally multiplied the weight of the container to accommodate 35 pounds of fuel. It's this way with thinking. Sometimes we set a ceiling on our minds that shouldn't be there. Sit down right now and apply a *"vision multiplier"* to your own situation. Increase everything in the following categories 10 times. You'll find the ideas they create are exciting...that they urge you onto greater action and achievement.

1. My present income is:
2. Now multiply by 10:

Here are actions I intend to take to get there:

1.

2.

4 Pitfalls to Avoid

1. **Spending time looking for a *"gold mine"* in the sky.** Success lies within you, not in external powers.
2. **Never looking inward.** The success-oriented individual knows him/herself. Examine your thoughts, your motives and your knowledge.
3. **Break the chains** that bind the mediocre person and strive for accomplishment, fulfillment and success.
4. **They don't make the mistake of blaming failures on outside forces.** Just as success exists within, so does failure. Mistakes are not the fault of other people. The dynamic person with vision, knows that mistakes will be made, but study them using them as building blocks for future accomplishment. You can't brood over challenges, but remember to avoid any recurrence.

Often minor obstacles stand in the way of our desires. We might want a certain position in the company. Our sights are set on getting this promotion, but when it comes down to it, you aren't willing to do what's necessary for you to get the promotion. So, many people give up, they forget their goal. The reasons are: the criterion is too high, the others are better qualified, or it wasn't really important in the first place. But, when you give up you are not true to ourselves. So sad, you must never give up. Keep on working to achieve your goal.

"The gem cannot be polished without friction, nor people perfected without trials."
-Confucius

Save water by sweeping your driveway or sidewalk rather than using the hose.

Have you ever leaned heavily against a brick wall, pushing with all your might, trying to get through it, around it, under it, by pushing it, accomplished nothing? Yet, you are working, expending tremendous amounts of strength. You might crawl over the wall, or you might dig a tunnel and go under it. If you can, you can go around it. But, pushing against it is useless. Unfortunately, this is the way many people spend their lives. They don't analyze their obstacles. They don't attempt to chart a course through the mine fields of failure. They never reach the few goals they set for themselves.

Shipping lines obviously couldn't operate in this manner. Each time a freighter sets out from port, its course is clearly charted. If some storm blocks the way, the course may be altered. Still, by one route or another it will reach its destination. If the ship hits a squall, the captain doesn't forget his route. It's called navigating around obstacles. Many transcontinental flights make altitude and direction changes while in flight. They fly above storms, or they revise their course to avoid weather disturbances. Still, they fly toward their original predetermined destination. When the pilot changes his plans, he computes the amount of fuel used in the change.

Obstacles To Prepare For

Being alone. Body changes. Car challenges. Children's challenges. Criticism. Death of a loved one. Death of a pet. Depression. Disappointments. Divorce. Exhaustion. Financial situations. Getting laid off job. Getting older. Major illness. Lightening speed of computer age. Litigation. Lost luggage. Miscarriages. Natural disaster. People lying to you. Someone says something unkind about your company. Spouse challenges. Stock Market fluctuation. Stress. Taking care of elderly parents. Upsetting news. Operations. Make up your own list.

Obstacles	Solution	Done

"When the sun announces the dawning day just flex your muscles and start on your way. Go over, or under; around, or through any obstacles or hurdles that challenge you. There's a new day coming. Cast aside the failures of yesterday. Forget the peaks and valleys that have paved your way. Wipe the sweat from your brow and the dust from your shoe. Take a breath and relax so that you may begin anew. There's a new day coming. Forget the burdens and obstacles that have held you back. Focus on your dreams and prepare a plan of attack. There are battles awaiting to challenge your success. Daring you to stand tall and to give it your best. There's a new day coming. No matter how great the journey, or how heavy the load, how steep the mountain, or how rough the road. When your arms grow weary and legs give way stop and rest for a moment, it will be okay. There's a new day coming. As shadows spring forth from the setting sun. Take a moment and savor the battles you've won. Sleep peacefully tonight and enjoy your rest. Awaken tomorrow and continue your quest. There's always, a new day coming."
-Mychal Wynn

The best time to plant a tree was twenty years ago. The second best time is now.

DON'T BROOD OVER THE PAST OR DREAM OF THE FUTURE; BUT SEIZE THE INSTANT AND GET YOUR LESSON FROM THE HOUR.

It is the idle people, not the great worker; who is always complaining that he has no time. Some people will make more out of the odds and ends of opportunities, which many carelessly throw away, than others will get out of a whole lifetime. Like bees, they extract honey from every flower. Every person they meet, every circumstance of the day, must add something to their store of useful knowledge or personal power.

There is nobody whom Fortune does not visit once in his life but when she finds he is not ready to receive her, she goes in at the door and out at the window.

> Life pulsates with chances. They may not be dramatic or great, but they are important to those who would get on in the world.

Open eyes will discover opportunities everywhere; open ears will never fail to detect the cries of those who are perishing for assistance; open hearts will never want for worthy objects upon which to bestow their gifts; open hands will never lack for noble work to do.

ETERNITY ITSELF CANNOT RESTORE THE LOSS STRUCK FROM THE MINUTE.

The Young Surgeon

The time comes to the young surgeon, when, after long waiting and patient study and experiment, he is suddenly confronted with his first critical operation. The great surgeon is away. Time is pressing. Life and death hang in the balance. Is he equal to the emergency? Can he fill the great surgeon's place and do his work? If he can, he is the one of all others who is wanted. His opportunity confronts him. He and it are face to face. Shall he confess his ignorance and inability, or step into fame and fortune? It is for him to say. If you are prepared, you should be ready.

Are you prepared for a great opportunity? Hawthorne dined one day with Longfellow and brought a friend with him. After dinner the friend said, *"I have been trying to persuade Hawthorne to write a story based upon a legend of Acadia-the legend of a girl who, in the dispersion of the Acadians, was separated from her lover and passed her life in waiting and seeking for him and only found him dying in a hospital when both were old."* Longfellow wondered that the legend did not strike the fancy of Hawthorne and he said to him, *"If you have really made up your mind not to use it for a story, will you let me have it for a poem?"* To this Hawthorne consented and promised, not to treat the subject in prose till Longfellow had seen what he could do with it in verse, Longfellow seized his opportunity and gave to the world Evangeline.

The time will come when you will hear me.

"The world each of us lives in every day, in the long run, is a mirror of ourselves; it is created by ourselves. Occasionally, it's a good idea to take inventory and ask ourselves, 'Do I like the world in which I live?' If not, I'm the one who's going to have to change."
-Earl Nightingale

I am Yesterday

I am Yesterday. I am gone from you forever. I am the last of a long procession of days, streaming behind you, away from you, pouring into mist and obscurity and at last into the ocean of oblivion. Each of us have our burden, of triumph, of defeat, of laughter, of bitterness, we bear our load from you into forgetfulness; yet as we go we each leave something in your subconsciousness. We till your soul's cellar. I depart from you, yet I am ever with you. Once I was called Tomorrow and was virgin pure; then I became your spouse and was named Today; now I am Yesterday and carry upon me the eternal stain of your embrace. I am one of the leaves of a growing book. There are many pages before me. Someday you shall turn us all over and read us and know what you are. I am pale, for I have no hope. Only memories. I am rich, for I have wisdom. I bore you a child and left him with you. His name is Experience. You do not like to look at me. I am not pretty. I am majestic, fateful, serious. You do not love my voice. It does not speak to your desires; it is cool and even and full of prudence. I am Yesterday; yet I am the same as Today and Forever, for I AM YOU; and you cannot escape from yourself. Sometimes I talk with my companions about you. Some of us carry the scars of your cruelty. Some the wretchedness of your crime. Some the beauty of your goodness. We do not love you. We do not hate you. We judge you. We have no compassion; only Today has that. We have no encouragement for you; only Tomorrow has that. We stand at the front door of the past, welcoming the single file of days that pass through, watching Tomorrows becoming todays and then enter among us. Little by little we suck out your life, as vampires. As you grow older we absorb your thought. You turn to us more and more, less and less toward Tomorrow. Our snows cumber your back and whiten your head. Our icy waters put out your passions. Our exhalations dim your hopes. Our many tombstones crowd into your landscape. Our dead loves, burnt-out enthusiasm, shatter dream house, dissolved illusions, move to you, surround you. Tomorrows come unnoticed. Today's slip by unheeded. More and more you become a creature of Yesterdays. Ours are banquet halls full of wine- soaked tablecloths, broken vessels and wilted roses. Ours are ghastly Pompeiian streets, rich galleons, a hundred fathoms deep, genealogical lists of sonorous names, mummies in museums, fragmentary pillars of battered temples, inscriptions on bricks of Nineveh, huge stone gates standing amidst the tropical landscape of Yucatan, Etruscan wine jars now dry and empty forever. From us comes that miasma of inertia that holds humanity in thrall; from us comes the strength of war makers, monarchs and all the privileged. We reach up long, sinewy, gray arms of custom and tradition, to choke Today and impede Tomorrow. We are the world's Yesterdays. If you knew enough to put your feet upon us, you might rise rapidly. But when you let us ride on your backs we strangle and smother you. I am Yesterday. Learn to look me in the face, to use me and not to be afraid of me. I am not your friend. I am your judge and your fear. Tomorrow is your friend.

Time is Money

We should not be stingy or mean with it, but we should not throw away an hour any more than we would throw away a dollar-bill. Waste of time means waste of energy, waste of vitality, waste of character in dissipation. It means bad companions, had habits. It means the waste of opportunities which will never come back. Beware how you kill time, for all your future lives in it.

> *"Let the past guide, the future cheer, while youth and health are in their prime; But, oh, be still thy greatest care - that awful point - the present time!"*
> -Edward Everett

2 Giant Success Goals

Under ordinary circumstances and with practical common sense to guide them, one who has these requisites will not fail.

1. Go-at-it-iveness is the first requisite for success.
2. Stick-to-it-iveness is the second.

DON'T HURRY. DON'T WORRY. YOU'RE ONLY HERE FOR A SHORT VISIT. SO DON'T FORGET TO STOP AND SMELL THE ROSES

Yesterday, Today, Tomorrow

There are two days in every week about which we should not worry. Two days which should be kept free from fear and apprehension. One of these days is Yesterday, with its mistakes and cares, its faults and blunders, its aches and pains. Yesterday has passed forever beyond our control. All the money in the world cannot bring back Yesterday. We cannot undo a single act we performed; we cannot erase a single word we said... Yesterday is gone. The other day we should not worry about is Tomorrow, with its possible adversaries, its burdens, its large and poor performance, Tomorrow is also beyond our immediate control. Tomorrow's sun will rise, either in splendor or behind a mask of clouds, but it will rise. Until it does, we have no stake in Tomorrow for it is as yet unborn. This leaves only one day. Today. Any person can fight the battle for just one day. It is only when you and I add the Yesterday and Tomorrow that we break down. It is not the experience of Today that drives people mad, it is remorse or bitterness for something which happened Yesterday or the dread of what Tomorrow may bring. Let us therefore, live but one day at a time.

"Goals are dreams and wishes that are not easily reached. You have to work hard to obtain them, never knowing when or where you will reach your goal. But keep trying! Do not give up hope. And most of all...never stop believing in yourself. For within you there is someone special...someone wonderful and successful. No matter what you achieve, as long as you want it and it makes you happy, you are a success."
-Rosemary De Paolis

Final Steps Leaving High School

"Take my hand and let us walk together through these hallways we've known so well. All seems quiet now, as we are the last to walk through these doors. The final bell scattering out friends into the awaiting world, still lingers in my mind. I think they forgot something. Our lessons weren't complete. They taught us many things, the art of words, the mystery of science, the essence of equations but something is missing. In all their haste they forgot to teach us the hardest thing to learn. We take our final steps through open door not knowing how to say it. Not knowing how to say...good-bye. We're being pulled apart, just like the child from the swings when it is time to go home. Just like that child, I'm crying out in pain. For, I'm not finished playing yet. I fear I'm losing you, like the child loses his youth. I want my innocence back. I want to take your hand again. The time has now come. The doors have closed and the world is waiting to take us in open arms. The road has branched off and we must now let go of this small part of our lives. My heart is tearing apart and I give you the piece you claimed so long ago. I don't know how to say it. I know the right words, but my soul will not release them, nor will it release you. The bond between us is rapidly withering. Before it fades into the night, look to the stars, close your eyes and I will see you in my dreams."
-Bill Heall

Time is like a handful of sand - the tighter you grasp it, the faster it runs through your fingers

The Champion Creed

*"I am not judged by the number of times I fail, but by the number of times I succeed. And the number of times I succeed is in direct proportion to the number of times I can fail and **keep trying**."*
-Tom Hopkins

Optimist: Someone who goes after Moby Dick in a rowboat and takes tartar sauce with him.

"You always do whatever you want to do. This is true of every act. You may say you had to do something or that you were forced to, but actually, whatever you do, you do by choice. Only you have the power to choose for yourself. The choice is yours. You hold the tiller. You can alter the course you choose in the direction of where you want to be-today, tomorrow, or in a distant time to come."
-W. Clement Stone

"An American figure skater had trouble getting up every morning at 5:00am to train...until she placed a photo of the Russian champion by her alarm. Under the picture were the words: 'Comrade, while you were sleeping, I was training'."
-Ron Gilbert

"Youth is not a time of life, it is a state of mind. You are as old as your doubt, your fear, your despair. The way to keep young is to keep your faith young. Keep your self-confidence young. Keep your hope young."
-Luella F. Phean

"'Come to the edge,' He said. They said, 'We are afraid.' 'Come to the edge,' He said. They came. He pushed them...And they flew."
-Bullaume Apollinarire

Who Am I?

"I am very accommodating. I ask no questions. I accept whatever you give me. I do whatever I am told. I do not presume to change anything you think, say or do; I file it all away in perfect order, quickly and efficiently and then return it to you exactly as you gave it to me. Sometimes you call me your memory. I am the reservoir into which you toss anything your heart or mind chooses to deposit there. I work night and day; I never rest, and nothing can impede my activity. The thoughts you send me are categorized and filed and my filing system never fails. I am truly your servant who does your bidding without hesitation or criticism.. I cooperate when you tell me that you are 'this' or 'that' and I play it back as you give it. I am most agreeable. Since I do not think, argue, judge, analyze, question or make decisions, I accept impressions easily. I am going to ask you to sort out what you send me, however, my files are getting a little cluttered and confused. I mean, please discard those things that you do not want returned to you. What is my name? Oh! I thought you knew! I am your subconscious."
-Margaret White

"Far away in the sunshine are my highest aspirations. I can look up and see their beauty, believe in them and try to follow them."
-Louisa May Alcott

chapter 12

Chapter Twelve

Awareness and Discovery

Awareness

If we know we want to succeed, but you are unable to see a direct path to our goal, chances are we have a couple of stumbling blocks in our way. The first step is to become aware of those stumbling blocks and of where you need to put your time so that you can help yourself clear the way to success.

Discovery

Once you are aware of the stumbling blocks between yourself and your goal, you can get depressed about the work and time it will take to change or you can discover what you can do to make the change. It is not too late for you to decide to do the latter of the two.

What would you truly do if you knew today was your last day to live? Watch television for a couple of hours? Probably not even for a couple of minutes. Most likely you would be busy all day making sure that your time on this earth has made a difference to somebody, somewhere — hopefully to many. You might call your family and friends to express love. You might write a letter to a friend you made an enemy long ago for a reason that was silly and is now long forgotten. *What would you do?* Riches are of no worth to the person who passes on. Knowledge and relationships will outlast any piece of gold. Mahatma Gandhi said it well when he said, *"Live as if you were to die tomorrow. Learn as if you were to live forever"*. You cannot relive and make right the errors of yesterday. Living in tomorrow is concerning yourself with events that you may never witness. See what you can accomplish by living this day as if it is your last! You will be amazed!

---

*"Your goals are road maps that guide you
and show you what is possible for your life."*
-Les Brown

Most likely as you read this you are sitting in the room with a light on. If this is correct, read on. Thomas Edison, among many other things, invented the light bulb. Today we enjoy the benefits of his work. What if he had discovered electricity and never done anything about it? Of work and application Edison said, *"I never did anything worth doing by accident, nor did any of my inventions come by accident; they came by work"*. Your chance to capture success is now in your hands and will simply take time and hard work. Edison said, *"Opportunity is missed by most people because it is dressed in overalls and looks like work"*.

*"Each of us makes his own weather,
determines the color of the skies in the
emotional universe which he inhabits."*
-Bishop Fulton Sheen

Have you ever been in a situation, perhaps at an office, when a person walked in, obviously in a bad mood and immediately started criticizing everyone and everything in the path they were traveling? The cruel words and glances send emotional lightning bolts, leaving in this person's path small fires of hurt that take hours to extinguish. Have you met a person with just the opposite effect? Their presence feels like a warm spring breeze, leaving everybody around rejuvenated and uplifted. Perhaps you have been like both of these people at different times in your life. Controlling your emotions doesn't mean that you'll always feel great. Greg Anderson said, *"You can't expect to prevent negative feelings altogether. And you can't expect to experience positive feelings all the time"*.

One day Alice came to a fork in the road and saw a Cheshire cat in tree. *"Which road do I take?"* she asked *"Where do you want to go?"* was his response. *"I don't know."* Alice answered. *"Then"*, said the cat, *"It doesn't matter"*.
-Lewis Caroll from <u>Alice in Wonderland</u>

The Law of Emotional Choice

The Law of Emotional Choice directs you to *acknowledge your feelings but also to refuse to get stuck in the negative ones.* Although circumstances around you may not change and tough times may be thrown in your path, you can choose to respond with a positive emotion no matter what.

LEWF

Four words that should make you cringe: Lazy, Evil, Weak and Failure. The first letter of each spells "LEWF".

Don't Be a Lewf

"I am not lazy," the Lewf said with a smile.
"It's all figured out, got it filed in my file.
If I spend all today relaxing I'll bet,
I'll be rested and ready tomorrow to sweat"
"Me, evil?" the Lewf said with a grin.
"How could you utter such nonsense, such sin?
Wait 'til the morrow, as idle minds would,
Be out of my system, tomorrow's for good. So my
productivity is down a little this month,
And last month, last year, haven't you had a slump?
Weak?" The Lewf questioned: *"You insult me today!*
I can choose to be strong, is tomorrow okay?
Success is the banner that hangs over my chair
I see it, I read it, I shout in the air..."
Can nobody hear me? I mean it this time!
A failure? No! Tomorrow, success will be mine!"
-Unknown

And so we hear such repetitive oration from Lewfs who love procrastination. But everyone knows the price they will pay, for when tomorrow is here it will still be today.

If you give a starving man a fish he will live a week. If you teach a starving man to fish he will live a lifetime.

"How many times have you called a technical support number and waited on hold for at least half an hour, all for a little (or not so little) guidance. While those calls may be necessary, we luckily have other types of guidance from good people all around us that come without holding at all. While we need to be careful about whose example and advice we follow, there is much to be learned from many. My advice about finding guidance from the other source...Hang up!"
-David Blanchard

Stay cool, calm and corrected

Get Some Rest

Go to bed early...wake up feeling great. Early to bed, early to rise, makes a man healthy, wealthy and wise. Sweet dreams.

When you reach for the stars, you may not quite get one, but you won't come up with a handful of mud either. How many of us wake up in the morning thinking, *I think I'll fail today!* Not one. But, have you had days where you wake up thinking, *I hope I make it through the day.* Plan on great things, to work for those things and if you come up a bit short at the end of the day, you still will have done very well!

"Hands that help are holier than lips that pray."
-Sathya Sai Baba

THE NOBLEST THING A PERSON CAN DO IS TO PLANT A SEED THAT WILL SOMEDAY GROW INTO A GIANT SHADE TREE TO GIVE SHADE TO THOSE THEY WILL NEVER KNOW.

An inch of time cannot be bought with an inch of gold.

The Little Engine That Could
-Watty Piper

One morning the little engine was waiting for the next call when a long train of freight-cars asked a large engine in the roundhouse to take it over the hill *"I can't; that is too much a pull for me"*, said the great engine built for hard work. Then the train asked another engine and another, only to hear excuses and be refused. At last in desperation the train asked the little switch engine to draw it up the grade and down on the other side. *"I think I can"*, puffed the little locomotive and put itself in front of the great heavy train. As he went on the little engine kept bravely puffing faster and faster, *"I think I can, I think I can"*. Then as it neared the top of the grade, that had so discouraged the larger engines, it went more slowly, but still kept saying, *"I-think-I-can, I-think-I-can"*. It reached the top by dint of brave effort and then went on down the grade, congratulating itself, *"I thought I could!"* To think of hard things and say, *"I can't"* is sure to mean, *"I won't even try"*. We must refuse to be daunted and say, *"I think I can"*. We will surely be able to join the little engine in announcing triumphantly, *"I thought I could!"*

When you just don't know where to start, start anywhere. Just do something! Get the ball rolling and then make corrections in its path.

We have enough youth, how about a fountain of smart?

"A man is not old until regrets take the place of dreams."
-John Barrymore

Where there's a will, I want to be in it.

"Nothing in this world can take the place of persistence. Talent will not; nothing is more common than unsuccessful people with talent. Genius will not; unrewarded genius is almost a proverb. Education will not; the world is full of educated derelicts. Persistence and determination alone are omnipotent. The slogan 'press on' has solved and always will solve the problems of the human race."
-Calvin Coolidge

"If you have built castles in the air, your work need not be lost; this is where they should be. Now put the foundations under them."
-Henry David Thoreau

So, get to work and dream on!

True happiness lies within you. Waste no time and effort searching for peace and contentment and joy in the world outside. There is no happiness in having or in getting, but only in giving. Reach out. Share. Smile. Hug.

I am a slow walker, but I never walk backwards.

Happiness is a perfume you cannot pour on others without getting a few drops on yourself.

Have intense desire for the use of your time rocket fuel for your goal

I'd rather change my mind and succeed than have my own way all the time and fail.

That which you resists persists.
Bypass resistance-gather assistance.

Forget Grudges

Carrying a grudge is like toting around a bag of bricks. Letting go will leave you feeling lighter and leave your hands free to receive others' forgiveness for your own small mistakes.

Always do Your Best

What you plant now, you will harvest later. Always seek out the seed of triumph in every adversity. Failure will never overtake you if your determination to succeed is strong enough. Take the attitude of a student, never be too big to ask questions, never know too much to learn something new.

"Beginning today, treat everyone you meet
as if they were going to be dead by midnight.
Extend to them all the care, kindness and
understanding you can muster and do it
with no thought of any reward.
Your life will never be the same again."
-Og Mandino

Ride the emergencies of life instead of being overwhelmed by them.

"The most valuable result of all education is to make you do the thing you have to do, when it ought to be done, whether you like it or not. It is the first lesson that ought to be learned. And however early a man's training begins, it is probably the last lesson that he learns thoroughly."
-Thomas Huxley

5 Ways To Use Time

WAY #1: Never Be Bored. Don't take life and all of its little mysteries for granted. Don't casually accept the ecosystem, communication, gravity. (Though, even if you don't accept that last one, you'll still be grounded.) Remember when you had to know why the sky was blue? Did you ever really find out? Reawaken the curiosity.

WAY #2: Get into reality. There's something breathtaking about life. Who wouldn't choose to experience love rather than watch it on the big screen.

WAY #3: Love criticism. Criticism is often seen as a personal attack. Think of what an Olympic athlete willingly endures from coaches! To reach your potential, seek constructive criticism. (Of course, if you want to avoid criticism you simply need to do nothing, say nothing and be nothing.)

WAY #4: Learn to do. The whole point of wisdom is to make a better life. There is no greater waste than to have a bunch of great ideas and not use them.

WAY #5: Learn from the wise person. An apprentice gains firsthand knowledge by watching how an expert works. So it is with wisdom. Don't only read about it in a book; find yourself an expert.

Confucius Ways to Wisdom

By three methods we may learn wisdom: First, by reflection, which is noblest; second, by imitation, which is easiest; and third by experience, which is the bitterest. Leave reflection to nobility. Bitter is for someone with less taste. Accept the invitation for imitation.

"If I can stop one heart from breaking,
I shall not live in vain;
If I can ease one life the aching,
Or cool one pain, or help one fainting robin
Unto his next again, I shall not live in vain."
-Emily Dickenson

10 Time-Tested Principles to Self-Management

What if YOUR business was made up of people who...

- Make and keep commitments.
- Face each day with a positive, upbeat attitude.
- Persist until they succeed.
- Capitalize on their strengths instead of weaknesses.
- Manage time to get massive results.
- Master their emotions.
- Overcome obstacles and challenges with ease.
- Find ways to multiply their value to the company.
- See needs and take action without being asked.
- Seek coaching.

When you've just been offended there's that one person who's always willing to commiserate? This is your pity party. If you are the source of the pity parties...stop. And when that person comes to complain to your sympathetic ear, try tactfully asking what good things are going on. Either the positives will begin to flow, or that pity party will party elsewhere. If you want to be depressed, you simply need to open your eyes, but to be positive, you must dig through the pile of *Woe, is me's* to find the precious and sincere *How lucky am I?*

Face the fear! Live your adventure!

"Life is either a series of adventures, or it is nothing."
-Helen Keller

Goal for today: Detox! Work to expel some of the toxins that are building up poisoning your body. Today drink a lot of water and your internal organs will have begun to purge those toxins out of your body. This is a wonderful first step towards the new you.

Trouble never leaves you where it found you

Troubles come and troubles go. Overlook the small ones and when the big ones are ready to move on, open wide the door and let them go.

How Exactly do we Put Off Happiness

Perhaps, you are not convinced that you do. Here are a few statements to determine your *I'll be happy when...*goals. Circle the letter you feel best completes each statement below.

Personally, I'll be happy when:
1. The children have grown up.
2. I have more free time.
3. I can finally relax.
4. I am chosen as a contestant on Deal or No Deal?

Relationally, I'll be happy when:
1. I find Mr./Mrs. Right.
2. I'm married.
3. She stops nagging/he listens to me.
4. I'm divorced.

Career-wise, I'll be happy when:
1. I get a raise.
2. I get a better job.
3. I have a better boss.
4. I retire in the Grand Cayman Islands.

Financially, I'll be happy when:
1. I have a house.
2. The house is paid for.
3. I have a bigger house.
4. I live among the stars in a Hollywood mansion.

How did you do? The answer key is simple. The answer to each question is actually a secret option:

I am already happy! Give up looking for future happiness. Find and enjoy it today!

George Carlin's View on Aging

Do you realize that the only time in our lives when we like to get old is when we're kids? If you're less than 10 years old, you're so excited about aging that you think in fractions. *"How old are you? "I'm four and a half!"* You're never thirty-six and a half. You're four and a half, going on five! That's the key. You get into your teens, now they can't hold you back. You jump to the next number, or even a few ahead. *"How old are you?" "I'm gonna be 16!"* You could be 13, but hey, you're going to be 16! And then the greatest day of your life...you become 21. Even the words sound like a ceremony... YOU BECOME 21. YES! But then you turn 30. OOOOhh, what happened there? Makes you sound like bad milk! He TURNED; we had to throw him out. There's no fun now. What's wrong? What's changed? You BECOME 21, you TURN 30, then you're PUSHING 40. Whoa! Put on the brakes, it's all slipping away. Before you know it, you REACH 50... and your dreams are gone. But wait! You MAKE it to 60. You didn't think you would! So you BECOME 21, TURN 30, PUSH 40, REACH 50 and MAKE it to 60. You've built up so much speed that you HIT 70! After that it's a day-by-day thing; you HIT Wednesday! You get into your 80's and every day is a complete cycle; you HIT lunch; you TURN 4:30; you REACH bedtime. And it doesn't end there. Into the 90's, you start going backwards; *"I was JUST 92"*. Then a strange thing happens. If you make it over 100, you become a little kid again. *"I'm 100 and a half"* May you all make it to a healthy 100 and a half!!

> *"She said she usually cried at least once a day, not because she was sad but because the world was so beautiful and life was so short."*
> -The Story People

How to Stay Young

1. Throw out nonessential numbers. This includes age, weight and height. Let the doctors worry about them. That is why you pay *them!*
2. Keep only cheerful friends. The grouches pull you down.
3. Keep learning. Learn more about the computer, crafts, gardening, whatever. Never let the brain idle. *An idle mind is the devil's workshop.* And the devil's name is Alzheimer's.
4. Enjoy the simple things.
5. Laugh often, long and loud. Laugh until you gasp for breath.
6. The tears happen. Endure, grieve and move on. The only person, who is with us our entire life, is ourselves. Be ALIVE while you are alive.
7. Surround yourself with what you love, whether it's family, pets, keepsakes, music, plants, hobbies, whatever. Your home is your refuge.
8. Cherish your health: If it is good, preserve it. If it is unstable, improve it. If it is beyond what you can improve, get help.
9. Don't take guilt trips. Take a trip to the mall, even to the next county; to a foreign country but NOT to where the guilt is.
10. Tell the people you love that you love them, at every opportunity.

> *Life is not measured by the number of breaths we take, but by the moments that take our breath away.*

Cross a threshold into the better life.

The Bridge of Tomorrow

There is a chasm in all our lives that separates us from the future. Standing at the edge of that canyon, you are the person of today, the sum total of everything in your past. Beyond is your potential, the person you are capable of becoming. Across that canyon of tomorrow are all the golden accomplishments waiting for you to mine. By reading this book you will help yourself bridge your canyon and move toward your success. The wisdom of *It's About Time*, can take you any place you wish to go. When applied strategically, the knowledge spans the chasm and creates the bridge into tomorrow, where the gold of achievement can be mined and refined. Challenge yourself now to reach for the objectives of your vision. The only limitations standing between you and those objectives are those that you yourself think. Step forward onto the bridge. Just like in Indiana Jones, when he stepped out into space and trusted that an invisible bridge would be there and it was. So is a beautiful future for you.

What you ardently desire and are willing to work for every day of your life, as long as it doesn't hurt your fellow mankind, must ultimately come to pass.

Aim for a Star!

"Never be satisfied with a life
that is less than the best,
Failure lies only in not having tried-
In keeping the soul suppressed.
Aim for a star! Look up and away,
And follow its beckoning beam.
Make each tomorrow a better
Today and don't be afraid to dream.
Aim for a star and keep your sights high!
With a heartful of faith within,
Your feet on the ground and your eyes on the
sky, some day you are bound to win!"
-Helen L. Marshall

The Bridge Builder

An old man going down a lone highway
came in the evening cold and gray
to a chasm vast and deep and wide
through which was flowing a sullen tide.
The old man crossed in the twilight dim;
that swollen stream held no fears for him;
but he turned when safe on the other side
and built a bridge to span the tide.
"Old man", said a fellow pilgrim near,
"you are wasting your strength with building here;
your journey will end with the ending day;
you never again must pass this way;
you have crossed the chasm deep and wide,
why build you this bridge at the eventide?"
The builder lifted his old gray head.
"Good friend, in the path I have come", he said,
"there followeth after me today
a youth whose feet must pass this way.
This swollen stream which was naught to me
to that fair-haired youth may a pitfall be;
he, too, must cross in the twilight dim;
good friend, I am building the bridge for him."
-Will Allen Dromgoole

I've Got to Find Myself

The other day, a man passed away at age sixty-seven. Forty years ago he was saying, *"I've got to find myself"*. Fifteen years later he was still saying, *"I've got to find myself"*. About a year before he died, he wrote a letter saying, *"I've got to find myself"*. We must all fight hard so that we do not make this mistake of spending all of our lives finding ourselves, for then there will be no time left to do anything about it. This year is a special year. It's the year to discover yourself, your future, your passion, your path and to become clear with what you MUST do from today on. Do not be denied a fabulous future. It's waiting for you on a silver platter. Come to the table of plenty. There is a place set for you. It's up to you to get there. Find yourself now.

The 8 Foot Fence Fable

Once upon a time two brothers who lived on adjoining farms fell into conflict. It was the first serious rift in 40 years of farming side by side, sharing machinery and trading labor without a hitch when the long collaboration fell apart. It began with a small misunderstanding, grew into a major difference and finally it exploded into an exchange of bitter words followed by weeks of silence. One morning there was a knock on John's door from a man with a carpenter's toolbox. *"I'm looking for a few days work, perhaps you would have a few small jobs here and there I could help with? Could I help you?"* *"Yes"*, said the older brother. *"I do have a job for you. Look across the creek at that farm. That's my neighbor; in fact, it's my younger brother. Last week there was a meadow between us and he took his bulldozer to the river levee and now there is a creek between us. Well, he may have done this to spite me, but I'll go him one better. See that pile of lumber by the barn? I want you to build me an 8 foot fence so I won't need to see his place or his face anymore."* The carpenter said, *"I think I understand the situation. Show me the nails and the post-hole digger and I'll be able to do a job that pleases you"*. So he helped the carpenter get the materials ready and then he was off for the day. The carpenter worked hard all that day measuring, sawing, nailing. About sunset when the farmer returned, the carpenter had just finished his job. The farmer's eyes opened wide, his jaw dropped. There was no fence there at all. It was a bridge stretching from one side of the creek to the other! A fine piece of work handrails and the neighbor, his younger brother, was coming across, his hand outstretched. *"You are quite a fellow to build this bridge after all I've said and done."* The two brothers stood at each end of the bridge and then they met in the middle, taking each other's hand. They turned to see the carpenter hoist his toolbox on his shoulder. *"No, wait! Stay a few days. I've a lot of other projects for you"*, said the older brother. *"I'd love to stay on"*, the carpenter said, *"but I have many more bridges to build"*.

Bridge Blueprints

Idea 1: Open your eyes. Don't limit yourself by stereotypes and first impressions. Look harder and deeper for the good in people you meet.

Idea 2: Think before you react. Nasty E-mails can be typed and sent or harsh words spoken before you take a moment to think about the recipient. Make allowances...even if you're right.

Idea 3: Listen to others. You'll discover things you never knew and find out just what you can to fulfill specific needs.

Idea 4: Plan. Make a conscious effort to create and heal relationships...at work, in your neighborhood, or with your family.

Idea 5: Give. While time is most precious, when busy, there's never a card or plate of goodies that goes unappreciated. And be yourself. A bridge that is built on anything but the truth will collapse as soon as an attempt to cross it is made. It's up to you. Build it!

Treasure every moment that you have. Treasure it more because you shared it with someone special, special enough to spend your time...that time waits for no one...so stop waiting until you finish school...until you go back to school...until you shed ten pounds...until you gain ten pounds...until you have children...until your children leave home... until you start work...until you retire...until you get married... until you get divorced...until Friday night... until after church...until you get a new car or home... until your car or home is paid off...until spring, until summer... until fall...until winter...until you are off welfare...until the first or fifteenth...until your song comes on... until you've had a drink...until you've sobered up... until you die... until you are born again to decide that there is no better time than right now to be happy...

No man is an island, no man stands alone.

Use your life time. Let your inner fire make a bonfire look weak.

Reach for Your Goals

"Whatever the goal we're pursuing,
  no matter how rugged the climb,
    we're certain to get there by trying our best
    and taking one day at a time.
Forever is hard to imagine,
  The Future:
    may seem far away,
      but every new dawn brings a wonderful
        chance to do what we can on that day.
As you reach for the goals
  you would like to achieve,
    may you find strength you will need,
    to meet every challenge one
      step at a time till the day when
        you proudly succeed!"
          -Larry Chengges

"I am the sum total of the genetic endowment with which I came into the world and all of the experiences which have made up my life. Some of them have been good, some bad, but all of them have been mine. What I currently am is what I deserve to be. My life, my reputation, my influence is the mirror of the choices I have made. If I am not everything I can be, it is because I haven't chosen to be more. I am determined not to live in my past, which I cannot change or to waste time waiting for the future, which I cannot guarantee, but to live in the emerging reality of the NOW, which is all I have. I cannot do everything, but I can do some things. I certainly cannot do everything well, but I can do some things well. I cannot guarantee I will win, but I can promise I will not allow losing to become a habit and if I fail, it will not be a failure of nerve. So I will stand tall, feel deeply, think large and strive mightily, remembering what I accomplish probably won't change the course of human history, but what I attempt will create the course of my personal history. Toward making this declaration a reality, I hereby commit myself!"
-John Compere

ℬelieve in the power you
have to control your own life, day by day.

ℬelieve in the strength that you have deep
inside and your faith will help show you the way.

ℬelieve in tomorrow and what it will bring,
let a hopeful heart carry you through.

For things will work out if you trust and
believe. There's no limit to what you can do!

Most people will make careful plans for small trips and none at all for their longest trip, that is, for their entire life. Think about that. Isn't it amazing that more energy often goes into planning a vacation than organizing an entire career? Millions of people stick with their first job until it's time to look for a help wanted sign again. They never plan their lives; they just react to emergencies.

Thomas Watson of IBM once wrote: *"Within us all there are wills of thought and dynamos of energy which are not suspected until emergencies arise. Then oftentimes we find that it is comparatively simple to double or triple our former capacities and to amaze us by the results achieved. Quotas, when set up for us by others, are challenges, which guide us on to surpass ourselves. The outstanding leaders of every age are those who set up their own quotas and constantly exceed them."* This statement has been true for innumerable great people. Study the philosophy behind it and the glow of success can be seen shining through.

Henry Ford, the founder of the great automobile industry, never made an important move in his business life without first finding a pencil and paper to write down the specifics of what he intended to attain. As he wrote, the ideas and fragment thoughts about the challenge he faced jelled in his mind into a clear-cut avenue of action. The decisions he made based on this dynamic method of pre-planning propelled his small company into becoming a giant in the world of commerce.

"Live your life each day as you would climb a mountain. An occasional glance toward the summit keeps the goal in mind, but many beautiful scenes are to be observed from each new vantage point. Climb slowly, steadily, enjoying each passing moment; and the view from the summit will serve as a fitting climax for the journey."
-Harold Melchert

"I think that you either follow the basic principles for creating success or you are going to get nailed. If you don't set goals, you don't get anywhere. That's so basic. The thing that I enjoy in my business is figuring out the overall mission, then establishing goals, developing the strategies, then the action plan and the calendar by which they must be completed."
-Mo Siegel, the founder of Celestial Seasonings

"After I made my first million dollars in sales I said, "Maybe I can make $10 million. After I made $10 million, my next goal was to make $10 million a year." Each year, Bo Pilgrim set higher goals until he made one million dollars each day. *"The key lies in having a management control system and having managers who understand those goals and perform in that direction. Set up a monthly award system where your compare actual performance versus goals. If your managers meet the goals, they receive a reward at the end of the month."*
-Bo Pilgrim, founder of Pilgrim Industries, a $300 million producer of chicken in the Southwest

Only You Can Make A Difference
"You alone can bring magic and humor and joy to the people you encounter. Anything you dream, by the very nature that you can dream it, makes it possible. The purpose of life is to help others. And if you can't help them, would you at least not hurt them? You can make things happen that you never thought you could! The greatest risk in life is to risk nothing. The person who risks nothing does nothing, has nothing and is nothing. To be is to do and to do is to do now because tomorrow might not be there. You have everything you need to be so much, don't settle for less! There is no end to human potential and there is so much more to learn. The time for action is now and only you can make a difference."
-Leo Buscaglia

I have observed, through a lifetime of study that all of us can be divided into 3 main classes.

1. **Those with will-power- THE LEADERS.** Read the biographies of the world's outstanding living or dead and in nearly every case one masterful trait stands out more prominent than all others. It is the real secret of their success. It is the indomitable, unconquerable WILL. Self declared refusal to yield an inch to the external forces which seek to thwart progress. Ask no one for permission to perform that which is within you to do. Boldly strike out upon you own initiative and do while the multitude stand by in mouth stretched awe. Pluck the prize while all others stand by and marvel at your daring. The greatest successes have been for those who have accepted the heaviest risks. The world is filled with the multitudes who dare not attempt big things. They worry about what others will say... *What will they say?* Forget this nonsense. Kick them into the scrap heap. The best successes are open to you if only you take the heaviest risks, balanced by cool, discerning decision making. Dare what no one else will dare. Seek to accomplish what no one else will attempt. Work out your own destiny on a grand scale. The price of success is the struggle to tower above belittlement, insult, jeer, sarcasm and insolence. Can you pay that price? Will you pay that price?

2. **Those with desire** whose intentions are good but who fail to put forth the necessary dominance and action to win out. They are the ones who wish instead of demand.

3. **Those of fate** who give up all the glory of human achievement because they say *It's all no use, things will never come my way.* And this is true. They certainly will never *come.* Between your birth and your death the hours and the days and the years will probably be many. Yet there is no cure for birth, no cure for death, so you may as well be happy with your allotted interval and live it with price, peace, honor, love and accomplishment. This very moment you have come to the crossroads of your life. Your destiny is in your hands.

You already possess all the tools and materials necessary in order to spend your time better. The greatest of all rewards of success, wealth, health and happiness are used through using your energetic qualities. Review these every morning, at the dinner table with your children every night and online with your friends. After you learn them and teach them you will have such a better time on your journey of life.

Separate yourself from the masses. Know that you are NOT a sheep who just nibbles dry grass following the herd as they wander across the wide open field. Separate yourself from all those average people so that you will be able to control your own destiny. What others think, say and do never need to influence what you think, say and do.

Live for today. When you awake put all of your efforts into what you need to accomplish today. Yesterday has gone forever and tomorrow is not here yet. Refuse to allow painful memories or your fears of tomorrow to take up your minutes. Go the extra mile. Work harder, longer and more intensely than anyone expects you to. Add value to who you are and what you are doing.

Look for the seed of good in every adversity. Every adversity that might happen to you today usually carries with it an equivalent or greater benefit that you will find when you seek it. When you suffer a setback, get in control of your emotions and ask yourself what possible good can come from what has happened. If one door closes, another door will open.

Never ever neglect the small things. The greatest difference between a failure and a success is that the successful person will do that which the failures won't do. When you work too fast and take shortcuts and do not pay attention to details, all will eventually cave in your career. Keep reminding yourself that if it is a part of your work, even if it is a small task, then it is important. In ancient battles that were lost, the reason could have been as small as a missing horse-shoe nail.

Don't spend your time in busy work. It takes just as much energy to fail as it does to be the success you wish to be. Don't waste your time being in a routine of remaining busy with unimportant busy work that can be an excuse to avoid meaningful opportunities that could change your life for the better forever. Your minutes and hours are your most precious possession. Waste not a moment.

Live today without allowing anyone to hurt you or to discourage you. The wounds to your inner self can be painful and long lasting whenever anyone criticizes you. Part of living a successful life is to realize that there will be people who will try to discourage you and who will attempt to drag you down to their level. This is just the way of humankind. Walk, no run away from those who discourage you. Envy always implies that the person who is discouraging you is inferior.

-Excerpted from Og Mandino

Use your life wisely, don't you think it's about time?

"Be avaricious of time; do not give any moment without receiving its value; only allow hours to go from you with as much regret as you give to your gold; do not allow a single day to pass without increasing the treasure of your knowledge and virtue,"
-Le Tourneux

SPURTS DON'T COUNT

"Time is the one thing that can never be retrieved. One may lose and regain a friend; one may lose and regain money; opportunity once spurned may come again but the hours lost in idleness can never be brought back to be used in gainful purposes."
-C. R. Lawton

*"Sow an act...reap a habit...
sow a habit...reap a character;
sow a character...reap a destiny."*
-George Boardman

"I will greet this day with love in my heart. For this is the greatest secret of success in all ventures. Muscle can split a shield and even destroy life itself but only the unseen power of love can open the hearts of many and until I master this act I will remain no more than a peddler in the market place. I will make love my greatest weapon and none on who I call can defend upon its force...my love will melt-all hearts liken to the sun whose rays soften the coldest day."
-Og Mandino

"When we die and go to Heaven, our Maker is not going to say, why didn't you discover the cure for such and such? The only thing we're going to be asked at that precious moment is why didn't you become you?"
-Elie Wiesel

"Blessed are they who expect nothing
for they are never disappointed."
-Alexander Pope

WHEN YOU COME TO A FORK IN THE ROAD, TAKE ONE.

"The only chance to start
at the top is to dig a hole."
-Og Mandino

"Most people die at age 25 but their
bodies don't catch up until they are 65
and can be buried together."
-Benjamin Franklin

television is a drug with a plug

"The end result of your life here on earth
will always be the sum total of the choices
you made while you were here."
-Shad Helmstetter

A whole lot separates a whiner and a winner.

Is this you: First I was dying to finish High School and start college. Then I was dying to finish college and start working. Then I was dying to marry and have children. Then I was dying for my children to grow up. Then I was dying to retire. And now I am dying and suddenly realized I forgot to live.

When you have come to the edge of all the light you know and are about to step into the darkness, faith is knowing one of two things will happen; either there will be something solid to stand on or you will be taught how to fly.

If you want to earn $100,000 in the next 12 months, that's $2,000 per week. Divide $2,000 per week by 40 hours, to get $50. Then, $50 per hour divided into 15 minute segments is $12.50. Is every 15 minute segment of your workday worth $12.50? Get into the habit of evaluating your productivity in 15 minute intervals of every work day.

Don't kill time, fill time.

The difference between failure and success is two well planned hours a day. Two well planned hours out of 24 is not very much.

What is the most important thing you can think about at this extraordinary moment in time?

"All things come to those who wait
provided they hustle while they wait."
-Thomas Edison

The TRAF Formula

High performance people are clear that some things are not worth their spending their valuable time on. Here is a formula to help you decide quickly what choices you have when deciding what to do with your time. **T**rash, **R**efer, **A**ction or **F**ile.

Keep away from people who try to waste your time who belittle your ambition and dreams. Small minded people always try to do that, but the really great people make you feel that you, too, can become great.

"There are some days when I think I am
going to die from an overdose of satisfaction.
-Salvador Dali

Seize the day!
The best is on it's way!

If you were given 28 hours per day for the rest of your life instead of the 24 you now have, what would you do with the four extra hours?

R2A2 Formula

When you are spending your time, learn to **R**ecognize, **R**elate, **A**ssimilate and **A**pply principles from what you see, hear, read, think or experience.

In five years you will be five years older.

If the dream is big enough, the facts don't count.

"If one advances confidently in the direction of his dreams and endeavors to live the life which he has imagined, he will meet with success unexpected in common hours."
-Henry David Thoreau

"I do not fear failure. I only fear the slowing up of the engine inside me which is pounding, saying, 'Keep going, someone must be on top, why not you?'"
-George S. Patton

Don't pout, profit

"Be willing to make a difference in each moment and your world will overflow with possibilities. Be willing to experience a life of richness and fulfillment and that is precisely how it will unfold."
-Ralph Marston

The nicest thing about the future is that it always starts tomorrow.

How come it takes so little time for a child who is afraid of the dark to become a teenager who wants to stay out all night?

Do you realize that in about 40 years we will have thousands of old people running around with tattoos? And RAP music will be the golden oldies!

You don't find time for important things, you make it.

Cutting Things Short

"I'm in the middle of something now..." start with *"I only have 5 minutes"...you* can always extend this, stand up, stroll to door, compliment, thank, shake clock-watching; on wall behind them.

What am I doing that doesn't really need to be done? What am I doing that could be done by someone else? What am I doing that could be done more efficiently? What do I do that wastes others' time?

Doing things at the last minute is much more expensive than just before the last minute. If you haven't got time to do it right, you don't have time to do it wrong.

Today work out how many seconds you have left to live. Here is the formula:
Average Life Expectancy is 79
Your Current Age x 31,536,000.
Now plan for each one of them.

DECIDE YOUR DESTINY= BUILDING A GREAT TOMORROW

Enjoy Yourself- It's Later Than You Think
-Frederic Loomis

For 21 years, Dr.. Frederic Loomis had been a busy obstetrician. For all of these years he had patiently listened to worried young wives, quieted their fears, given them advice and comfort and delivered their babies. He was a kind and understanding gentleman. He so completely devoted himself to his patients and their challenges that there had been little time for a life of his own. In 1938, Dr. Loomis came to an important decision. The time had come to retire, to think and reflect on the wisdom he had learned in his experience. He decided to make some notes in his journal. One of the first things he wrote was *"In a Chinese Garden"*, the story of a letter that completely changed his way of life and which has since changed the lives of thousands of others. I have told many times the story of a certain letter, which I received years ago, because the impression it made on me was very deep. And I have never told it, on ships in distant seas, for by quiet firesides nearer home, without a reflective, thought response from those around me.

The letter:

Peking, China

Dear Doctor:

Please don't be too surprised in getting a letter from me. I am signing only my first name. My surname is the same as yours. You won't even remember me. Two years ago I was in your hospital under the care of another doctor. I lost my baby the day it was born. That same day my doctor came in to see me and as he left he said, *"Oh by the way, there is a doctor here with the same name as yours who noticed your name on the board and asked me about you. He said he would like to come in to see you, because you might be a relative. I told him you had lost your baby and I didn't think you would want to see anybody, but it was all right with me"*. And then in a little while you came in. You put your hand on my arm and sat down for a moment beside my bed. You didn't say much of anything but your eyes and your voice were kind and pretty soon I felt better. As you sat there I noticed that you looked tired and that the lines in your face were very deep. I never saw you again but the nurses told me you were in the hospital practically night and day. This afternoon I was a guest in a beautiful Chinese home here in Peking. The garden was enclosed by a high wall and on one side surrounded by twining red and white flowers, was a brass plate about two feet long. I asked someone to translate the Chinese characters for me. They said:

ENJOY YOURSELF, iT iS LATER THAN YOU THiNK.

I began to think about it for myself. I had not wanted another baby because I was still grieving for the one I lost. But I decided that moment that I should not wait any longer. Perhaps it may be later than I think, too. And then, because I was thinking of my baby, I thought of you and the tired lines in your face and the moment of sympathy you gave me when I so needed it. I don't know how old you are but I am quite sure you are old enough to be my father and I know that those few minutes you spent with me meant little or nothing to you, of course, but they meant a great deal to a woman who was desperately unhappy. So I am so presumptuous as to think that in turn I can do something for you too. Perhaps for you it is later than you think. Please forgive me, but when your work is over, on the day you get my letter, please sit down very quietly, all by yourself and think about it.

Marguerite

Usually I sleep well when I am not disturbed by the telephone. But that night, I woke several times seeing the brass plate in the Chinese wall. I could not believe I was so disturbed by a letter from this woman who I couldn't even remember. I finally dismissed the idea from my mind and not too long afterwards, I found myself saying: *"Well, maybe it is later than I think; why don't I do something about it?"*

The next morning I went to my office and told them I was going away for three months. It is a humbling experience to think you are important in your business to leave it for a few months. The first time I went away on a long trip, some years before this letter came, I felt sure that everything would go to pieces, even though I had a very competent associate. When I returned I found there were just as many patients as when I left. Everyone had recovered just as fast or faster and many patients did not know I had been away. It is humiliating to find how quickly your place can be filled, but it is a good valuable lesson.

Today, many years have been added to the average expectation of life but each person's fate is still a hazard. The most valuable people around us have lived largely for others. This seems the time to remind them that they will have more years and happier ones, to do good for others if they start right now to do something for themselves to go places and do things which they have looked forward to for years; to give those who love them the happiness of seeing them enjoy some of the rewards which they have earned; to replace competition with a bit of contemplation.

The story of the unexpected letter from China, how it altered Dr. Frederic Loomis's way of life reached out to influence the lives of those about him and has become an inspirational classic. A simple, human story, charged with emotion, has made countless men and women look to the future with suddenly altered vision, has encouraged them to put aside their burdens for a while and enjoy themselves...before it's too late.

NASA TIME

Are you aware that the space shuttle uses more fuel during the first few minutes after lift off than it uses during it's entire trip into orbit? Do you know why? Because at the beginning of the trip, the space shuttle needs to overcome the incredible gravity of the earth. As it does, though, the shuttle becomes easier to fly. Think about how that relates to you and your lifetime. Getting started toward your goals can be the hardest at the beginning. It takes time to stop letting your habits control you. There will be plenty of time to sleep when you are dead.

> *"Your eyes show the strength of your soul."*
> -The Alchemist

YOU CAN'T STROLL TO A GOAL.

Once you have done your best, let go and let life do the rest.

At the end of life, the multi-billionaire gets buried and ends up as dust. It's about time to have fun starting right now.

Time heals what reason cannot.

Worrying does not empty tomorrow of its troubles, it empties today of its strength.

If you have decided it's about time to reach your goals, face the fact that the higher and more unusual your goals, the more others will try to discourage you from them, even in jest. Have a strong purpose and the heart to pursue what you want with all of your heart, even when other people give up or quit.

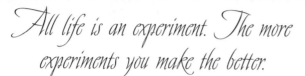
All life is an experiment. The more experiments you make the better.

"Anyone can stand tall on the high peaks. It is the people who survive the valleys between the peaks who will emerge the strongest. These survivors will be our leaders, the ones who are mentally tough and have the perseverance to keep going."
-Preston Pearson

Dare to dream.

Dare to start a new way of life, here and now.

Debate only yourself.

Decide to begin and then decide to keep going.
Don't waste a day.

Dreams give rise to desire, desire gives rise to the daring to do, the daring to do gives rise to the deciding to begin and the deciding to being gives rise to the deciding to try seriously.
Flourish in life.

Follow that rainbow. Get a sense of urgency. Get going, start growing and keep glowing.

GET THAT FAMILIAR TINGE OF WONDER. I CANNOT SLEEP FOR THE ANTICIPATION OF WHAT LIES AHEAD.

People are defeated in life not because of lack of ability but for lack of wholeheartedness.

What will you no longer settle for...what do you have to give up to get it?

And They Call it "Luck"

He worked all day and toiled by night. He gave up play and some delight. Dry books he read, new things to learn and forged ahead, success to earn. He plodded on with faith and pluck; and when he won, people called it luck.

Your fabulous future starts today!

"When I was in the batter's box, I felt sorry for the pitcher."
-Roger Hornsby

"Most time is wasted, not in hours, but in minutes. A bucket with a small hole in the bottom gets just as empty as a bucket that is deliberately emptied."
-Paul Meyer

"Each of us thinks our watch is telling the right time."
-Gandhi

"If one less person had put out one less percent we would have lost."
-Tommy Prothro UCLA football coach

Your Living Situation:

Make a list of the five things you are tolerating about where you are living and what the solution could be to change it. This could be the location, size, design, messes, unorganized closets, carpet needs cleaning or replacement, walls need new paint, appliances need updating, mortgage is way too high, rooms too small, furniture needs updating.

1._____

2._____

3._____

4._____

5._____

Your Family/Community:

Make a list of the five things you are tolerating about your family or community and what the solution could be to change it. This could be communication needs to improve within the family, shouting, pouting, moaning, criticizing needs to stop. Need to get better in replying to my children instead of reacting. My friends don't reciprocate, I am the one making all of the effort. I need to be kinder to my neighbors. I need to relax when driving and not be a jerk.

1._____

2._____

3._____

4._____

5._____

Your Life Work:

Make a list of the five things you are tolerating about your work or professional life and what the solution could be to change it. This could be working for someone who is a jerk, hating what you do, stressing out, always needing a vacation, not enough pay, unpredictable future, not enough training, need to know more about what I am doing to improve.

1._____

2._____

3._____

4._____

5._____

Don't let your surroundings assault you. Blaring iPods, glaring lights, loud colors and bold patterns attack your senses. Arrest demanding sights and distracting sounds with CALM alternatives. Reform your environment with soft music, candles and soothing color.

DON'T allow dinner to be disturbed by phone calls. Let your voice messaging pick up your calls.

⌐ TWINKLE ⌐
TWINKLE

Your daily cares will slip away as you scan the night sky. You won't miss the tranquil twinkling of a star.

Certainty/Comfort

Everyone is searching for these certain needs. If you are in business and can provide these certain needs, you will be successful. No matter what you try or do, if you do not meet these needs for yourself and others, you will stay upset, mixed up, craving these needs and not discovering what you need to do to satisfy them. We all want to be certain that the floor will be under our feet when we get up in the morning.

Variety, Significance, Connection, Contribution

Seek variety in cultures and traveling the world. Be so busy giving significance that you don't need it any more. Work hard to have the money to stay connected with your children forever. Charity and contribution begin at home. If you come from worrying what a crowd thinks of you, you will not be invited back. If you come from contributing to make those in your audience satisfy their human needs, they will love and appreciate you. Contribute to your relationships. Don't wait for others to contribute to your happiness, contribute to theirs.

Will Have to Spend Money to Achieve My Goals?

Achieving your goals may mean additional costs to you, but the revenues of success are more than enough to compensate for whatever expenses you accrue. Set those goals, get your map. Know where you're going.

MAKE A DECISION TO LIVE FIVE MINUTES AT A TIME.

"It is estimated that 98 out of every 100 people who are dissatisfied with their world do not have a clear picture in their minds of the world they would like for themselves. Think of it! Think of the people who drift aimlessly through life, dissatisfied, struggling against a great many things, but without a clear-cut goal."
-W. Clement Stone

"All men seek one goal: success or happiness. The only way to achieve true success is to express yourself completely in service to society. First, have a definite, clear, practical idea - a goal, an objective. Second, have the necessary means to achieve your ends - money, wisdom, materials and methods. Third, adjust all your means to that end."
-The Greek philosopher Aristotle

STAY COOL, CALM AND PROTECTED.

Did you ever hear of someone
on their death bed say:
"I wish I'd spent more time at the office!"

Count down
everything you do....
10, 9, 8, 7, 6, 5, 4, 3, 2, 1...
dinner is served...
I am getting in the car...
I am going to make
a phone call...
have fun with your time.

MY NEED 1:
Certainty/Comfort

MY NEED 2:
Uncertainty/Variety

MY NEED 3:
Significance

MY NEED 4:
Connection/Love

MY NEED 5:
Growth

MY NEED 6:
Contribution

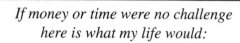
If money or time were no challenge here is what my life would:

Look Like:

Smell Like:

Sound Like:

Feel Like:

If I knew I couldn't fail, here would be my perfect vision for how to use my time:

This one set of questions can change your life. They will get you to focus on the fact that you want to achieve your goals early in life so that you can enjoy the fruits of your labors and the lifestyle of the rich and famous! Just set goals and stay focused.

Important questions to answer before you proceed to deciding where you are going to put your lifetime:

In 10 years...	
How old will I be?	
How old will my children be?	
How old will my spouse be?	
How old will my parents be?	
How old/out-of-date will my clothes be?	
How old/out-of-date will my car be?	
Will I want a new home?	
Will I be paying for college education?	
Will I be upgrading my computer/appliances?	
Will I have money to pamper myself?	
Will I have money in case of emergencies?	
Will I have money to travel?	
Will I have money to retire comfortably?	
How much money will I have if I keep doing what I am doing right now?	
Am I ready to make a change in my life?	

"We are not living in eternity. We have only this moment, sparkling like a star in our hand and melting like a snowflake."
- Marie Ray

Set up a program of daily time targets for completion each day:

Set up a program of daily time targets for completion each week:

Daily Goals to Complete	Done
Sunday	
Monday	
Tuesday	
Wednesday	
Thursday	
Friday	
Saturday	

My Weekly Goal	Done
Week #1	
Week #2	
Week #3	
Week #4	

8 W's Rule

Work
Will
Win
When
Wishy
Washy
Wishing
Won t
Work

Set up a program of immediate targets
for completion this month.

My Monthly Goals	Done
January	
February	
March	
April	
May	
June	
July	
August	
September	
October	
November	
December	

Set up a long range calendar.

List all the steps to help you reach your goal.
Don't linger too long.
This doesn't have to be exact.

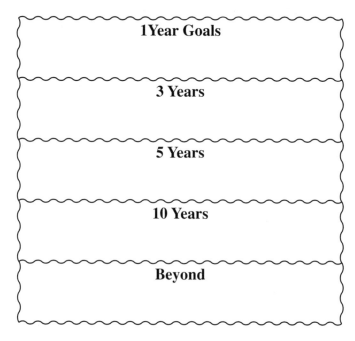

1 Year Goals

3 Years

5 Years

10 Years

Beyond

This exercise pushes you to think.

Now add them all up, all the 1 years, 3's, 5's, 10's.
How many goals do you have in the next year?

_____

How many goals do you have in the next 5 years?

_____

Now go through your next year goals and
identify your 4 major 1-year goals.

1.

2.

3.

4.

What would you like to have, do and be?

What do you really, really want, the very most in your lifetime:

Determine the major goal of your future on the basis of your individual needs. Isn't it time for you to dream some magnificent dreams? Now, get real, what is it that you really and truly want in life...get totally honest...now.

Here is my major #1 goal of my future being totally honest with myself:

Set goals several years out				
	20__	20__	20__	20__
Major Goal				
Plan				
PROGRESS				
30 days				
60 days				
90 days				
Stretch Goal				

Would people who have achieved what you wish to accomplish give you an "A" for effort and another "A" for accomplishment?

Specifically answer these in writing:
What you are doing now
to focus on your goals?

What you are saying vs.
what you are doing?

Focus on what you are willing
to work for and make a list:

I am willing to work for: Done

All About Me			
How well can I predict the responses of other people?			
	Excellent	Good	Poor
Have I set my personal goals for the future?			
Am I sticking to them?			
Do I apply myself to the tasks to accomplish my goals?			
Am I improving my performance from day to day?			
Do I get along with others?			
Do I refuse to bow to challenges and use them to spur me on?			
Am I clear time is fleeing?			
When greeted with a new idea, do I always examine it without prejudice?			
Do I look at challenges from every possible point of view?			
Do I respect others?			
Do I recognize needs and attempt to fulfill them?			
Do I use my time wisely?			
Am I doing everything that I can to ensure my personal advancement?			
Do I have a program of Self-Improvement?			
Do I have the philosophy of Constant and Never Ending Improvement?			
I am going to quit sitting at my desk and just shuffling papers without getting any work done?			
I will find ways to save time.			
I will try new things			
What can I simplify?			

MY CHORE CHART

NAME: _____

MYSELF	S	M	T	W	T	F	S

CLEAN ROOM	S	M	T	W	T	F	S

HOUSE CHORES	S	M	T	W	T	F	S

OTHER	S	M	T	W	T	F	S

Time-Wasters are Everywhere

In the floor of the gold-working room in the United States Mint at Philadelphia, there is a wooden lattice-work which is taken up when the floor is swept and the tiny particles of gold-dust, thousands of dollars yearly are thus saved. So every successful person has a kind of network to catch *the raspings and parings of existence, those leavings of days and wee bits of hours* which most people sweep into the waste of life. He who hoards and turns to account all odd minutes, half hours, unexpected holidays, gaps *between times* and chasms of waiting for unpunctual persons, achieves results which astonish those who have not mastered this secret.

What do you want to get accomplished today, tomorrow, this week, this month, this year?

_____

_____

_____

In what order of importance?

_____

_____

_____

Over what period of time?

_____

_____

_____

What is the time available?

_____

_____

_____

What is the best strategy for application of time to projects for the most effective results?

_____

_____

_____

The "I" Pie

Picture your time as a pie about you. Cut your pie into 3 slices. Decide what is most important to you.

Material Wealth-Having:

_____%

Work-Doing:

_____%

Relationships/Family-Being:

_____%

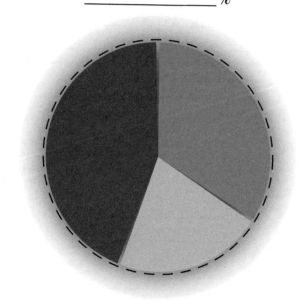

I Will Focus More On:

_____

_____

_____

I Will Focus Less On:

_____

_____

_____

Isn't it about time you get happy with what you are doing and enjoy life?

You are going to live a beautiful, abundant, prosperous life. It is the only life you get to live. One in which those people who love you will cherish their time with you and possibly the rest of the world will remark about what you did with your one magnificent lifetime. Your time depends upon you, so start going after your dreams with all you've got. It's about time.

Take charge of your time, you will be so happy you did!

Work like you don't need the money.
Love like you've never been hurt.
And dance like no one is watching.

I have a premonition, it soars on silver wings, I dream of your accomplishments and other wondrous things. I do not know beneath what sky that you will conquer fate, I do know it will be high and I do know that you will be great!

Grow old with me, the best is yet to be...

Now that I have stimulated your desire to take charge of your time, now it's time to take action. Don't be part of the herd, step out into your own magnificence and take charge of your time. What are you going to do with your precious future? Go for greatness, be the best you can be...after all it's about time!

Seize the Day! Carpe Diem!

I just wanted to let you know that I value your time and any moment spent with you is a moment I treasure!!!

So, it's about time my friends, Don't be average, be a champion!

Thanks for your time...

Let forever begin,